ANATOLE FRANCE

David Tylden-Wright

WALKER AND COMPANY
NEW YORK

To Di

Tous que je découvre de ma fenêtre, l'Arc de Triomphe, la Seine, la terrasse des Tuileries, le Louvre, le vieux et vénérable Paris avec ses tours et ses flèches – tout cela c'est ma vie, c'est moi-même, et je ne serai rien sans ces choses qui se reflètent en moi avec les mille nuances de ma pensée et m'inspirent et m'animent. C'est pourquoi j'aime Paris d'un immense amour.

Le Crime de Sylvestre Bonnard

Illustrations

Preface

THIS BOOK has taken me far longer to write than it should
have done. For this, the main fault was undoubtedly my
own – the result of a basic inability to resist putting second
things first – but a contributory cause was the nature of the
subject. Evasive in life, disliking extremely being cornered
by commitments, by circumstances, or by the demands of his
fellow-men, France is no less elusive to a biographer. Or so
at any rate I found. Time and again I thought I had him
cornered – only to find that an entirely contradictory side
of his character came to the surface to upset all my ideas.
It took me some time to realize that the essence of France's
character lay in these contradictions, and that a great deal
not only of his creative, but of his staying power, came from
them also. They kept him young.

Looking back now over France's life, as it has shaped
itself in this book, it seems to me to contain an unexpected
element of humility. France did not like judging other
people – even as a critic he would only consent to do so on
the clearly stated understanding that his opinions were
personal and as such open to doubt, discrepancy and dispute – and he was no keener to judge himself, even to the
extent of distinguishing between his virtues and his weak-
nesses, even to the extent of disciplining his character into a
consistent and cohesive whole. But because he did not spurn
the services of any of the many sides of his character, he had
at his disposal an unusually varied band of helpers. The results were often surprising. For someone who approached
life so doubtfully and sceptically, France managed to capture
and convey an astonishing zest for living; for someone

admittedly self-centred he gave up an astonishing amount of his life to social concerns in which he had no personal interest; for someone who declared himself to be temperamentally and incurably lazy, he produced an amazing volume of work.

I wanted to write this book for various reasons, chief amongst them the desire to pay attention and tribute to a writer who since his death has, I think, been unjustly neglected. Although France would never have thought of himself as a member of 'the Establishment' – on the contrary he often went to great trouble to dispel such an impression – he was a prominent Parisian figure for so long that inevitably over the last years of his life he was looked upon as part of the established order. The violent reaction against his work, which followed his death, was, in part at least, based on a desire for change, for new methods and new masters. Such a reversal is a normal process of literary life and nothing to be surprised at. But what is surprising is the little interest that has been shown in France's work, the little effort that has been made to assess its permanent value, in the forty-odd years since his death.

For this neglect, the main reason may, I think, be the diverse nature of his work. France left no single monumental work such as Proust's *À la Recherche* by which to be remembered. His talent is scattered over not only many books, but many fields of writing. No more in death than in life can France be classified conveniently into a single compartment of literature. Nor have most of his books remained untouched by time. Particularly during the period when he, like most Parisians, was preoccupied with the Affair, his works show his concern with the topical issues of his day. The interest of such passages has inevitably passed with that of the events they reflect. France, too, was given to introducing long conversational set-pieces into his novels. They may have talked in such a way in Mme Arman's salon, but they certainly no longer do so around the dinner-tables of our own times. This, too, considerably dates his dialogue. From his journalistic training, France had, also, acquired an episodic approach to his work, and some episodes are noticeably better than others. All of which simply means that a reader today has to be selective in his approach, even within the covers of a single book.

Yet if one pieces together the various elements of France's work which have outlasted the swing of disfavour they build up into an *œuvre* of remarkable richness. *Les Dieux ont Soif* stands alone among his novels, the only one untouched by time, because it has always been timeless, the analysis not only of the French Revolution, but of human experience. But there is also the brilliant satire of the early part of *l'Ile des Pingouins*; the convincingly authentic appeal of his love story in *Le Lys Rouge*; the conscious but still uncloyed charm of much of *Sylvestre Bonnard*. In other fields there are his essays for *La Vie Littéraire*, still as fresh as when they were written; and the wry wisdom and courageously defiant gaiety of the two admittedly autobiographical volumes *Le Petit Pierre* and *La Vie en Fleur* which he wrote at the end of his life. There is much else besides. Few writers, of his time or ours, can offer so varied and satisfying a feast.

But I wanted to write about France, not only because of a desire to remove the mould of neglect that has collected on his work since his death, but also because of the obvious challenge of a highly complex personality. In one of his most famous phrases – the only one, curiously, to find its way into the *Oxford Dictionary of Quotations* – France described 'the good critic' as 'he who relates the adventures of his soul among masterpieces'. It was partly for the adventure it seemed to offer that I wanted to follow up the track of France's life.

Finally, there was a more personal reason. No one has ever written more fondly or more beautifully about Paris, the city in which France was born and brought up, and in which, save for holiday absences, he lived the whole of his life. It was partly to catch the reflection and the spirit of a city for which I, too, have a strong personal affection, that I chose to study the writer who, of all, is surely the most passionately Parisian.

I am greatly indebted to M. Lucien Psichari, the grandson of Anatole France, both for his personal help and for permission to use letters and the *carnets* of his grandfather. The letters of France to his grandson, quoted at the end of my book, are from *Ma Suzon Cherie*, a selection of France's letters privately published by M. Psichari.

I would also like to thank Mme André Maurois – the granddaughter of Mme Arman de Caillavet, Mme Jacques Lion, M. Jacques Suffel, M. Pierre Castaing and Mr. Roger Senhouse for helping me in various ways at various times.

The quotations from France's own works, which include passages from *Le Crime de Sylvestre Bonnard*, *Le Livre de mon Ami*, *Les Désirs de Jean Servien*, *La Vie Littéraire*, *Le Lys Rouge*, *Pierre Nozière*, *Les Dieux ont Soif*, *Le Petit Pierre* and *La Vie en Fleur*, are printed by permission of MM. Calmann-Lévy.

I also gratefully make acknowledgement to the following for permission to quote from the works named after them – Messrs. Chatto & Windus for part of a letter from Proust's *Correspondence* edited by Mina Curtiss; Mr. C. D. Medley for extracts from George Moore's *Confessions of a Young Man* and *Memoirs of my Dead Life*; Librairie Gallimard for extracts from *La Jeunesse d'Anatole France* by George Girard – c Libraire Gallimard, 1925; Flammarion for extracts from the Journals of the Goncourts and for an extract from *Les Goncourts* by M. André Billy; Librairie Plon for extracts from *Souvenirs* by Marie Scheikevitch; and Librairie Imprimieres Réunies for extracts from *Leconte de Lisle et ses Amis* by Fernand Calmettes.

I would also like to thank Mrs. A. Ball for coping miraculously with a hand-writing that was described by my tutor at Oxford some twenty years ago, as an 'interesting example of medieval script' – and which has not improved since.

I

MANY PEOPLE COME, and always have, to the *quais* of
Paris for many reasons. There is the river, which brings
into the city not only a breath of fresh air, but also a sense
of spaciousness, even a feeling of excitement, for at no point
does the Seine seem far from the sea, and from the sea opens
out the whole world of adventure. There are the bookstalls,
lining both banks. There are, grouped particularly on the
Left Bank, the bookshops, the shops of antique and picture
dealers, shops full of every sort of curiosity. There are the
buildings, which for a variety of reasons have risen beside
the river. The *quais* were the seat of the Court when there
was one; they are still that of Government, with the
Chambre using the river as a barricade between itself and
the noisier, more turbulent part of the city from which come
most of its problems. They are still, as they have long been,
centres of Culture, with the Louvre on one bank and the
Institut on the other; of the Church, with Nôtre Dame rising
proudly on the larger of the two linked islands lying like an
outsize battleship in the middle of the river; and of Justice,
whose *palais* rises like the bridge of the battleship on the
same island as the cathedral. Yet of all the reasons for which,
over the centuries, people have come to the *quais*, the best
is still, as it has always been, simply the pleasure of being
there.

For an intelligent and receptive child to be brought up on,
or near, the *quais*, is obviously a great stroke of luck. Or so,
at any rate, thought a bookseller's son, Anatole François

Thibault, born at No. 19, quai Malaquais, on the 16th April, 1844. Some forty years later he was to write that in his opinion it did not seem possible 'that one could have a completely ordinary mind if one was brought up on the *quais* of Paris, opposite the Louvre and the Tuileries, near the Palais Mazarin, in front of the glorious river of the Seine, which flows between the towers, the turrets and the spires of ancient Paris. There, from the rue Guénégard to the rue du Bac, the booksellers, the antique dealers, the sellers of old prints, spread out a profusion of the most beautiful forms of art . . . Since there are trees as well as books, and since there are women passing by, it is the most beautiful place in the world.'

It was chance rather than design that prevented Thibault becoming one of the famous names of French literature. In the days of his fame, Anatole France explained how it happened to a journalist who asked him why he had chosen to adopt a pseudonym – 'I did not choose a pseudonym. Properly speaking I have no pseudonym. The name of France is a nickname older than I am. I come from an old family of Angevin vignerons. My father was named François-Noël Thibault. In his own country he was known by the diminutive of his Christian name, France. It is the name he kept during the eighty-five laborious, modest and honourable years of his life. Habit, stronger than love, imposed on me in my turn the name of France which I carry, as he carried it.' In his early years the bookseller's son was generally known as 'Le petit France' – his father becoming, now that he had earned the title, 'Père France'. The name of his bookshop had been similarly simplified by usage. In 1840, when it had first opened – then at No. 6, place de l'Oratoire du Louvre – it had carried the top-heavy title of the 'Librairie Politique Ancienne et Moderne de France-Thibault', but successive moves had pruned it to the point when, by the time it reached the *quais* by way of the rue de Seine, it was simply – if somewhat ambiguously – known as the 'Librairie de France'.

In several ways the Librairie de France was no ordinary bookshop. For one thing it specialized in works of, or about, the French Revolution. For another, it was the last *librairie à chaise* in Paris. Chairs were spread about the room to encourage customers to settle with the books they had pulled down from the shelves, to browse as well as to buy, to chat amongst themselves or with the proprietor. It was a pleasant, convivial arrangement, and gave to the bookshop something of the appearance and atmosphere of a club, which in the evening it really became, for a group of Père France's customers, who were also his friends, habitually met there.

Amongst the most regular of daytime visitors, although their evenings were spent in company far more distinguished than the bookshop could provide, were the brothers Edmond and Jules de Goncourt. When eventually Père France retired, somewhat prematurely, largely on account of the incomprehensible refusal of his son to follow him in the family business, and sold the bookshop, its passing was to be noted in an entry of their Journal for January 1867 – 'A symptom of our time. The bookshop no longer has chairs. France was the last *librairie à chaise*: and the last shop to allow a little leisure between business. Now one has to buy books standing up. A question and a price; nothing more.

'This is the point to which the devouring business activity of today has led bookselling; hitherto surrounded by leisure, by dawdling, and by much talkative and friendly browsing through books.'

Some years later, Edmond de Goncourt, smarting from the sting of an unfavourable review by the bookseller's son, then launching out on his career as a critic for *Le Temps*, was to remember him in the bookshop as a 'young wretch who seemed to have a perpetual cold in the head'.

France also remembered the Goncourts – 'monocle in eye, moustache in the air, they scrutinized quickly and well'.

The bookshop specialized in the French Revolution mainly because that was the particular preoccupation of Père France's patron, the Comte de La Bédoyère, a man of intelligence, rank and wealth who had the perception to see that the Revolution was the most crucial period in modern French history – the watershed, in fact, between the old France and the new – and as such wanted to know as much as he could about it. It was, in fact, a watershed which had divided his own family, for his brother had been executed for raising Grenoble on behalf of Napoleon during the Hundred Days, while he himself was staunchly true to the original Bourbon line, under whom after the Restoration, he served as an officer in the King's Guard. It was there that he had met Père France, who was serving in the ranks. At the time of the deposition of Charles X in 1830 the Comte was Colonel of the Guard, while Père France had risen to the rank of corporal. The relationship of the colonel and the corporal shows the system of patronage at its best. Liking the efforts of the at first entirely illiterate guardsman to better and educate himself, the Comte had used his influence when Père France left the army to get him a job with one of the best bookshops in Paris where he could serve his apprenticeship and learn a new trade. When his protégé became knowledgeable and courageous enough to seek to set up on his own, the Comte put up most of the money that enabled him to do so. Thereafter, he remained Père France's best customer, and his open commission to take anything of interest that would add to his immense collection of Revolutionary material was for many years an essential financial prop to the bookshop. The value of this support can be judged from the fact that after the Comte's death in 1861 his collection – the cataloguing of which was one of the few professional jobs in which the bookseller and his son collaborated – was sold complete to what was then the Bibliothèque Imperiale, and is now the Bibliothèque Nationale, where it forms the basis of their immense and invaluable collection of Revolutionary material.

But it is not only historians of the Revolution who owe the Comte de La Bédoyère a considerable debt. So, too, do all lovers of French literature. For the books that he read, the talk that he listened to about the Revolution in the bookshop, left a rich deposit in France's mind, from which was to come, some sixty years later, *Les Dieux ont Soif,* the best novel ever written about the Revolution and one of the few historical novels effectively to telescope time. In it, past and present come very close together, and for France, of course, so far as the Revolution was concerned, that had always been so. From his childhood he was as familiar with its events as with those of his contemporary world; its scene was that of his everyday life.

In July 1844, Père France moved his two-month old son, together with his other possessions – including his bookshop – from No. 19 to 15, quai Malaquais. There he and they were to remain for the next nine years in an apartment of four rooms on the first floor reached by a winding staircase which started at the side of the concierge's lodge. For this and the use of a cellar below, Père France paid a rent of 550 francs, increased to 750 francs in 1849 when he took a smaller flat on the floor above for his mother-in-law and her erring and errant husband.

Despite the disadvantage of not opening directly on to the street, the bookshop was well placed to attract those who would appreciate its unusual amenities. It was close to the line of bookstalls on the *quais,* and thus its chairs were often a boon to footsore booklovers, weary of sorting their way from stall to stall. Also, the *quais* were the natural habitat of those who would appreciate the bookshop's quiet, restful undemanding atmosphere, a survival of the more leisurely way of life generally associated with the *ancien régime.*

21

It was, too, close to the Institut, and many of the Academicians, on their way to and from séances at the Palais Mazarin,
used it as a refuge or a rendezvous, or simply as a pleasant
place in which to while away some spare moments of their
day.

For these various reasons, the bookshop built up a diverse
and distinguished clientele. As well as the Goncourts, the
younger Dumas frequently went there. So, too, did the
Baron de Barante, famous for his immensely popular
Histoire des Ducs de Bourgogne; Cheron de Villiers, biographer of Charlotte Corday; Jules Janin, Desiré Nisard,
Paul de Saint-Victor – three eminent and powerful critics;
Jacques-Charles Brunet, a famous bibliographer whose
works still carry authority; Paul Lacroix, better known as
the 'Bibliophile Jacob', after whom a short street tagged on
to the end of the rue de l'Université was – and still is –
named; his brother Antoine, well-known as a dramatist.

There were others, too, valued not so much for what they
wrote as for what they were; the Comte de La Bédoyère:
the Comte Dubois-Dubais, more generally and simply
known as 'M. Dubois', an expert collector and connoisseur
who was to exert a considerable influence over the bookseller's son as he grew up; Louis de Ronchaud – the *grand
ami* of Mme d'Agoult – a pleasant poet but an even more
pleasing personality; Jacques Charavay, France's godfather,
a one-time lawyer from Lyons who had followed his love
of books to Paris where he had started a bibliographic
business that is still one of the best there.

The sight, and more particularly the sound, of visitors
such as these, immensely impressed the bookseller's son.
Their talk was some of the first he heard, and the remembrance of it lasted the length of his long life. In his sixties
he told his secretary that these learned and loquacious,
courteous and generally kindly 'old gentlemen', whose conversation he had listened to as a child had seemed to him
then 'the personification of glory', and that at that time he

had not been able to imagine anything more 'splendid' than to be one of them.

But if in terms of distance the bookshop was close to the Institut, in terms of achievement an immense gulf separated them. Even Père France in his wildest dreams – and according to his son, he was a man of dreams who rarely looked directly at anything – cannot have imagined that his son would succeed in crossing it. Yet when, fifty years later, France was elected to the Académie française, thus becoming an 'Immortal', his achievement was in reality no greater than that of his father in becoming a successful and respected bookseller.

For Père France, born on Christmas Day, 1805, was the fifth and last child of a cobbler, who worked in the market town of Saulgé l'Hôpital, that stands roughly half way between Angers and Saumur. At the age of fourteen he had started work as a farm labourer for a widow called Samson who proved a kindly employer and with whom he remained in touch long after he left the district. All the same it was a hard life from which it was difficult to escape. Père France only managed to do so by enlisting in the army. He was tall and his farm work had given him a good physique. So, when in 1826 he came to Paris as a raw country recruit, he was taken into the Garde Royale of Charles X. At that time he could neither read nor write, even to the extent of signing his name.

Yet during his years of military service, Père France managed to educate himself so well that on leaving the army he was able to take and hold down successfully the job as an apprentice bookseller which the Comte de La Bédoyère had got for him. Few places are less conducive to study than a barrack-room, and something of the resistance and ridicule which Père France encountered in the effort to better himself seems to show in a passage of one of his son's books, in a snatch of conversation between Monsieur de Gerbois, a one-time officer of the King's Guard and Leclerc, an armourer who had once been a guardsman – 'Ah, Leclerc,' says the Marquis, 'those were the good old days.' 'Yes, M. le Marquis,' replied the armourer quietly, continuing the polishing of a blade, 'Yes, those were the good old days in a sense; but all the same I was made wretched because my room mates had found a grammar in my kit. For I must tell you that I had wanted to learn French while in the regiment and I had bought a grammar out of my pay, but the others made a mock of me.' 'They weren't so far wrong,' replied Monsieur de Gerbois, 'in your position, my friend, you had no need to learn grammar.' But in fact, Père France, or Corporal Thibault, had every need if he wanted to escape from the prison of illiteracy.

Although forced by the Revolution of 1830 to change kings, the Comte de La Bédoyère refused to change masters. Since he would not give his oath and allegiance to Louis Philippe, he was struck off the strength of the Guard in 1833. Père France may well have left the army at much the same time and for much the same reason. He certainly served out the short length of Charles X's reign, and was present at a farewell parade held in the courtyard of the Château de Maintenon on the 4th August, 1830. A small piece of white silk, part of the royal standard torn up and distributed on that occasion, was to remain one of his most treasured possessions.

Edmond de Goncourt recounts an episode which also recalls this period of Père France's service. 'I found myself,' Goncourt writes in the Journal for 15th February, 1862, '. . . chez France, the bookseller. A man came in, bargained for a book, bargained for a long time, went out, came in again, bargained again. He was a fat man with a square face and the gait of a horse-dealer. He gave the address to which his book was to be sent – M. — at Rambouillet. "Ah," said the bookseller, as he wrote it down, "I was there in 1830 with Charles X."

' "I was too," replied the fat man, "I had his last signature. Twenty minutes before the deputation from the provisional government arrived, I was there with my cabriolet. . . . Ah, he needed money badly. He was selling his silver, and not at all dear . . . I had fifteen thousand mouths to fill – those of his Guard. I was their purveyor."

'Chance had brought them face to face; the old soldier of the guard of Charles X and the purveyor who had profited by a moment of royal misfortune to buy the silver of a king at bay.'

At this time the tracks of Père France's life disappear. He may have gone straight into civilian life when the old Guard was disbanded, or, since it is easier for a wealthy colonel to retire than for a penurious corporal, he may have signed on for a further engagement. Either way, by the time one picks up his trail again – in 1837 – he was working for Techener, one of the best-known, most erudite and respected of Parisian booksellers. The following year Techener made him the manager of a branch at 4, place de l'Oratoire du Louvre, which, a year later, with the Comte's financial aid, he was able to buy. The year after that he gave his name not only to the bookshop, which he moved to 6, place de l'Oratoire du Louvre, but to Antoinette Gallas. In 1841 the couple had a still-born son; and then, three years later – two years after the bookshop had reached the *quais* – another son, Anatole-François – Anatole France – who thus became, and remained, their only surviving child.

Dependent though he was on his Comte's financial support, Père France was not content simply to act as his patron's scout. He set himself to learn his subject, and on his son's evidence, succeeded so well that many of his customers would sit down before him and 'leaf him over like a dictionary. Pamphlets, newspapers, posters, notices, the whole curious museum of '93, he knew it all.' There is other than filial authority for the respect and admiration that Père France won for himself both as a bookseller and as a man of learning. The catalogues of a big book sale in 1859 refer to the help in classifying those items concerned with the French Revolution of 'M. France, whose name by itself is a guarantee'. In a short story by Gerard de Nerval, 'Le Faux Soulier', the lover of the Queen of Sheba is looking for a rare book. 'We have still,' he says, 'to visit the learned bookshops – there is France, there is Merlin, there is Teche-ner.' So, in the opinion of the Queen of Sheba's lover, and no doubt of many others, Père France by then came first in his field.

Something of the cost of the study and effort needed to effect this transformation showed in the bookseller's grave and sombre manner. France was thinking of his father when in *Pierre Nozière* he described Dr. Nozière bending over the supposedly sleeping form of his son, his face lit by 'the sad and exquisite smile of a man who smiles rarely'. 'The master of the house,' wrote the son of the house on another occa-sion, 'upright, rather dry, very stiff behind his black cravat, looked pretty inflexible, and in fact was so. But without bending his conviction before that of others, no one knew better than he how to conserve the goodwill and the sym-pathy of the visitors.'

In the family photograph, seated at his supposed ease but in obvious discomfort, opposite a table on which a beautifully bound book is precariously balanced in front of a top-hat, symbols of the position of eminence and respec-tability he had won for himself, Père France shows as a strong, stern-faced character, with a long nose and a fringe of beard. In his son's more revealing portrait he appears as an idealist whose faith in human nature made him an opti-mist but whose naturally serious temperament rendered him gloomy. 'Enveloped in a sort of poetic melancholy he was truly a man of his time, both in his attitude and appear-ance. The gentlemen of that time wore their hair *en coup de vent*. Doubtless a skilful brush created this disorder; but it always seemed as if they had just been exposed to the storm and the north wind. My father, unpretentious as he was, had his share of *coup de vent* and of melancholy.'

From the matching photograph in the family album, France's mother looks out with a likeable face of extreme plainness. A long nose with a blob on the end of it, a wide slit of a mouth, bushy eyebrows – the eyes beneath them kind – there is nothing in her appearance to suggest the legendary beauty of the love-child, which should have been hers. Yet in spite of her illegitimacy her background by country standards had been reasonably well-to-do. Her mother's father was a miller and on his death, Amable-Antoinette Gallas, France's grandmother, inherited a half-share in a mill. Her illegitimate daughter, France's mother, was born on 1st November, 1811. Not quite a year later, in September, 1812, Amable-Antoinette married a civil servant, François Reynard, who died eighteen months later. However, Reynard's successor in the *bureau d'enregistrement* soon became his successor in his bed and his home.

Unfortunately, Jean Dufour, Amable-Antoinette's second husband, was a man of a very different type. He was a good-looking, idle, ex-soldier of the Empire, whose service had in fact been much shorter than the stories he liked to tell about it. His step-grandson was later to write that in fact he had only taken part in one battle, but that on the strength of that one day's gallantry he considered society to be ever afterwards in his debt. On his marriage to Amable-Antoinette, Dufour hung up his coat, resigned his job and settled down to live on his wife's fortune. The mill and the money lasted a number of years, but finally there was nothing left, and France's grandmother, from a state of reasonable affluence, was reduced to one almost of penury. She had six children by Dufour but none of them – save possibly a son of whom the trace was early lost – survived childhood and her only child by her first marriage, a son, died when he was eleven; so that France's mother, also named Antoinette, was in the end her only known surviving child.

On her this decline into poverty was particularly hard, for having known the easy independence of a country upbringing in the early years of her youth, she was suddenly sent out into service. Unlike her future husband, she found the experience harsh and it had a lasting effect on her character. 'Ma mère,' wrote France, in *Le Petit Pierre*, 'had a charming spirit, a fine mind, a generous heart, and a difficult character . . .' For the hardships of her life France's mother sought consolation in religion, and for her natural warm and affectionate nature she found an outlet in a passionate preoccupation with the problems and the progress of her son. Fortunately, however, her obsessional interest in him grew only as he did and in France's earliest recollections she appears simply as a warm supporting figure to whom he could run in case of need. 'Ma mère,' wrote France in *Le Livre de mon Ami*, 'had the divine patience and joyous simplicity of those souls whose only business in this world is to love.'

No. 15, quai Malaquais, France's home for the first nine years of his life – except, of course, those first two hardly conscious, hardly considerable months – was typical of many Parisian houses in that, like an iceberg, its external appearance gave little idea of its size, the bulk of the building being placed around an inner courtyard. It stood next to one of the great houses of Paris, the Hôtel Bouillon, later to become the Hôtel Chimay, built by Mansard in the middle of the seventeenth century, altered in the eighteenth for the Duchesse de Bouillon, the friend of La Fontaine, and still one of the most beautiful and imposing houses on the *quais*, now part of the École des Beaux Arts. At this time the owner of both houses was Léon Pellapra, a financier. Pellapra's wife had been a mistress of Napoleon and his legal daughter was openly admitted to be Napoleon's. In fact late in life she published her memoirs as such. By way of compensation to the injured, but far from outraged, husband, Napoleon in 1809 had made him Collector of Taxes for the district of Calvados, a position he held with dishonour until 1815. Changing sides successfully at the time of the Restoration, Pellapra changed only the districts of his tax-collectorship, holding first that of the Allier and then that of the Meurthe. By this time his fortune was immense. He bought the Hôtel Bouillon in 1825 and remained one of the richest financiers in Paris for the further twenty-nine years of his life.

France wrote about Pellapra as 'M. Bellaguet' in *Le Petit Pierre*. In spite of his wealth, Pellapra ran his properties himself, arranging the tenancies, collecting the rents, supervising the repairs. According to France, not a roll of wallpaper could be hung except in his presence. Pellapra was respected by his tenants, not only for his wealth and the way he looked after it – since, as France put it, 'What one respects in rich people, is their richness. The avarice, which increases their wealth, makes them more respectworthy; while their liberality, which diminishes their fortune, diminishes at the same time their credit and their reputation' – but also because he made himself genuinely the central point of their community. Pottering about his properties in his house-cap and dressing-gown, Pellapra was a fatherly figure where rents and repairs were not concerned, and obviously a personage of considerable importance in France's childhood world as well as that of the community which he owned and ran.

Unsavourily associated with every form of public and private financial scandal, Pellapra was scrupulously careful in his dealings with his tenants, and in his selection of them. They ranged from country gentlemen and civil servants in the more spacious and expensive lower apartments, to penurious artists, craftsmen, shopkeepers in the small, draughty, ill-equipped rooms under the roof which originally had been those of the servants. There were two bookshops already in the building when the 'Librairie de France' came there, but these were unlikely to offer much competition since both were scientific and technical.

The life of the considerable community, which the tenants formed, centred on the courtyard. It was a courtyard in which there was always something going on, always something to watch, a courtyard that in France's description was ever 'gay' with the movement of servants, tradespeople, the tenants themselves, the various animals they kept as their pets. A gnarled and spindly vine covered the wall at the entrance; above it a sundial, from which years of hard weather had erased the figures, dripped its stain into the stone. In a child's memory even insignificant details hold hard, and forty years later, France could still in his mind's eye, see the vine and the sundial with perfect clarity. When he wrote of the courtyard then, he contrasted its spaciousness which allowed room for light, life, and which enabled it to play a proper part as the core of the community which enclosed it, with the wretched 'wells' of the buildings then going up – 'four yards square with a pocket handkerchief of sky' at the top. France was a born spectator and was to retain throughout his life much of the insatiable curiosity of a child to see whatever happens to be going on. But that he awoke so early to the pleasure of simply watching was certainly in part due to the fact that in the great and gay courtyard of No. 15, quai Malaquais there was always something to watch.

France's early years passed mainly in the care and the company of the family servant whom he later characterized as 'Mélanie'. Mélanie came from the country, but had been in service in Paris all her working life. She was already old when France was born, but her 'radiant innocence made up for her lost youth and gaiety'. As well as her care and attention she gave France the gift of her natural, vigorous speech. Without effort or forethought, expressions 'savorous as the fruits of our orchards' flowed to her tongue. It was Mélanie, France considered, even more than his mother, who formed his speech – and not only his speech. It was Mélanie, France believed, who gave him his first idea of morality, which was considerably sounder, he later wrote, than most of those he acquired later. Most afternoons Mélanie would take France for a walk, sometimes to the Jardin des Plantes, sometimes to the Trocadero, then a hill covered with grass and bushes; sometimes to the Gardens of the Luxembourg or those of the Champs Élysées, where there was a perpetual fête, with roundabouts, goat-carts and grand guignol; sometimes simply along the banks of the Seine. Paris, then, was surprisingly countrified. Most of the houses had gardens with trees and bushes, whose branches hung over the walls, and some of the long streets which ran on to the *quais*, such as the rue Notre Dame des Champs, at their other end emerged into open country.

But France's legs were short and Mélanie's old. They did not often venture far along such streets. Yet each walk, however short, was an adventure for an imaginative child such as France, who when he was bored and alone would make up plays for himself with his fingers and thumbs for the actors, and whose bedroom walls at night were over-run with a succession of strange pictures that had tumbled out of his imagination. There were two houses in what was then the place d'Enfer – now by a curious transformation of name the place Denfert-Rochereau – linked by an iron grill. This, for France, was one of the entrances to a secret world. Another was a niche in the walls of the Tuileries that housed a marble goddess entwined by a serpent. France was sure that if one rolled away a stone below the statue one descended straight into the underworld.

The peaceful progress of France's walks with Mélanie, and of his childhood, was interrupted by the Revolution of 1848. France was not yet four when he awoke one morning to find himself being lifted out of bed by his mother to kiss his father who was wearing the uniform of a National Guard.

On the *quais* the bugles were sounding, the sounds of horses' hoofs were ricocheting round the narrow streets; in the distance France heard the crackle of musket-fire. The February Days had begun and the *bourgeois* monarchy of Louis-Philippe was about to fall.

France did not see much of the fighting. He was not allowed out until it was over and all the windows of his parents' flat looked inwards on to the courtyard. But even inside the building the excitement was immense. France's mother and Mélanie joined the other tenants in rolling bandages for the wounded. Few battle casualties seem, in fact, to have come their way, the only victim that France actually remembered treated being a portly neighbour who had caught a chill when an urchin had poured a bucket of water into the baggy pockets of his uniform. One evening France was taken into one of the larger apartments on the entresol which looked out across the river, and saw a blazing carriage dragged out from the Tuileries and tipped over the side of the Pont de la Carrousel into the river. For the first time, too, he heard the mob and for the rest of his life the sound echoed in his mind.

More important at this age, however, than the change of régime without, were the changes of régime within. Mélanie was growing old. For some time she had been losing her sight and her memory. Finally she retired to the country. Her going caused France the first real grief of his life. With her went 'the sweetness and joy of early childhood. My mother, who respected Mélanie, had the generosity not to be jealous of the love which I gave my old nurse. If this love was not as great or as respectful as the love I felt towards my mother, it was perhaps more tender and certainly more intimate . . . Mélanie had a heart as childlike as mine, and we were very close to each other in the simplicity of our thought.'

France was now put in the care of his grandmother, Mme Dufour, for whom Père France in 1849, had rented the flat

France at the age of 17

Madame Arman as she was when France met her

above theirs. Of his grandmother, France has painted two very different portraits. She was undoubtedly the original of the enchanting 'Grandmère Nozière' of *Le Livre de Mon Ami* – 'Grand'maman was frivolous; grand'maman had an easy morality; grand'maman had no more piety than a sparrow . . . she laughed at the seriousness with which my mother looked on the affairs of this world and of the other. She easily forgave my faults, and I think she was a woman to forgive faults greater than mine.' But she was no less certainly the formidable Mme Mathias of *Pierre Nozière* – 'with sunken cheeks, smouldering eyes beneath the grey locks of her hair . . . dark, dry, silent, her broken, disillusioned mouth, menacing chin and mournful silence afflicted my father'. France may not have been falsifying his memory in painting two such contrasting portraits. France's maternal grandmother lived a long time, until she was close to a hundred. He may simply have been depicting her at the two ends of their acquaintanceship – as he first remembered her while she retained something of her natural gaiety and as she became when the effect of her hard life with Dufour caught up with her.

Whether Dufour himself also lived in the flat above the Librairie de France is uncertain. He was certainly there some of the time; he was equally certainly not there much of the time. Yet however much or little Dufour came into the apartment of No. 15, quai Malaquais, he certainly had his place in France's life, for he often comes into his books – as Mathias in *Pierre Nozière*, as the swaggering Captain Victor of *Le Crime de Sylvestre Bonnard* who 'inspired me with much respect by his frogged coat and still more by his way of turning the whole house upside-down when he came into it.' – and as Uncle Hyacinthe of *Le Petit Pierre*, who was 'the terror and the shame of the family'. Despite his many misdeeds and misdemeanours, Jean Dufour seems to have introduced a needed element of rascally gaiety into a family circle that had perhaps become too closely constricted

c

by circumstance. Certainly, between the bogus, bibulous old soldier of the Empire and the bookseller's son, there seems to have been, if not a natural affinity, at least some natural affection. It was one afternoon when left in the charge of 'Bon-Papa' Dufour that France conceived, but did not carry out, one of his first literary projects – that of writing his autobiography. He was then eight. When at twice that age he did for the first time achieve print, his father flattering a prize-winning school effort by publishing it 'chez France, libraire', it appeared with a magnificent title-page that had been inscribed in the beautiful copper-plate hand of the old soldier, who earned the occasional sou as a professional letter writer.

Père France had done well with his bookshop, although in his son's opinion he was far more suited to reading books than to selling them, but even so, in the days of France's childhood there was little money to spare. France as a child never knew want, but there were many things that he wanted and could not have. Looking back from the detachment of his old age, France considered this no disadvantage, for 'to live is to desire' – yet at the time he may not have taken so philosophical a view of the advantage of being relatively poor.

On the social level, too, France's position was a difficult one. For Père France, in making his mark as a bookseller, and in the learned world which centred on the Institut, had raised the social level of his family. He and his wife were conscious of this and careful to maintain their position. As a result, France's childhood seems to have been more constricted and confined than most. For various reasons he was forbidden to mix with many of the other families who also lived at No. 15. He was not allowed to play with Alphonse, his natural companion, on the grounds that Alphonse had bad manners, bad habits and used bad language, but the real reason of the ban, one would think, was that Alphonse had bad social connections, in that he was the son of Pella-

pra's cook. To the credit of France's parents they also for-
bade him to play with the son of a Councillor of State,
because he was cruel to animals. Thus, for one reason and
another, as France summed it up, 'few people were judged
suitable to mix with me'.

His best friend at this time, as for most of his life, was
Étienne Charavay, the son of Jacques Charavay. But Étienne
was four years younger than France, and although such a
difference between them when they were grown-up was
negligible, at that age it was enormous. A child of eight does
not play with one of four when he has plenty of friends of
his own age. Much of the detail of France's early childhood confirms his own description of himself as 'an only
child, used to playing by myself, and always absorbed in
some reverie, living very much in the world of dreams'.

In 1853 the lease of the flat at No. 15, quai Malaquais ran
out and Père France either could not, or would not, renew
it. So the bookshop made the last move of its career – to the
neighbouring quai Voltaire, where at No. 9, Père France
rented a larger shop, and the flat above it. Here the Librairie
de France was to remain for the further thirteen years of its
existence. The move made little difference to its character
or clientele. It was still a *librairie à chaise*, it was still conveniently close to the Institut, and it was still something of a
club as well as a bookshop. France was to describe this last
halt of the bookshop in one of his first journalistic articles as
'a low shop, pretty large, neither very clear nor absolutely
sombre, very little decorated, having as its only luxury blue
paper on the shelves'.

Over the period of the move, France was sent to a
boarding-school in Versailles. On his return he started as a
day-boy at the Institution Sainte-Marie in the rue Bonaparte, just round the corner from the quai Voltaire. Two
years later, in October 1855, at the age of eleven, he entered
the senior school with which the Institution Sainte-Marie

was affiliated – the Collège Stanislas. It was here over the next seven years that he spent the remainder of his schooldays, which in his case proved to be far from the happiest of his life.

The Collège Stanislas, which had recently moved into the Hôtel Mailly, a great mansion in the rue Notre Dame des Champs, a short street's length from the Gardens of the Luxembourg, was run by Jesuits. As well as being one of the largest religious schools in Paris – it had some thirty masters, 200 boarders, as well as numerous day pupils, of whom France was one – it had the reputation of being one of the best. The social and economic level of most of the parents was considerably higher than that of the bookseller and his wife. The difference showed most markedly on special occasions when the pupils wore a blue uniform which for those with wealthy parents had been well cut by expensive tailors, but which for France had been made by a local tailor whom his mother knew to be down on his luck and in need of work.

France's tunic, by his own description, looked like a 'bell'. It had no shoulders, a dropped chest and left an inviting opening in the back of the neck down which his schoolfellows delighted in pouring pebbles. When France appeared in the school playground, wearing it for the first time, there was almost a riot. Even the abbé in charge, who had hitherto befriended France, could not face the ridicule of associating with so absurd a figure. 'Seeing me rigged out in this grotesque uniform, the Abbé Samler smiled discreetly and held me at a distance. He was an excellent man, but only a man; he did not like the idea of being included in the ridicule which I carried with me, nor to compromise his *soutane* with my tunic . . . This disgrace caused me some distress.' The distress was deep felt and long lasting. The pain still showed clearly twenty-five years later when France wrote about it in *Le Livre de mon Ami*. The feeling of inferiority and the resulting resentment which such incidents

ANATOLE FRANCE

produced did not help to make France a willing or respons-
ive pupil, and most of his masters found him obtuse,
apparently disinterested and very disinclined to work. Over
the years his reports varied from bad to worse – 'lack of
discipline . . . idleness', 'extreme nonchalance . . . negli-
gence', 'carelessness and frivolity . . . he sneers all the time.
A fly distracts him.'

The day of the *rentrée*, the beginning of the school year,
became one which France long dreaded; and long remembered. At the age of fourteen it provoked a passionate out-
burst in his diary . . . 'It has come at last, this day of terrible
memory . . . was there ever in heaven as good cause for
tears? Yes, there has been one year by year for the past
three years and there will continue to be one for the next
four.' When he was forty, the falling leaves and broken sky
of autumn could still bring back painful associations.
Crossing the Gardens of the Luxembourg in the first days
of October at that time of year 'when it is sadder and more
beautiful than ever . . . when the leaves are falling one by
one on the white shoulders of the statues', he would see in
his mind's eye the small figure of himself as a schoolboy
'hopping like a sparrow. Twenty-five years ago he used to
cross the beautiful gardens before 8 o'clock. His heart was
heavy. It was the *rentrée.*'

Stanislas left his mark on France in many ways. France
himself believed that having been 'a very intelligent child',
he 'became stupid' in the course of his schooldays. His
masters' reports and the fact that he failed several times the
examination for his baccalaureat, only finally passing it at
the advanced age of twenty, bear this out. France's stulti-
fying experience left him with a deep resentment of authority
and since authority at Stanislas was represented by the
Jesuits, his hatred of school spread into a deep distrust of the
Church also. Much of France's later anti-clericalism undoubtedly stemmed from unhappy and useless hours in the
classrooms of Stanislas.

37

But if at school France seems to have learnt little, on his way to and from it he seems to have learnt a lot. His masters at Stanislas had at least introduced him to the classics in which he immediately found a delight which lasted his lifetime. 'At seventeen,' he wrote later, 'I adored Virgil and I understood him almost as well as if my teachers had not explained him to me. On holiday I always had a Virgil in my pocket.' Earlier he had fallen under the spell of Homer – 'for six months I could not get out of the Odyssey'. Then it had been the turn of Sophocles and Euripides who 'opened to me an enchanted world of heroes and heroines, and initiated me into the poetry of misfortune'.

France formed the habit of reading and reciting parts of the classics to himself on his way to and from school. As he walked along immersed in his world of gods and heroes 'it often happened that I felt suddenly on my cheek the warm breath of some wretched horse, pulling its cart. Reality did not at all spoil my dreams, for I loved well the old streets of the faubourg, whose stones had seen me grow up. I remember, one evening, reading some verses of Antigone by the light of a chestnut-seller's brazier, and now after a quarter of a century I cannot repeat those verses . . . without seeing the old Aurergnat blowing into his paper bag, or without feeling at my side the heat of his stove on which the chestnuts were roasting . . . This was the way in which I studied the humanities.'

But it was not only the humanities that France studied on the way to and from school – he also studied humanity itself – 'Nothing is better than a street scene to enable a child to understand the social machine. He must see in the morning the milkmen, the water-carrier, the coalmen; he must press his nose to the windows of the grocer, the butcher, the wine-merchant; he must watch a column of soldiers passing with a band at its head; he must, in fact, have inhaled the air of the street to know that the law of work is divine; and that everyone has his task in this world.'

Fortunately, too, France's dislike of school does not seem to have clouded his love of books. Outside his home there were the long lines of the bookstalls on either side of the *quais* – few men, France would say later in his life, had had at their disposal in their youth a library three-quarters of a mile in length. Inside his home there were all the books of his father's stock. By contrast with Père France, who, according to France, had no interest in the books themselves, only in what they contained, France even as a boy was an ardent book-lover in the fullest sense of the word. 'There is no true love,' he wrote in *La Vie Littéraire*, 'without some sensuality. One can only find true happiness through books if one likes to caress them. I can recognize a true bibliophile by the way in which he handles a book.' In his father's bookshop France learned to handle books as well as to read them. At that age they were his playthings as well as his teachers. Jottings in his notebooks show him as a boy of fourteen playing at being a bookseller, speculating that the stock of this or that book, this or that writer, would rise or fall, sometimes using his pocket-money to back his judgement – not always successfully, so that on occasion Père France had to be called to the rescue. Not always did he let his son off lightly. There was the time when France got stuck with a book and suggested that his father should buy it off him. 'M. France valued it at five francs. I asked for ten.' In the end it was put on sale in the bookshop on France's behalf. 'So it is settled and sometime I will put it in order and make a card for it. But not today. I am in too bad a temper.'

He was also already a collector. Taking advantage of his father's somewhat vague supervision of his stock, he would sometimes sneak off with a dust-covered volume from the back of the shelves. But again Père France did not always prove to be as gullible and unobservant as his son liked to imagine. Once he had designs on a *Guide Archéologique*, but 'Papa was suspicious and hid it'. Another time he was

39

alarmed to find Père France querying the whereabouts of a book he had removed only the night before. So he had quickly to slip it back on the shelves.

France did, however, read as well as play with, the many books that passed through his hands. He learned also to bind and repair them, which remained a habit and a hobby throughout his life. Even in old age, often when he saw on a stall a set of a favourite author – Voltaire, Racine, Montaigne – in a bad condition, he would buy it, repair it as well as he could, and then give it away to any friend who would provide it with a good home. To see good books in a bad state seemed to France an indignity, an insult to his craft. It was almost as bad as if he had found Voltaire himself crouched on a corner, holding out his hat.

As well as books to read and to play with, the bookshop supplied France with conversations to be listened to – quite as important an influence at that impressionable stage in his life. If the evening group of Père France's customers and friends who met in the bookshop did not include the more distinguished of the daytime visitors, all those who gathered there were fond of books, of conversation and of the good things of life.

Not all of the talk was about books. There was much about people and, particularly, politics. The Parisians of that time had, France was to remember, 'a healthy sense of ridicule', which 'for an empire of reasons' of which the chief was probably the Second Empire itself with its oppressive system of censorship, he considered they afterwards lost. Any public figure at that time had to accept the fact that he was inevitably also something of a figure of fun. France was born, he considered, 'in the golden age of caricature'. It was from the lithographs of Charivaria and from the mocking remarks of those he listened to in his father's bookshop, that he formed his idea 'of public life, which still seemed comic, in spite of the riots and revolution amongst which I was brought up'.

Thus, if France's time in school seems to have given him little of value, his schooltime as a whole was far from being a complete loss. Books, his father's friends, life on the *quais* and in the streets leading off them, taught him as his masters were apparently unable to. Like other distinguished writers, France was educated much more away from school than at it.

Within his family circle, France's character developed under the dual influence of an affectionate opposition to his father and of an irritated devotion to his mother. France was fond of his father, yet their characters were in frequent conflict and contradiction, possibly because basically they were in many ways much alike. 'In all things by nature I opposed him,' wrote France of his father. 'Because he was optimistic and melancholy, I became pessimistic and joyful . . . As a romantic he took pleasure in the vague and indeterminate. I took it upon myself to like the ornate reasoning and beautiful judgement of classical art. Throughout the years these contrasts were accentuated and made conversation a bit difficult between us, without altering our mutual attachment. I owe this excellent father some qualities and a lot of faults.'

France's early devotion to his mother was such that at the age of eight he wrote her this birthday note – 'if you knew how much I love you and knew how much confidence I have in your love for me. Isn't it true that you will pardon me all the troubles I have caused you. I know well that if they continue they will lead you to the tomb. You must take more notice of this compliment than you did of my New Year one.'

But as he grew older, his love for his mother was limited by his irritation caused by her obsessive passion for her son. 'Ma mère,' wrote France in *Le Petit Pierre*, 'would have preferred me not to grow up so that she could hold me closely to her. And while hoping I was a genius, she rejoiced that I was without spirit and that hers was necessary to me. Everything which offered me a little independence

and liberty, was to her cause of offence. She would imagine
in terror the dangers that I ran without her, and I never
came back from a walk without finding her with a crimson
face and wild eyes.'

Where her son was not concerned, his mother was clear-
minded and reasonable, her outlook supported by a sturdy
country common sense which, much more than her excessive solicitude, drew her son to her. At table she would cut
through her husband's rhetorical flights by the 'unexpected
sallies of a very Voltairean wit'. She ran her house well and,
throughout the pages of her son's recollections, she shows
as a person of genuine kindness of heart. At France's death,
Paul Bourget was to remember her across a gap of sixty
years – 'that excellent mother, so refined in appearance, so
gentle in manners. Visibly, her son was all her joy, all her
pride, all her hopes. He felt it . . .'

The person, however, who, over the period of France's
late youth and early adolescence, probably influenced him
more than any other, certainly more than either of his parents, was not a member of his family at all. 'M. Dubois', the
Comte Dubois-Dubais, was not one of those who met most
evenings in the bookshop. He was not gregarious by nature;
on the contrary, he was something of a recluse. But he was
a frequent visitor to the bookshop in the daytime, and at all
times a constant caller at France's home, having a particular
attachment to France's mother, mainly because her serious
nature made her the perfect butt for his kindly, but mocking,
cynicism.

M. Dubois had served in Napoleon's armies, fighting
throughout the Russian campaign, but had left them in
1814 with an abiding hatred for the one-time emperor. In
spite of being, in France's words, *'ami des livres et des
femmes'*, he was rich and a bachelor. When he died in 1878,
he left over two and a half million francs to charity. He
lived alone, except for the company of a drunken housekeeper, in a beautiful old house in the rue Sainte Anne,

which he had inherited from his parents, and where the room in which his mother had died was left exactly as it had been at the time of her death.

M. Dubois devoted his leisure hours, which comprised the greater part of his life, to the cultivation of his taste, and the more he refined it, the more it turned his interest away from the present to the past. His aristocratically astringent attitude towards contemporary life, contemporary art, and his contemporaries in general, did much also to turn the awakening attention of his young protégé away from the present to past glories. By the time France met him, M. Dubois was a confirmed classicist. He would tell France – one must allow that over the gap of sixty years France's recollection was not word perfect, but the temper rings true – 'It was given to the Greeks to carry art to perfection. It was the privilege of a talented race, living in a good climate, under a clear sky, in a harmonious landscape, on the edge of a blue sea, practising the principle of liberty.'

Since M. Dubois was something of a recluse, an invitation to visit his house and see his collection was a rare privilege and, for France, a great occasion. The day when he went there was gloriously fine. On his way along the *quais*, the fresh breeze, the subtle, ever-changing colours of the river, the laughing sky, filled him with gaiety. 'I loved my great city . . . I loved my royal river, the Seine, so sage, so self-contained . . . I loved the great, famous and familiar *quais* . . . In those days they were enveloped in calm and beautiful silence, those beautiful *quais*.' An hour or so later, France came out of the house in the rue Sainte Anne, his head whirling with the glories of the past. Yet outside, the breeze still blew, the sun still shone, and not all France's admiration for M. Dubois' collection could dim his pleasure in the present. The pattern of this exceptional day seems, in a way, to symbolize that of France's life. For, however much he delighted in the past, he never forgot – he never could forget – that he was living in the present.

As well as forming and firming France's taste, M. Dubois influenced him in another way. Mr. Dubois believed in a quiet life. To do anything out of the ordinary, to write or to paint, to show in any way that one had talent was, in his view, to risk bringing on one's head the malicious envy of one's contemporaries which could shatter the peaceful flow of one's existence. Far wiser, he considered, to develop one's taste instead of one's talent, to watch rather than to work. When he aired such views, M. Dubois may not have intended himself to be taken seriously. His delight in teasing the mother, may at times have extended to the son. Yet he was taken very seriously indeed by his protégé, whether he intended to be or not. As it turned out, France was to go against his advice and to write a great deal: but there was always one side of his character which beckoned him towards the quiet shady grove of an indolent obscurity to which M. Dubois had shown him the path. Had he also possessed a title, a fortune of two-and-a-half million francs, and a charming old house in the rue Sainte Anne with a beautiful garden, with or without the drunken house-keeper, who knows whether France, too, might not have chosen to collect books rather than to write them.

France was over thirty when M. Dubois died. As a young man he did not see so much of him as he had as a youth, possibly for the reason he put forward in *La Vie en Fleur*, that once the soft wax of France's adolescent mind, in which M. Dubois had delighted to impress his thoughts, had hardened, it ceased to give him pleasure to communicate, particularly to 'a great oaf who often contradicted him, sometimes without respect or restraint'. Even so, at the end of a life which was almost as long as that of his mentor, France remembered M. Dubois as the most intelligent man he had ever known.

Looking back at it from the other end of his life, France was to see not only the place, but the people, of his childhood, mantled with affection. Since then, he considered, life on the *quais* had lost something of its charm and character. 'If I am not mistaken, there reigned on the *quais* at that time, a *douceur de vivre*, a familiarity, a friendliness of both people and things . . . an intimate charm, which do not exist today. It seems to me that people were closer to one another in those days. Perhaps it is simply that my childhood sympathies make it seem so.'

Perhaps it was. Yet France may have been born not only in an exceptional place, but at an exceptional time. The Revolution had cleared the air and removed much of the dead wood of the *ancien régime*. Napoleon had imposed an Empire whose lasting greatness lay in its efficiency rather than its military glory. Both these experiences were to contribute greatly to the make-up of the modern France. Yet at the time, many of the most valuable features of the old France still lived on. People were valued for what they were as well as what they did. The world was still small, life was slower. There was still time to spare – not so much of it as there had been, but a great deal more of it than there was to be in the future. Ephemeral things – good conversation, good taste, style of living – were valued as highly as other works of art more obviously made to last. It was to be the particular task of writers of France's generation to capture these qualities before they fled, to carry forward into the new France that was forming around them, the best of the old. Thinking, from the other end of his life, of men such as M. Dubois, who left nothing behind by which they could be remembered except their own remembrance, France was to write that their example made him suspect that 'some of the greatest of human values have perished without trace'. Much of France's life was to be spent seeking to express, and to recapture, the value of what he had seen and heard, the sense of values he had acquired, during the years of his childhood and youth on the *quais*.

Chapter

2

————◆◆————

'I LIVED several happy years,' wrote France in *Le Livre de mon Ami*, looking back from his middle age to his youth, 'before I began to write. I lived then a contemplative life of which the recollection is infinitely sweet to me. At that time, since I studied nothing in particular, I learned in general a great deal.'

France was writing of the period between 1862, in the summer of which he left Stanislas, and 1866, when his father sold his bookshop, thus forcing France to face up to the distasteful task of earning a living. It was not strictly true that France did not write at all during those years. He wrote quite a lot of verse, as did most young men with literary aspirations. Nor was his life either as completely contemplative or solitary as he suggests. For one thing he still had to pass his baccalaureat, and working for it took a good part of his time during his first years after he left school. For another, his father's customers and friends, all the people who came into the bookshop, provided him with much company, some encouragement, and a few odd jobs. His main concern, however, during these years, was coming to, and carrying through, the difficult decision that he did not want to become a bookseller like his father, and to carry on the family business.

It was a big decision to take. France had no illusions about the difficulties and dangers of the outside world, and grave doubts about his ability to make his way in it. Thought of the future, he later remembered, made him, at that time, worried and anxious. 'Straight away I had a presentiment that I would not easily find a place in a society in which, to succeed, one had to be prepared to elbow oneself forward. It was an art of which I knew nothing. I perceived that I was different from the others, without knowing whether it was a good or a bad thing.'

A photograph of him at the age of nineteen shows that there was some foundation for his fears. Adolescence is seldom an attractive age, and in France's person it seems to have been particularly unprepossessing. A long, equine face, very like his mother's; the hair cut *en brosse*, emphasizing the plainness of the face beneath; a receding chin falling away from a wide, non-committal mouth, whose edges were turned neither up nor down; even the fineness of the eyes seems at this age nullified by the fishy incomprehension of their stare. There is a touch of youth in the spotty cravat tied in the shape of a starfish, a touch of pretension in the watch-chain that creeps in and out of the crumpled waist-coat; and more than a touch of pathos in the baggy, ill-fitting suit – surely made by the same tailor who produced his school uniform. And yet in the midst of this adolescent waste-land, there was a core of character and courage sufficient to deflect France from the safe, secure life which opened before him into a hazardous and uncertain world full of perils and problems – if also of possibilities.

Why did France refuse to become the bookseller that his father so much wanted him to be, and that all his friends, and more particularly his father's friends, expected him to become? All the circumstances of his past, and all practical considerations for his future, pointed him towards the book-shop. He would have been able to start his career as a book-seller at the point where Père France left off – with, at his disposal, all the assets – a sound business, a firm reputation, a distinguished and dependable clientèle, many of whom were friends as well as customers – that it had taken his father most of his life to achieve. He would have been able to continue to live on his beloved *quais*. He would have spent his life among the books he already loved with passion; and if circumstances demanded that he should sell as well as read them, that would only have entailed a continuation, in rather more serious surroundings, of one of his favourite childhood games.

France himself would probably have said that in this he was simply following the line of most resistance, and that he did not want to become a bookseller mainly because his father wanted him to be one. Yet there was a lot more to it than this. A desire to prove himself, to escape from the parental cage, his mother's exaggerated but encouraging belief in his genius – all these played their part in his decision. But perhaps the most powerful spur of all, was the feeling that words, which were already his friends, might one day become his servants.

Ever since France had learned to write, words had come easily to his pen, more easily than to his lips, for he was a shy and hesitant speaker, at times afflicted with a slight stammer. Aged seven, he had produced his first work 'Nouvelles pensées et maximes chretiennes par Anatole', in which he demonstrated the goodness of God – 'Story; I was walking with someone who was talking foolishly: I said a little prayer to myself and he stopped talking. See how good is God.' As befitted so solemn a work, it ended with this ponderous pulpit injunction – 'My dear friends, follow this advice and you will go to Paradise. Listen to the counsels of this booklet, and pray evening and morning.'

At school it was only by his literary compositions that France in any way distinguished himself. One of them, a *Méditation sur les Ruines de Palmyre*, was placed in the Livre d'Or of the college. Another, *La Legende de Sainte-Radegonde*, written when France was sixteen, was crowned by a jury made up of the best pupils. This was the work which his father proudly published for him, 'chez France, libraire – 9, quai Voltaire'. France was always addicted to

short works, but this was one of his shortest. It ran to six
pages.

In his early teens, France went through a purple patch –
his holiday letters to his parents from Normandy are full
of wild winds, mournful churchyards, oppressive skies.
A little later on he became bogged in a slough of sentiment.
'I love. I need to love,' he noted in his journal of 1861, 'It
is towards the college that I turn my eyes. They do not
think as I do but they see as I see and perhaps sometime they
will understand my thoughts.' He added some character
sketches of his friends. Martel had little wit or talent but
was good-looking and had a good tailor – 'I do not despise
Martel in saying that. How often one sees people with less
intelligence than he who have neither good manners nor
good clothes to hide their stupidity.' De Lachenais he
respected while in his presence, but as soon as he went out
of sight he went out of mind. It was on Cazeaux that his
affections centred – 'Louis has a lot of friendship for me, and
shows it often enough. And for that I am grateful. It would
be unfair to ask anything else of him. It is not his fault if I
love him.' A subsequent mood of ill-temper condensed
these reports to – 'Martel, idiot; De Lachenais, empty-
headed; Homburg, false; and Cazeaux, egoist.' All of which
showed a lot of schoolboy sentimentality, but also some promise for France's future as a novelist.

After he left school, France's taste turned to poetry as his
thoughts turned to a more appropriate love. This time it was
a distant, essentially hopeless passion for an actress. France
had early shown a marked susceptibility to the theatre. On
his first visit, taken by his parents as a reward for a rare
scholastic success, he had fallen madly in love with the first
actress who walked on to the stage. His first love, however,
was not a long one. As he went to more plays, he fell in
love with more actresses – Isabelle Constant, Blanche
Pierson – but the most powerful passion of all was lit by
Élise Devoyod, an actress of the Comédie Française, some

six years older than France, who played Émilie and Phèdre in 1865, the year in which France came of age. During that year he wrote at least thirty-eight poems with Élise Devoyod in mind and heart – poems full of a romantic yearning for a grand amour, of some pretty painful passages, but poems which also showed here and there a natural feeling for words and a sense of rhythm which promised that their author might some day produce something worth while – if probably not poetry. About this time France started, and completed three scenes, of a poetic drama, built around a Falstaffian figure called 'Sir Punch'. All in all, in one way or another, France produced over the years of his childhood and youth, ample evidence to show that he was quite right in wanting to write books rather than to sell them. Yet it was still an immense and a courageous decision to take.

France filled in the time while he made up his mind to take the plunge and made up his father's that there was nothing he could do to prevent it, in various ways – working for his baccalaureat, doing odd jobs for his father and other booksellers, reading a lot, and, of course, wandering about, looking at people and things.

This time Père France coached his son for his baccalaureat, and since France opened his mind to his father and his father's books as he never had to his teachers at school, he was successful. In July 1864, at the age of twenty, in the company of Étienne Charavay then aged sixteen, France finally became a 'bachelier'. In the days of his fame, when he could afford to do so, France would laugh about his painfully prolonged efforts to pass an examination that should not have overtaxed anyone of even moderate intelligence, but at the time it can have been no joke, either to France or his parents.

It was in the year that he left school that France helped his father catalogue the library of the Comte de La Bédoyère who had died in 1861. The catalogue grew and grew, to become finally a volume of 700 pages. France wrote the notes on many of the individual items, and also much of the preface, since Père France already admitted, and modestly stood down before, his son's stylistic superiority. This was a job after his own heart. However, the more routine jobs, such as a period of clerking for another bookseller, Nottet, France found tedious, so much so that he grumbled that having looked forward to his freedom all through the years of his schooldays, he now found himself far less free than he had been while at school. But in reality he had a great deal of time to himself, the more so since his first ventures into the adult social world were not a conspicuous success – in fact, were not a success at all.

At this most vulnerable stage of his social growth, France was handicapped by his lack of looks, of assurance, and of a good tailor. Even the modest parties thrown by his father's friends and by his friends' fathers, into which he now ventured, placed many pitfalls in his path, few of which he managed to avoid. He was extremely shy and at any moment was liable to find himself tongue-tied, particularly when placed in front of any reasonably pretty woman. As a result, at any party he went to, he usually found himself, to his mute and muffled fury, anchored to the plain and unprepossessing, the only ones to whom he could talk.

Alternating between fits of paralytic shyness and compensatory bouts of rather ungracious garrulity, France cannot have been a very rewarding guest, and he was not often invited to be one. This left him a lot of time in which to read and to wander about. A generation later, France saw something of Proust, nearly thirty years his junior, then in the full flight of his butterfly youth. Proust, long an admirer of France's style, was also very impressed by France's learning, and once asked him how he came to know so many things. 'It is quite simple, my dear Marcel,' replied France, 'When I was your age, I was not good-looking like you. I was never asked out, but stayed at home reading, reading endlessly.'

This 'endless' reading, although at the time it may have seemed a poor substitute for the gayer activities of his more socially successful friends, was, in fact, the most valuable part of France's education. At this stage, he read without discrimination or restraint, without particular care or calculation; from curiosity as much as from a desire to acquire knowledge. In this choice of books he preferred the old. As well as the Greek classics, he delighted particularly in the works of French eighteenth century writers – here, as always, frequenting the by-ways as much as the main roads, so that lesser known figures such as Bouffon and Lesage became his friends as well as Voltaire and Beaumarchais – but he did not overlook the new. These were exciting publishing years in Paris. The first translation of Darwin's *Origin of Species* appeared in 1863 when France was nineteen, and a year later Michel Lévy published Renan's *Vie de Jésus*. Both of these books worked a long spell on France's mind. Ten years later, France still referred to the works of Darwin as his 'bible'. When Renan died in 1892, France wrote in a letter, 'Something of ourselves disintegrates with his death' – and it was true. Renan had kept so strong a hold on France over the years that in the end he had become virtually part of him.

Although he cannot have realised it at the time, this period of omnivorous reading was, in fact, to prove to be the first stepping-stone to his success. France was ultimately to become famous mainly for his style and his charm, but these were qualities which he developed relatively late in life. With his diffident, late-maturing temperament, he might never have reached a position in which he was able to do so, had he not earlier become invaluable to editors and publishers because of his immense store of literary knowledge, which enabled him to tackle virtually any subject they set him. France became a writer by way of becoming a journalist; and he became a journalist by way of being a publisher's hack.

But France not only read, he also looked – in shop windows, at the Seine, whose seasonal changes of scene always stirred some strain of his country ancestry, at pictures, but most of all, at the statuary in the Louvre, so conveniently close at hand. Here he was conscious, not only of the thrill of beauty, but for the first time, of its inspiration. Long afterwards he recalled that it was in the Louvre that he had first felt the desire to create beauty as well as to look at it, and that the satisfaction that he found in these Greek statues was one of the sharpest spurs behind his desire and decision to write.

Pleasant and valuable though they were, however, these formless but formative years could not be continued indefinitely. France's parents were not rich enough to support him for long and he had to think about earning a living. This he found disagreeable and difficult. If he was quite sure that he did not want to become a bookseller, he was far from certain what he did want to be. Even his wish to write was, at this stage, a nebulous inclination, which he might well have been able to satisfy in the margin of some other career. At the suggestion of his friends he considered several of them. He was put off medicine by watching an elderly medical student go through a public examination under the mocking eyes of a corpse stretched out on a slab, and of the examiners, stretched out in their armchairs. He was put off the Civil Service by his belief that the examination was simply a farcical formality to eliminate those who were not socially well-connected. He considered retiring to the country to cultivate his land, but was put off by the fact that he had not any land. He was thought, also, about this time, to have attended l'École des Chartes where Charavay and another friend, Édouard Pelletan (to become well-known as the publisher and printer of rare books) were studying to be archivists, but this he later denied – 'Ah, no. I was much too lazy for that. The truth is I often went to l'École but it was to pick up Étienne and Pelletan.'

As often happens, France's first proper job came apparently accidentally and quite unexpectedly. One Saturday afternoon, probably in late 1865, he was walking along the *quais* – it was, he was to remember fifty-five years later, exactly half-past four in the afternoon – when he met Louis de Ronchaud, the poet to whose conversation he listened with such delight in his father's bookshop. At the time of their meeting on the quai de la Conference, 'M. de Ronchaud was no longer young, without yet being old. Friends of his will know that in fact he was old in no time of his long life, for he never ceased being fond of things and people.' They chatted inconsequentially – about a Roman mosaic that had just been discovered at Lambessa, about the book that happened at that time to be the talk of the town. They parted. Then, struck by an after-thought, Louis de Ronchaud turned back. 'I was going to ask you to come and see me,' he said, 'I wanted to talk to you. Some friends and I are preparing for a well-known publisher . . . a Dictionary of Painters, to succeed that of Charles Blanc, which is no longer adequate.' He suggested France might take over the editorial part of the work. The publisher would pay him a salary and provide a room in which he could work. 'Three days later I was holding this extremely pleasant position which, while it would not last my whole life, would at least enable me to obtain . . . other work to my taste.'

The publisher was Bachelin-Deflorenne, whose premises were on the quai Malaquais only a few houses away from France's birthplace. The Dictionary of Painters was never, in fact, completed, but France, as he had hoped, found himself helping with other similar tasks, and was soon taken permanently on to the pay-roll as a part-time editorial assistant, with a monthly salary of between 100 and 150 francs. This, although it would allow France to grow neither fat nor rich, was a very reasonable wage in those days for a part-time job.

With this behind him, one would have expected France,

dilatory and disinclined as he seemed to be at this stage to look for work, to have rested content for a while. But, in fact, in the autumn of that year, on the eve of the sale of the bookshop – and perhaps spurred on more by his parents' concern than by his own – he applied for a job as an assistant librarian at the Bibliothèque du Sénat. The post did not carry with it a great deal more money than he was getting from Bachelin-Deflorenne, but it involved very little actual work – it was mainly intended as a sinecure for aspiring or exhausted writers – and it would have given France an entrée into a wide stretch of the literary world round which opportunities of making friends, money and possibly a name, might in time accumulate. But fate, which had opened the front door to an easy life by offering him his father's bookshop – only to see it soundly slammed – was not going to allow him to sneak in by a side entrance. France applied for the position in the autumn of 1865 and again in January 1866, but although his applications were backed by the Baron de Barante, Paul Lacroix, and other distinguished friends of his father, they were turned down. France was eventually to get the post, but not for a further nine years – by which time a lot of ink had flowed from his pen.

At the end of June, 1866, the bookshop was sold to someone called Simon, who has otherwise sunk without trace. For many, its sale must have been a sad occasion – particularly so, of course, for Père France, for whom it meant not only the end of his life's work, but the end of his life on the *quais*. He moved first to a temporary lodging in the rue de Seine, then to a more permanent one in its prolongation, the rue de Tournon. Thirty-six years before, Balzac had lived at No. 21. Père France now took a small flat on the fourth floor of No. 5.

Apart from Père France, those who grieved the most, were the group of friends who regularly met there of an evening. One of them, Antoine de la Tour, showed his sorrow in a letter to Père France – 'I cannot resign myself to seeing you leave the fine little bookshop which framed you so well . . . where one breathed the atmosphere of classical integrity as well as of fine books. I had hoped to see it not change its name but simply to be rejuvenated, and I regret that things did not turn out that way.'

The Goncourts mourned and marked the sale of the bookshop as the end of an easier, more leisurely epoch of social life, and for France, too, it was the end of an epoch, but a more personal one, that of his childhood and youth on the *quais*. But for him the end was also a beginning, the beginning of his independence. For when Père France and his wife left the quai Voltaire for the rue de Seine, France did not go with them. Exactly where he did go is not known, but for at least a year and a half, possibly two years, he lived on his own. In April 1867, a telegram telling him of the death of his godfather, Jacques Charavay, Étienne's father, found him at 3 bis rue des Beaux-Arts. The following year he lived for a while at No. 4 rue du Pré-aux-Clercs. But by August of that year, and possibly earlier, he was back with his parents in the rue de Tournon.

A few weeks' absence from home would probably indicate only a temporary arrangement to cover the inevitable disorganization of a move, yet that France prolonged his absence long after the dust had settled, seems to show that it was a real attempt to stand on his own feet – possibly, too, that the atmosphere in his home over the months preceding the same had become so strained that it was thought best he and his father should separate for a while. France himself admitted that, over this period, while remaining as timid as ever in public, he had become 'insupportable' in the privacy of his own home.

Père France, on his side, had good grounds for feeling resentful towards this obstinate and opinionated son who spurned the offer of a secure and satisfying life, simply because of what his father looked upon as a disastrous liking for 'blackening paper'. In fact, a feeling of pique and general disgruntlement at his son's mulish behaviour may well have played its part in leading the bookseller into what appears to have been a premature, and regretted, retirement. At the time of the bookshop's sale, Père France was hardly sixty, in excellent health – he was to live through a vigorous old age until he was eighty-four – and there seems, on the face of it, to have been no practical reason why he should not have continued to sell, talk and live books on the *quais* for many more years – no matter what his son decided to do, or not to do.

Freed of the cares of the bookshop, Père France does not seem to have found it easy to fill the hours they occupied. He continued to give expert advice to other booksellers when it was needed – for a period he was his son's colleague at Bachelin-Deflorenne – and to do a certain amount of cataloguing, but these tasks were not enough to fill more than a part of his time. The rest he tried valiantly to occupy by learning Hebrew, Copt and Egyptian. Like his son, he also tried his hand at verses, before – sensibly – settling for bowls.

In later life, France rarely referred to this time on his own, and his silence about it – since he talked, and wrote, at length about most other periods of his life – seems to show that he looked upon it as something of a failure. But he mentioned it once to Brousson, his secretary, one afternoon nearly forty years later when they were strolling in the area of the Val du Grace, which is also that of the rue du Pré-aux-Clercs. Caught in a circling current of time, France's mind was carried back to those days of youthful independence, and he told Brousson that he had a particular liking for the quartier through which they were walking since he had lived there for a while in his youth. He had then been very poor. 'I lived . . . in a garret, up under the roof. It was about as big, and as comfortable as a swallow's nest. To write, I had to push my table out on to the gutter, which wasn't at all convenient when it rained. In bad weather I had to work in bed. But when it was fine, as I scribbled away in my vertiginous gutter, I perceived the shadows of birds and of clouds flit across the page . . . and then, mon ami, I had neighbours. Ignorant as I was, I gave them lessons. They gave them to me also. Their knowledge was far the greater than mine: their great subject was love. From our bed we could see the cupola stolen from Sainte Génévieve, to cover the remains of the Republican saints. Was it the decor? I have never felt such ardour . . .'

Yet in retrospect, the experience probably appeared more romantic than it had seemed at the time. There can have been little glamour in a garret, hot in summer, cold in winter, with nothing that could be called a convenience, let alone modern. As well as the discomfort, there was the loneliness, and the boredom of fending for himself – and no-one was ever less suited to looking after himself than France. All through his life he was notoriously bad at coping with the small practical matters of day-to-day existence. At the age of sixty, he still had the greatest difficulty in dealing with such things as changing a shirt, taking a ticket for a journey, or paying a bill. There is no reason to think he was any better at such things in his youth. His mother's profound, but possessive, love, had not helped him in this, since even when he was grown-up, she delighted to do everything for him.

These months on his own, if they revealed to France some of his personal limitations, may also have opened his eyes to some of the larger problems of life. For the first time, France rubbed shoulders with real poverty and distress. By his own standards he may then, as he told Brousson, have been 'very poor', yet he had his salary from Bachelin-Deflorenne and his parents would see to it that he was never seriously in want. But around him there were many whose lives were pared down to the minimum of existence. France, in later life, was always compassionate towards genuine poverty, although he sometimes turned his face away from it. It was probably at this time that he acquired his understanding of what poverty really meant. In his first novel, *Les Désirs de Jean Servien*, written some four years later, France put his hero into a position of youthful susceptibility and through a period of experimental independence very like his own. In it he showed Servien at one moment surveying the street scene while his aunt chatted with a friend. As Servien did so, 'the savour of humble, human existence, a particular feeling for the miserable, inactive and resigned lives of insignificant people, moved powerfully the plebeian blood in his veins. In that moment, between these two old women, the colour of stone, whose only life was that of the street, sometimes sombre and solitary, sometimes sunny and thronged with people, the young man learned more about life than he ever had at school.' So perhaps did France during the time that he lived in a garret in the rue du Pré-aux-Clercs.

Life in the raw, however, is often something of a shock. From his garret window, France looked out at a very different angle from that to which he had been accustomed in the safe security of his father's bookshop. The shadows of swallows might flick across his page on a sunny day, but always beside him was the vertiginous drop to the street below, reminding him how close he stood himself to the poverty and failure he saw around him.

About this time there was a considerable change in France's attitude. The idle apprentice suddenly decided to work. The truculent, rather tendentious youth, in revolt against authority, whether it took the form of a schoolmaster or his father, suddenly decided to accept the world's terms rather than to seek to impose his own. Was possibly the cause of this change the shadow of fright that fell across his mind at the same time as the shadows of the swallows flicked across his pages?

For whatever reason, or reasons, France decided to return to the nest – a touch of fright, a dislike of discomfort,

a resurgence of affection for his family, free to flow again
now that he had had his own way, and most probably a
mixture of all three – he was back there by August 1868,
for on the 28th of that month, Père France wrote a letter to
a bookseller friend, Bossange, which shows clearly that not
only was his son again living at home, but that while the
ex-bookseller still disapproved of his decision to write, and
foretold that only disaster would come of it, he now left him
alone to go his own way – 'What I feared most since his
childhood . . . has happened. He has always been absorbed
by this idea that has made him throw away his career. I
have given up struggling with him, for fear of making him
leave home. Will he have enough talent to live? Alas! Alas!'

In fact, for all his father's predictions, and his own pre-
monitions, of disaster, now that France had decided to accept the world's terms, he did not find them so hard. Once
the bookshop was sold, his father's friends were eager to
help him if they could and often they were able to. His life-
line remained his job with Bachelin-Deflorenne, but at the
end of 1866 another publisher, Roudiez, whose shop was in
the rue Dauphine, put him in charge of a bibliographic periodical, *Le Chasseur Bibliographe*, whose appearance had
hitherto been so periodic that there had been a gap of several
years since its last issue. Now under France's guidance, it
ran for a further three issues and three months, from
January to March, 1867. France was not only its editor and
secretary, he also wrote dramatic criticism as Anatole
France, book reviews as A. Thibault, and the article on his
father's bookshop entitled 'Un foyer s'éteint', which he
signed 'Un bibliophil'. To one issue, his father contributed,
out of the vast fund of his Revolutionary knowledge, an
article on Marat's *Ami du Peuple*; and in another, the last,
France included an immense poem of his own, La Legende
de Sainte-Thais, which ran to 274 verses – interesting historically as the precursor of one of his most famous works, but
possibly a reason, amongst others, for the abrupt return of

Le Chasseur Bibliographe to the limbo of unpublished periodicals.

In May of that year, France wrote his first article for another bibliographical journal, *l'Amateur d'Autographes*, run by France's godfather, Jacques Charavay. It was his only contribution that year. But in the same year, Jacques Charavay died, and Étienne, his son and France's closest friend, found himself at the age of nineteen, having to assume responsibility for a large family – he had two sisters and two brothers – for the family business, and, indirectly for *l'Amateur d'Autographes*. Charavay bore manfully the many burdens laid so prematurely on his shoulders – although they nearly cost him his degree as an archivist, for he passed out of l'Ecole de Chartes bottom of his batch. But it was only natural that to help him run *l'Amateur d'Autographes*, he should turn to France, not only because of the friendship between them, but because France's background and upbringing had already put a large fund of bibliographic knowledge and experience at his disposal.

From 1868 until 1875, few issues of *l'Amateur d'Autographes* appeared without containing some contribution from France. In its pages he tackled a wide range of critical and bibliographic subjects, and this for France was an invaluable experience, not only because it gave him confidence that what he wrote was printable, but also forming his ideas and style. On the wider stage that *Le Temps* was later to provide, France might not have been able to perform with such skill and assurance had he not earlier rehearsed his role so well before the few readers of *l'Amateur d'Autographes*. For Charavay, France's collaboration changed what otherwise would have been an arduous and worrying responsibility into something of a game shared between friends. France and Charavay used at this time to frequent the Procopé, a café in what was then the rue de l'Ancienne Comédie, that Voltaire had once used and where there was still a table at which he was supposed to have been served.

There the two of them would talk far into the night, shaping the future of the world, and the next issue of *l'Amateur d'Autographes*.

If, in spite of his forebodings, France's literary career seemed to have got off to a good start, it was still contained in what was little more than an extension of his family circle, for Bachelin-Deflorenne, Roudiez, Nottet and, of course, the Charavays, were all firm friends of his father; and their shops, offices, houses, all lay close to that enchanted area on the *quais* which, all through his life, France was to look upon as particularly his own. It therefore symbolized a real step into the outside world when, sometime in April 1867, France crossed the Seine and, if he followed the direct route, skirted the buildings of the Tuileries, many of which were to be destroyed four years later in the fighting at the time of the Commune, passed by the Théâtre de Comédie Française, along the narrow ravine of the rue Richelieu to the grim, prison-like building of the Bibliothèque Imperiale, before side-stepping through a criss-cross of small streets to the Passage Choiseul, a quiet arcade in which the shop of Alphonse Lemerre, an up and coming young publisher, lay submerged in a soft, subdued, sub-aqueous atmosphere. With him, France brought an introduction from his father and some of his own poems. Lemerre seems to have been impressed by both, for he gave France some odd jobs in his office, and published two of France's poems in his *Gazette Rimée* – to which, however, they brought no more luck than had France's contributions to *Le Chasseur Bibliographe*. *La Gazette Rimée* also folded up before the end of the year.

But even if *La Gazette Rimée* disappeared, France stayed, a habit of his when he was in a place where he wanted to be. In fact, though, it was no more calculated than the walk along the *quais* on which he met Louis de Ronchaud, he could not have come to the Passage Choiseul at a luckier time.

For Lemerre, an assertive, assured man of business with a profitable penchant for poets – he was described by one of them as a stockily built man with a vast chest (shortly to be supported by a vast stomach) shoulders and arms of a boxer and a face which combined something of a Roman Pro-consul with a touch of a cattle-dealer – was in himself and in his own line, something of a prodigy. Only six years older than France – that is to say, when France went to work for him in 1867, he was still in his twenties – he had already made his mark and an impressive place for himself in the world of publishing. He had started a few years before as an assistant in the shop he now owned, which then specialized in religious books. Managing to raise enough capital to buy out his former employer, he had overnight transformed the shop into a publishing house, concentrating on poetry at a time when no other publisher would touch it; his first venture being an edition of the famous French poets of the sixteenth century. From the first, his sails caught the wind of both fashion and fortune; but even so, his business was some time gathering way. During these lean years, it was largely supported by the earnings of a dress shop on the other side of the arcade run by his newly-married wife. Over this period, every sou in the till of the modiste's had to be hurriedly taken over to the other side of the Passage Choiseul to balance the books or pay a printer's bill.

It is a charming picture – the young couple joining hands across the arcade and backing their faith in their poets with the francs they made in the dress shop. But there was nothing sentimental about Lemerre's approach to his authors. Those poets that he agreed to publish had themselves put up the cost of the initial 500 copies. These expenses were returned to them three months later, if all went well; but while the subsequent glory was theirs, the subsequent profit was Lemerre's. This was an arrangement they did not always appreciate, and in later years his relationship with many of his authors was often to founder on financial bickerings.

But during this first period of beanstalk growth, everything that the happy and successful young publisher touched, seemed to turn to gold. When, out of the profits from his poets, Lemerre bought a country villa at Ville d'Avray, he found in the summer house, four original frescoes by Corot, which when sold, more than paid for the cost of the whole property. Yet, while Lemerre was undoubtedly close-fisted in his dealings with his authors so far as money was concerned, in other ways he gave them much. He kept more or less open house – his lunches soon became famous, even in so gastronomic and gregarious a city – and to a group of poets who previously had been wandering somewhat aimlessly in the wilderness, he gave not only a cohesion and a unity they had hitherto lacked, but a platform, a meeting-place and even a name. They had been thinking of calling themselves 'les formalistes', but after the publication by Lemerre of the first volume of 'le Parnasse contemporain', a collection of their verse, they were simply 'le Parnasse'. Every evening between five and seven, they met in Lemerre's shop, in the small entresol, whose half-moon windows looked out on to the arcade, reached by a spiral staircase on which the late arrivals had to sit.

The publication of 'le Parnasse contemporain' in 1866, a year before France came to work of Lemerre, brought to a head, and to the notice of the public, a movement of poetic opinion that had, for some time, been gathering weight, ammunition and adherents in the cafés, bars and 'boîtes' of Montparnasse. For a while it was the talking and arguing point of literary Paris. In its inspiration it was a movement of reaction against the long run of romanticism. In its theory, it was a movement of reliance on art for its own sake. In its character, it was a movement of detachment that suppressed individuality, discounted personality and depended for doing so on rigid technical rules which removed the author as far as possible from his work.

It was a hard school and it had a hard master, for although there were several who disputed the honour of founding Parnasse – notably two young litterateurs of France's age, Louis Xavier de Ricard and Catulle Mendès – the undoubted and undisputed pivot around which it revolved, was Leconte de Lisle. A small but formidable figure much older than most of the group, and more than twice France's age, born and brought up in the strange stratified society of the Ile Bourbon, now Reunion Island, Leconte de Lisle mingled in his veins the pride of the patrician, the arrogance of the colonial estate owner and a touch of Creole laziness that made him inherently ineffective and impractical in the smaller things of life, such as making a living.

At this time, Leconte de Lisle was just emerging from a long spell of penurious obscurity, during which he had often been close to starvation, and during which he had had little else to sustain him but his pride as a poet. This period of poverty, and possibly of humiliation, had left its mark. One would think that it was chiefly as compensation and consolation for the hardships that he had been through that his position in Parnasse was so important to him. It made up for much that he had now gathered around him what was virtually a band of disciples, to whom he was indisputably 'cher maître'. In Parnasse his judgement was final, his word law. One suspects that this authority was what mattered most to him – more than the movement of poetic force he headed, or, even, the poems that he wrote. His ancestors had set their slaves to work to produce sugar and vanilla. He set his to produce verses.

Before France was allowed to join the group which gathered most evenings in the room on the entresol, he had to serve his apprenticeship in the shop below. But it was not long before Lemerre realized that France wrote with a particularly pleasant pen, and that he could back it with a

surprisingly wide range of literary knowledge. In consequence, he soon admitted France to his friendship and his
patronage, allowing him to stay on after his work so that
he could listen to all that was going on.

A great deal always was. For, having caught the ear of
the public, there was no lack of poets, men of letters, and
artists of all sorts, wishing to speak into it. Apart from
Leconte de Lisle, Ricard and Mendès, the most prominent
of these early Parnassiens, were Sully-Prud'homme, a
delightful, devoted man of letters, of whom France was to
become increasingly fond, with a charming lyrical gift
which was to be sadly blanketed by Parnassian theory;
José-Maria Heredia, a benevolent, indolent Cuban, of half-
Spanish, half-French descent, who devoted his life to the
perfecting of 118 sonnets, finally published in 1893 as *Les
Trophées*; the warm-hearted François Coppée, soon to de-
sert Parnasse for more popular and profitable fields; and
Villiers de l'Isle Adam, an aristocratic vagabond vowed to
poverty by his extravagance and romantic ideas. Baudelaire
had contributed his *Nouvelles Fleurs du Mal* to the first
collection of le Parnasse contemporain, but was to die the
year after its appearance.

The movement also had the blessing of such senior and
influential figures in the literary world as Théophile
Gautier and Théodore de Banville. Gautier, whose
daughter subsequently married Mendès, much against her
father's will, had, with his impersonalized poems, provided
Parnasse with its point of departure; and it was Banville, a
versatile poet and distinguished dramatist, who had first
shepherded the, as yet, incohesive flock of poets to Lemerre.
But it was the younger generation of Parnassians who were
to be touched most generously by fame. Mallarmé, Verlaine
and Paul Bourget, as well as France, were to serve their apprenticeship there. There were others, also, who were not to
hold the place of importance for posterity that they had in Lemerre's shop – Léon Dierx, Louis Ménard, Mérat, Henri

Cazalis, who wrote under the name of Jean Lahors, André Lemoyne, amongst them. Nor was it only writers and poets who came to the evening meetings in the entresol. Manet was the most famous of several artists who regularly climbed to Parnasse by way of the spiral staircase.

At first the Parnassians showed little interest in France or his work. They admitted his presence – they could hardly do otherwise since he worked for Lemerre and they met in Lemerre's shop – but they did not notice it. Even Xavier de Ricard, who for the next three years was to be a close friend, admitted that France was only reluctantly allowed into their meetings, that it was a long time before they would acknowledge him as being 'de la maison'.

But during the first half of 1868, several factors were to force the Parnassians to take more notice of France, whether they liked it or not – and, fortunately as it turned out, they did. In February, Lemerre started a new periodical, *La Gazette Bibliographique*. France contributed two articles to the first issues and in later ones had his own column. Coincidentally rather than competitively, Bachelin-Deflorenne started in May *Le Bibliophile Français Illustré*. France was one of the editorial committee and as well as writing several important articles – one about his father's patron, the Comte de La Bédoyère – contributed a regular column of 'Books of the Month'. With so much journalistic space at his disposal, France became someone worth knowing.

Yet even while they admitted his presence and his usefulness, the Parnassians might not for a while yet have admitted that he was really one of themselves, but for the publication in May by Bachelin-Deflorenne of France's first book, a study of Alfred de Vigny. This was his proper passport to Parnasse.

France clearly intended that it should be. As such, there were several reasons why the choice of de Vigny as a subject should particularly commend itself. Not only was he a perfect example of the gentlemanly, detached poet, devotedly following his Muse regardless of the vicissitudes of everyday life, but he had been the close personal friend of Xavier de Ricard's father, a Napoleonic general, now enchained by ill-health and old age to his Paris apartment. De Vigny was also the acknowledged model and master of Leconte de Lisle. In his text, France managed adroitly to pay tribute to both by writing, '(de Vigny's) influence was apparent when the Academie crowned Leconte de Lisle's *Poèmes Antiques*, one of the greatest works of modern poetry'.

The seriousness of France's intentions, which he bared in his preface, carried echoes of 'Nouvelles pensé es et maximes Chretiennes par Anatole' – 'We have tried to tell the simple story of a great poet, but also a gallant man, because it seems to us instructive to seek out under what conditions great works are produced . . . we have tried to produce the example of a fine life from which have emerged fine works.'

Yet although France followed faithfully enough his original plan to be certain of Parnassian approval, his book did not come out as he expected. In fact it showed some encouraging signs of a life of its own. Comments such as this on de Vigny's schooldays – 'His schoolfellows beat him because he was weak. The reason was excellent and childhood has an implacable logic,' – had a bitter ironical twist drawn, one would think, from his own experience, rather than from that of his subject. There were also signs of a growing sense of style, a more mellow, more mature use of words – 'Alfred de Vigny dans son enfance, avait dévouré beaucoup de memoires et de chroniques, et depuis n'avait cessé de respirer cette pousière du basse, incéssament remuée autour de lui' – and some of considerable insight – 'M. de Vigny understood the historical novel in a strange way, it was for him the opportunity of substituting for real people, types and almost abstract symbols who took their names from their clothes. Under the name of Richelieu the author showed Ambition. Friendship was called De Thon.'

In spite of France's deliberately eulogistic approach, his heart does not seem to have followed his head and one has, throughout, the impression that, on closer acquaintance, France liked De Vigny much less than he had expected to. However, the Parnassians were content to read along the lines and not between them, and after the publication of *Alfred de Vigny*, made France one of themselves.

Now that he had been admitted into their circle, France was able to mix with the younger Parnassians on more or less equal terms, for he was of much the same age. Verlaine, Ricard, Mendès, Heredia, Coppée and Mallarmé were all born within two years of himself. Some years later, in *La Vie Littéraire*, France was to remember and refer to these companions and colleagues of his literary youth – Coppée, 'a natural poet. As such he is also unique, for the natural in life is the rarest of all things'; Mendès, 'in the whole of Paris, the man the most devoted to literature, and the least prone to envy and petty ambition that I know'; Herédia, the only one who could afford to dress 'as a young gentleman and to smoke cigars. His cravats had as much éclat as his sonnets. But we were only jealous of his sonnets'; Mallarmé, 'this proud and gentle spirit, inflexible and generous'; Louis Xavier de Ricard, 'with his apostle's brow, his inflamed eye, his aesthetic thinness . . . the doctrinaire of impassivity' who 'did not write a single verse that is not a violent expression of his political, social or religious passions'; Verlaine, not yet 'le sorcier de village', as France was later to see him 'with his bald, bronzed head, battered like an ancient cauldron . . . a Socrates without his philosophy and without his self-possession', but at that time living 'like the majority of the Parnassians . . . a modest and monotonous existence favourable for dreaming and the patient work of versifying, the prisoner of an office'.

To these newly-won friends, France now added Fernand

Calmettes, recently a student at the École du Chartes with Charavay, whose sister he was soon to marry. Calmettes was one of those talented and promising people who cannot stick long enough at any one task to find either satisfaction or success. Having given up thought of becoming an archivist, he now aspired to be an artist. Later he was to try his hand at writing. France introduced him – and also Charavay – to Parnasse, of which, forty years later, he was to write an account under the title, *Leconte de Lisle et ses amis*. France's success, or perhaps Calmettes' lack of it, was ultimately to sour their friendship, although Calmettes' son Pierre was, over the last twenty years of France's life, to be a devoted follower – virtually a member of France's household. But for the time being, France, Charavay and Calmettes formed a close trinity that gave a comfortable feeling of personal support amidst much that was still strange and insecure.

Of the Parnassians proper, France seems, during these years, to have come closest to Louis Xavier de Ricard. In the late summer of 1868, the two of them collaborated in writing a one-act play, *Le Valet de Mme. la Duchesse*, which they submitted to the Comédie Française, where it was forgotten until it was unearthed thirty-five years later by the then director, Ginesty. Since France was by then famous, it was at that time seriously considered for production, and only an anguished letter from France imploring that they should not reveal and ridicule the shortcomings of his youth, put it back on the shelf.

Together France and Ricard also conceived the idea of bringing out an *Encyclopédie de la Revolution*, a mammoth work designed to cover all aspects of the Revolution in twelve quarto tomes. They even went as far as drawing up and arranging an extremely distinguished list of contributors that included Michelet, Edgar Quinet, Louis Blanc, as well as Leconte de Lisle; and published a prospectus in *l'Amateur d'Autographes*. Financial support was to be provided by a banker, Joublin, who was to advance a quarter of a million francs. But when it came to the point, no funds were forth-coming, so neither was the Encyclopaedia.

They did, however, contribute to another encyclopaedia – the immortal work of reference which Larousse was com-piling in the rue St. André des Arts, a long sinuous street running parallel to the quais Voltaire and Malaquais. Ricard has described how every Saturday morning he would pick up France at his home, and how they would go on together to Larousse's office, to join the queue of other con-tributors hoping for commissions or payment – 'Regularly every Saturday we made our way to the rue St. André des Arts to appear before Larousse, the compiler of the great dictionary of the nineteenth century. I can still see the small courtyard with the large staircase on the left and on the first floor, the room full of books where everyone anxiously awaited their turn. He was a thoroughly good fellow, Père Larousse: all the same, we never approached him without a qualm; he had his bad days when he was moody and defiant, and one was always so afraid of having to go down again without the small sum one was hoping for, and for which possibly one was not the only one hoping. The young of today do not know how providential was Larousse for the young that we were.'

Larousse paid two sous a line, not a great deal, but more than some editors and publishers allowed, for in those days opportunity was more plentiful than payment. Many editors and publishers allowed their authors little or nothing more than the pleasure of seeing themselves in print. These were the hard facts of the literary life, underlying the super-ficial charm of an apparently easy-going existence, and they forced out of even so senior, so well-respected, and pre-sumably well-paid a writer as Théodore de Banville, the indignant and anguished cry, 'In Paris, d'you hear, one needs to be a genius to earn ten sous.'

France himself was by now better placed than most. In the summer of 1869, Lemerre took him permanently on to his pay roll as a part-time editor, at 120 francs a month, slightly less than he was already getting from Bachelin-Deflorenne. He also quickly enlarged his journalistic contacts. In November 1869 he started a series of articles of general literary criticism for *La Rappel*; and in the spring of the following year, began a regular column in which he was mainly concerned with drama and history in *La Vogue Parisienne*, which he continued for several years. There were also occasional jobs that must have brought him in reasonable remuneration as well as repute. One such, arranged in the autumn of 1868 by his father, whom it particularly pleased since, as Père France wrote to a friend, 'only made men were engaged in this work', was to contribute an article on Greek mythology to Hachette's *Dictionnaire d'Antiquités*.

The key that opened Parnasse to France, also unlocked many other doors. Paris at this time was a city of salons, ranging from select social soirées to the nightly meeting of habitués in certain cafés, where the right of admission was bought for the price of a cognac or of a cup of coffee. Now that Parnasse was popular, the poets who composed it were widely welcome and France, as one of them, had his share of social as well as literary success.

The Parnassians themselves also had their own gatherings. Louis Xavier de Ricard and his mother gave regular receptions at No. 10 boulevard de Batignolles, receptions at which the high spirits of the guests sometimes contrasted with the infirm presence of the aged general. Catulle Mendès also entertained in the rue de Douai. But, as one would expect, the most serious meetings were those which took place every Saturday evening in the small fifth floor flat at No. 8 boulevard des Invalides, the home of Leconte de Lisle. These were not so much convivial gatherings as councils of war of an attacking literary movement. With the sole exception of the diminutive hostess, it was entirely a 'salon mâle'.

As a host, or commander-in-chief, Leconte de Lisle made

a formidable figure. He was small in stature, but none the less dominated proceedings. Any presumptuous or unruly guest was quickly frozen into silence by an autocratic stare from the eye-glass which he wore to disguise a squint. France, at this stage, was so over-awed by his companions and the exacting atmosphere that he hardly opened his mouth, and, according to Calmettes, spent most of the evening on the edge of his chair at the edge of the room as if 'intimidated by these people who imposed their superiority on his still unformed character'.

Calmettes has left a detailed description of France as he remembered him at this time – 'Wishing to extend his amiability, the young France dilated his eyes, so that they seemed about to pop out of his head . . . he spoke with his hand under his chin, cupping the palm as if to stop his words falling to the ground . . .; he stammered, searched long for his words . . . From his education at Stanislas he had picked up a habit of inclining his body forward; also of forcing his smiles so that one thought him obsequious.' If some of the detail of this description was clearly etched by the acid of Calmettes' resentment, there is no reason to fault the general impression of awkwardness and unease.

Some of the sharper edges of France's character were, however, removed in the course of his visits to a salon of a very different sort. Together with many of the other Parnassians, France went regularly, possibly by way of light relief after the exacting sessions in the boulevard des Invalides, to the 'salon des ratés' – the salon of failures – of Nina de Callias, a young heiress whose purpose and pleasure in life was to entertain. To belong to Nina's 'salon des ratés' one had, theoretically, to have written, painted or composed, some work too advanced, too abstruse or simply too unlucky to have caught the popular taste. 'You have no need of evening dress chez moi,' Nina would say, 'a sonnet will suffice.' Sometimes, to the alarm of her guests, she exacted her sonnet, but in general her hospitality was as easy as her ways, and one only had to be a friend of a friend of Nina's to be welcome.

George Moore, who was living in Paris during the heyday of Parnasse, was also one of Nina's guests. Moore does not seem to have cared a great deal for the Parnassians or for their work – he described the effect upon him of Leconte de Lisle's poems as that of 'a walk through the Law Courts, with a steady but not violent draught sweeping from end to end' – but he does seem to have liked Nina, or at any rate her evenings, and he described one of them under the title of 'Ninon's table d'hôte' in *Memoirs of My Dead Life*.

That evening Moore was particularly struck by the size of the garden on which Nina's windows opened and he wandered out into it. 'I walked about the pond, interested in numerous ducks and cats, and in the company of macaws and cockatoos which climbed down from their perches, until I came upon a badger and her brood, but on my approach they disappeared into an enormous excavation. Behind the summer-house I came upon a bear asleep, and not far off some chained apes strove hard to gain my attention which I yielded to them until I heard Augusta Holmes singing her opera; singing all the different parts, soprano, contralto, tenor and bass. At that time we were all talking about her and I was standing by the window listening when Nina's cat suddenly misconducted itself. I raised the window, but the ventilation did not prove enough and a company of women came forth in flowered gowns and scarves about their shoulders.'

One of them was a cousin of Nina's, just up from the country, her eyes wide with wonder, who asked Moore to point out the celebrities to her, ' "Who is he who slouches towards the pond? That one wearing grey trousers and a black jacket – oh!" my companion's exclamation was caused by a new sight of Verlaine; he walked, his hat in hand (the evening being warm), and his great bald skull hanging like a cliff over eyebrows shaggy as furze bushes, frightened her. We continued to watch him, "How bored he seems. And why does he walk apart like that talking to nobody? Does he look upon us as too stupid?" my companion asked, and almost at the same time, Verlaine caught sight of me and coming forward, he engaged me in conversation, remarking as one might say, "it's a fine evening", "If I were in love with a young girl or a young man." A look of alarm spread over my companion's face, and drawing me aside, she whispered, "You must not leave me alone with him." '

Later, when they had got rid of Verlaine, Moore pointed out a man fumbling with his shirt collar – 'The celebrated Villiers de l'Isle-Adam. "He has no talent – only genius, and that is why he is a failure." '

Moore does not specifically mention that France was present that evening, but another of Nina's chroniclers, André de Bersaucourt, also reconstructs a typical evening and in his version, France is very much part of the picture – 'Imagine Léon Dierx declaiming his *Filaos*; Anatole France, Mérat and Valade gossiping in a corner, Charles de Sivry improvising at a piano, Dumont playing Hungarian airs on a zither, and Francés, the remarkable comic at the Palais Royal, reciting a monologue, and you have an adequate idea of Nina's soirées.'

Nina was welcoming to all her guests, but she seems to have been particularly so to France. She had literary inclinations and it was supposedly France who knocked into shape Nina's contribution to the second issue of Le Parnasse contemporain, collected in 1869. It was certainly France who collaborated with Nina on a short one-act play, *La Dompteuse*, also, like *Le Valet de Mme. la Duchesse*, unsuccessfully submitted to the Comédie Française.

This literary collaboration seemed to be leading to, and may actually have arrived at, a more intimate association, when it was nipped, possibly in the bud, possibly in the bloom, by another claimant for Nina's attentions.

Charles Cros was a mysterious member of Nina's entourage. A poet and a Parnassian, he acted also as Nina's secretary and manager – Nina's temperament as well as her affairs needing constant managing. He was thought to be her lover also, but about this many were never quite certain. His behaviour towards France, however, leaves little doubt.

One evening, Cros, France and a number of other Parnassians were sitting in a cafe on the Left Bank, when Cros suddenly assaulted France, saying he was going to strangle him. France beat a hasty retreat, but it was not hasty enough. He was caught and pinioned to the ground by his pursuer who was only prized off by the combined efforts of the others present. This was altogether more than France had bargained for. As far as he was concerned, it was the end of the affair. His ardour for Nina was replaced by a venomous, unforgiving hatred for Charles Cros. Several years later when he was one of the three editors selecting the third and final selection of Le Parnasse contemporain, he threatened to withdraw his own contributions if any poems of Charles Cros were included. He never again attended Nina's soirées. Yet even if France's scuffle with Cros bruised his self-esteem as well as his neck – he should at least have been grateful to Nina for an experience which knocked some of the more irregular edges off his character.

France's further progress in Parnasse, and the progress of Parnasse itself, was halted by the outbreak of the Franco-Prussian war in July, 1870.

THE RISE of France's star coincided and contrasted with the decline of the Second Empire. It was fashionable amongst the Parnassians, as amongst most vocal literary groups, to raise their voice against authority – and particularly an authority which, in the effort to hold together the rapidly disintegrating fabric of the Empire, was tightening its hold in various displeasing ways, which included literary censorship. France joined the chorus of protest as soon as he joined Parnasse, and the poems ('Denys, tyran de Syracuse' and 'Les Légions de Varus') which he contributed to Lemerre's *Gazette Rimée* shortly after his arrival in the Passage Choiseul, were so thickly studded with allusions to the contemporary situation, and contained so thinly veiled a criticism of the Emperor himself, that they undoubtedly contributed also to the sudden demise of the paper in which they appeared – Lemerre fearing that he had allowed his new protégé rather longer a rein than was either healthy or advisable in such circumstances.

The outbreak of war, however, took the wind not only out of Parnassian sails, but also out of Parnassian lungs. This was not only because in time of war Parisians had graver matters to think about than problems of poetic theory, but because one of the more curious secrets of the Tuileries to be brought into the light of day by the overthrow of the Empire, was the fact that Leconte de Lisle, despite his overt republicanism, had, over the last six years, been receiving a very considerable pension, of 300 francs a month, from the Emperor's Privy Purse. However severe the official policy of censorship, it says much for the Emperor's personal tolerance that despite Leconte de Lisle's often sharp and personally-pointed criticism, he should have suppressed neither de Lisle nor his pension during the period of gathering storm. Since, however, Parnasse was moulded so closely round Leconte de Lisle's proud, if as it proved, unpredictable, personality, when his reputation went under a cloud, so too did that of the movement he headed. He made matters no better by remarking when Heredia, at that time his principal lieutenant, reproached him for concealing the existence of his pension – 'When one goes to the lavatory one does not boast about it.' France, too, whose political views were swiftly turned about by the wind of war, renounced his republicanism and was the probable author of a poem which appeared in *La Vogue Parisienne*, to which he had been regularly contributing, over the signature 'France' on 7th January, 1871, which deeply lamented the fall of the Emperor.

Throughout the autumn and early winter of 1870–71, France and his parents, together with two million other Parisians, were besieged by the Prussians. So far as supplies were concerned, the siege was not effective enough nor did it last long enough to create conditions of starvation or even of any great shortage. In this way France and his parents were put to no great test of endurance. They were troubled considerably more, however, by the bombardment which began early in the New Year. The Prussians had by now come close enough and their guns had a long enough range – over four miles – to be able to shell most of the Left Bank as far as the river. One of their favourite targets was the area which enclosed the rue de Tournon. One evening the house next door was hit and France and his parents had to seek refuge for the night in the near-by house of the Charavays – 22, rue des Grands Augustins. After that, Père France decided to seek safety for himself and his wife on the other side of the Seine, and rented a room in the rue Richelieu, quite close, as it happened, to Lemerre's shop.

France seems to have stayed on with the Charavays, but was in any case away for a considerable part of this time on duty. Together with all other young men, he had found himself, on the outbreak of war, liable to military service. Unlike Étienne Charavay, who fought at Champigny and Buzenval, he did not show any particular eagerness to get to the front. On the contrary, enrolled in the National Guard, he and Calmettes went to considerable pains to get, on the 4th January 1871, an exemption on grounds of 'constitutional weakness' from any service other than that of guard-duty on the ramparts of Paris.

France did, however, on two occasions at least, come within sight and sound of the fighting, although on neither does he seem to have been greatly stirred. In *La Vie Littéraire* he was later to recall that 'during the battle of the 2nd December, placed in reserve under the fort of La Faisanderie, we (he and Calmettes) read Virgil's *Silenius* to the sound of the shells which fell in the Marne in the front of us. While on the horizon of the grey and bare countryside the Prussian batteries drew white clouds above the hills, the two of us sitting on a slope, close to our stacked rifles, bent our brows over a little Virgil of Bliss, which I have still and which is dear to me.' On another occasion, France told of a sortie made by his company, which came to nothing before even they got near the enemy when their commander was thrown from his horse and killed.

The armistice at the end of January 1871 put an end to the short term of France's very unmilitary service. Shocked and humiliated though they were by the obliterating defeat, most Parisians must have thought the worst of their troubles were now over. But, in fact, the trials and tribulations they went through in the course of invasion and defeat by a foreign power, were to prove as nothing compared with the suffering inflicted and the damage done in the short but savage period of internecine struggle which followed. The Commune was born out of the chaos of defeat. It achieved power in the middle of March. It was suppressed by the end of May. The events of the two and a half months which intervened, and 'the bloody week' of reprisals which followed, cost Paris more casualties than the whole of the French Revolution, caused more damage to her buildings and beauty than any other event in her history and left an undercurrent of bitterness that was to come to the surface again in later social struggles – notably the Affair.

Even to those such as France and Calmettes who had taken the Prussian siege relatively casually, the Commune from the start, was a very different matter. Calmettes quickly sought safety in his parents' house at Ville d'Avray, close to Versailles. Charavay, too, who had returned to Paris and civilian life at the end of the Prussian war, conscious now of his responsibilities as head of his family, left with them for Lyons. France stayed on in Paris until the beginning of May, but was as antagonistic to the Commune, and as apprehensive of their designs, as any. In a letter to Mme. Charavay of the end of March, he referred to them as 'the committee of assassins', and in one to Calmettes dated 3rd May telling him not to come back to Paris he gave him news of friends, mostly other Parnassians – Coppée was thinking of 'sudden flight', Bergerat had fled via Bercy at the bottom of a barrel – France had hidden Bergerat, a young Parnassian poet, for a while in the Charavay's flat, where he made such a mess that Mme. Charavay never really forgave France for having arranged and allowed his stay. France then went on – 'Some days there are real massacres. Those who are not dead, sing and fight, dead-drunk. It will last another six weeks. In six weeks they will have blown-up half Paris.'

France must have got to Ville d'Avray almost as soon as his letter, for, understandably scared that he might be caught up in the death-throes of the Commune, he left Paris and his parents on either the 5th or 6th of May, furnished with a false passport which described him as Henri Gillis, a Belgian, 'fair with a round face, forty-seven years old and small in stature.' Since France, in fact, was on the dark side, had a thin equine face, was twenty-seven years old and tall, he must have approached the Communard post with some misgiving. But, in fact, those on duty were too drunk to notice any discrepancies between the passport and its bearer, and France got safely through to Calmettes' house, already overcrowded with earlier refugees. There he and they remained, leading a life of, in the circumstances, rather surprising convivial rusticity, while the final act in the drama of the Commune was played out.

At first communications were still possible with Paris and France profited by this to correspond with his parents – even to get a parcel of clean linen sent out from his mother – but as the Government troops closed in, so the gaps in their lines were closed up, and for the last ten days of the fighting, France was totally out of touch. Most evenings, he and his friends went to the higher ground of near-by Versailles to watch the bombardment, almost by way of entertainment. Since at first the bulk of the shelling fell on the area of Passy and Auteuil and the higher ground around the Trocadero, some way from the Left Bank, France at that time probably felt no particular personal anxiety. But one can imagine his feelings on the night of 24th May when the whole of Paris seemed on fire, and the brightest glow of all, from the burning Tuileries fired by a fanatic Communard determined to remove 'the last vestiges of the monarchy', hung over the district in which France knew his parents were sheltering. By the 31st May all was over. France could not immediately get into the city, but he early received a note from his mother saying she and his father were safe, and sent a reply by return which shows his relief – 'You have survived and surmounted everything. I would not have dared ask so much of fate; there are no ruins for me where you and père are safe and sound.'

But, in fact, there were a great many ruins, for France, as for everyone else, in the Paris to which he returned on the 4th June. The Tuileries was a shell, a wing of the Louvre housing the Ministry of Finance was burnt out – the main part of the Louvre itself with its priceless collections, had only just been saved – the Hôtel de Ville was gutted, the Palais de Justice, the Prefecture of Police, the Cour des Comtes, a large part of the Palais Royale, had all been destroyed. Père France himself had seen, as he noted down 'with grief', flames coming out of the windows of the Palais Luxembourg, and elsewhere and everywhere, signs of an insane incendiarism. Whole areas of houses, shops and buildings had been burnt or pulled down – notably in the rue Royale, the rue de Rivoli, the rue de Lille, and on la Butte itself where the Communards had made their last desperate and despairing stand. Some of this had been done to clear lines of fire, some – but relatively little – was the result of Government shelling, but by far the greater part of the destruction had been caused by the urge to destroy to which many Communards succumbed when they realized that they themselves were soon to be destroyed.

But if the Communards in their last week of power did more harm to the appearance of Paris than centuries of revolution and war, it was the returning Government who did the greatest hurt to its soul. The Communards had been brutal in their treatment of prisoners; cruel, capricious and callous in their executions, which included that of the Archbishop of Paris; they had at times let their blood-lust run riot through the streets to the cost of anyone out in them – yet their barbarities were as nothing compared with the ordered and organized massacres which followed the end of the fighting. In the Government reprisals, most of which took place in the first 'bloody' week of peace, between twenty and twenty-five thousand Communards, or suspected Communards, who were, after all, Parisians like their captors, were executed. On the individual level vengeance was just as savage. Alphonse Daudet saw two cavalrymen come up to a laggard in a column of prisoners, attach tethers to his arms, and then set off at the gallop, dragging their victim between them until he was a bleeding mass of flesh, when they finished him off with the butts of their carbines. An English witness saw an old couple in another such column come to a halt – 'The woman was a cripple. She said, "Shoot me. I cannot walk any further." The husband stood by her. They were shot down after thirty shots of revolvers.'

Between them, the Commune and the Government had produced one of those moments of incomprehensible horror which haunt the human memory.

On the surface, France seemed to have come through the experience of invasion and civil war, relatively unscathed. His home and his parents were safe and unharmed. He himself had seen no service more active than an occasional stroll round the ramparts. Yet within a few months of his return to Paris, he wrote a novel – his first – full of a youthful disillusionment and a despairing anger against society that was quite as clearly a product of the times as the burnt and broken stones of the Tuileries.

France did not publish, or seek to publish, this novel for ten years. Then he only produced it when cornered by an angry publisher with a contract from which he could see no other means of escape. When, finally – reluctantly and rather apprehensively – France pulled the manuscript out of the drawer in which it had been lying all those years, he found that either he or it had changed almost out of recognition. He had to re-write a great part, but even so, the hard core of the original version remained, and that core was so hard that it shocked him in the more mellow frame of mind he had by then acquired. 'It has something bitter and hard about it,' he wrote in the preface with which it was published in 1882, 'which shocks me now. I would today have more gentleness.'

France called the novel *Les Désirs de Jean Servien*, but he could just as well have entitled it *The Youthful Fears of Anatole France*, for if the detail is different, the central figure is clearly his own – or rather, it is that of the France who might have been, the failure he might have become had he not possessed through his father an entrée into the literary world, had he not been gifted with a genuine talent; had he not, none too soon, decided to work; had he not, on the whole, been lucky.

France made Servien the son of a bookbinder, not a bookseller, and placed him one degree, or one generation, closer to the poverty-line than he had been himself – but he showed him, like himself, raised up by the affectionate aspirations of his parents on to a higher social level than the origins, status or financial circumstances of his family really justified. Servien's mother died while he was a baby, but France gives us a brief glimpse of her, imagining the brilliant careers of which the choice awaited her new-born son. In turn she saw him as a fashionable man of the world, the centre of a sparkling circle of wit and beauty; as a brilliant advocate, pleading and gaining the cause of some famous or infamous client; as a victorious general directing the battle on his curvetting steed; finally, and this was the image closest to her heart, as a priest raising the Host to Heaven. At this vision, 'she groaned like the mother of a god, this poor, ill, working-woman whose sickly child languished near her in the bad air of the back of the shop.'

Partly from a desire to realize the dreams and desires of his dead wife and to honour her memory, partly because of his own affection and ambitions for his only child, the bookbinder spent his savings sending his son to an expensive school, where Jean learnt, not so much how to adapt himself and be happy in this new world, as how to be discontent in the old. Returning from visits to his friends' homes, Jean found himself unutterably disparaging and scornful of the drab but worthy conditions under which his father lived and worked.

An outing at the fair of Saint-Cloud also had a disastrous effect. Taken by a friend's mother – a Mme. Ewens, a beautiful *femme du monde* living in considerable luxury and somewhat dubious circumstances – there was no sign of a M. Ewens and a minor tycoon in the butchery business was persistently and importunately hanging around – Servien's head was turned, not only by the noise and excitement of the fair, but by the intoxicating presence of Mme. Ewens herself – and by her reckless spending, incredible to Jean, accustomed to the necessarily careful circumstances of his own home, where every sou counted, and probably was counted several times. Thereafter, for the rest of his youth, Servien prostrated himself before the image of a sophisticated woman of the world, such as Mme. Ewens, an ambition at that age hopelessly beyond his reach and his means, and in consequence spurned the shop-girls and seamstresses who would have been far more accessible, far more use, and far more fun.

At the end of his schooling, Servien, unlike France, took his baccalaureat without difficulty; but then found that for someone without money and without connections, there was no sign of the reasonable job that he had been led to believe went with it. Drifting from one miserable makeshift occupation to another, Jean became increasingly bitter about, and resentful of, the society and circumstances which had filled his head with illusions, pretensions and desires, none of which he was able to satisfy, and at the same time, deprived him of the small practical and physical pleasures which would at least have made life tolerable. Finally, caught up in the whirlpool of the Commune, Servien, although sympathizing with the Communards, was mistaken by a marauding band for a Government spy and summarily executed.

It is the example of an entirely futile and frustrated life, to which Jean's execution by the Communards might seem to come as an entirely fortuitous climax. Yet the two, in fact, are directly and indissolubly linked, for the conditions which produced Servien were also those which produced the Commune. France showed, by the fact that he locked the manuscript away for ten years, that he wrote Servien more from a personal desire to exorcise a youthful fear of failure, and to rid his mind of the shadow which the events of the Commune had cast upon it, than with any practical thought of publication. Yet although his first, *Les Désirs de Jean Servien* is far from being the worst novel France ever wrote. It has an integrity and an interest of its own, revealing a side of France that rarely shows in his work, an insecure and un-certain side, full of fears and forebodings, of bitterness and resentment – a side, the knowledge of which makes it easier to understand the course of his further progress in Parnasse.

Parnasse had survived the two wars, but not without casualties. Louis Xavier de Ricard, a supporter of the Commune, had had to seek refuge in Switzerland. So, too, had Nina, who, caring little whom she entertained so long as she entertained someone, had made the mistake of asking the Communard leaders to her house. Verlaine was ex-cluded from the movement because of his Communard sympathies. Louis Ménard excluded himself, in disgust at the severity of the measures of repression, and in anger that the Parnassians should condone them. Parnasse had suffered, also, some loss of face from the revelation of Leconte de Lisle's Imperial pension and considerable loss of impetus from the standstill that the war had imposed on all literary activities. Now, far from being *avant-garde*, it was much more *arrière-garde*, having to defend its poetic position against the attack of symbolism. However, enough ad-herents and interest in the movement remained to make it still a considerable force in the literary world. In this changed and, on the whole, chastened Parnasse, France was a figure of far greater importance and influence than he had been before.

The main reason for this sudden rise in his stock and his status, was the fact that France had been one of the few Parnassians who, throughout the war, save for the months when he was at Ville d'Avray, had continued regularly to visit Leconte de Lisle in the deep dudgeon and disgrace into which the revelation of his pension had cast him. At this time Leconte de Lisle was so conscious of his isolation that the sight of a friend on his threshold was liable to make him burst into tears. France, one of his few frequent visitors, was quickly admitted into his intimacy. France realized this himself, for in his letter to Calmettes of the 4th May, he wrote 'Leconte de Lisle . . . takes me into his confidence.' Nor was it only on the social plane that France drew close to the sadly diminished and downcast 'Maître'. In the lean literary months which followed the end of the fighting when writers even of eminence had to turn their hand to anything that was going, and little enough of any sort was, the two of them collaborated on a *Dictionnaire de Cuisine*, a task which, France wrote to Charavay, he thought might cover him with gold but give him 'cerebral paralysis into the bargain'.

When Leconte de Lisle started his salon again after the war, now in a flat overlooking the gardens of the Luxembourg, in the boulevard de l'École des Mines, France more than held his new-found position of favour, so much so that a new recruit, Paul Bourget, later recalled that when he first got to know France, 'shortly after the war of 1870 . . . he was still young but already accepted by his juniors as a master.' Another friend of the time, Frédéric Plessis, a quiet classicist whose poetic works were never to achieve the range of recognition his friends thought they deserved, showed, in a letter of 27th June, 1871, the respect, and even devotion, which France could already inspire – 'I believe – in you, above all! – and before all!'

France, described at this time by a more clear-sighted onlooker, Virginie, the daughter of the painter Jules Breton, as 'tall and thin, with sloping shoulders, a long, pale face, close-set black eyes, chestnut-coloured beard and very short hair cut *en brosse*', was most conscious and jealous of his growing authority and quick to cut down any contenders. Of these Bourget, who although eight years younger than France, had already shown the glint of an unusual talent, enhanced by the sparkle of his absurd but amusing dandyism – he sent his laundry to London because he considered English washerwomen washed whiter – was now the most formidable. There were at first several tiffs between them. One such occurred after Bourget had read a poem of his to the assembled Parnassians. At the end there was general applause and Leconte de Lisle gave his approbation by murmuring gently 'Beaux vers.' 'Mon cher,' snarled France 'I noticed a pleonasm – "deceptive mirage" – a mirage is always deceptive.' Bourget, refusing to accept the correction and the rebuke implied in it, the argument became so heated that Leconte de Lisle had to intervene – 'Mes enfants. You are both right, but the verse is too delicate to be corrected. There are some flowers which wilt when you touch them.'

Subsequently France subdued Bourget in the best possible way – by taking him under his wing. Bourget became one of the group of close friends with whom France regularly wandered of a fine evening, or on a wet one sat in one of the innumerable cafés of the Left Bank. Fifteen years later France was to remember and remark in *La Vie Littéraire* – 'Five or six of us carry in the recollections of our youth the memory of those evening meetings under the great lime-trees of the avenue de l'Observatoire, of the interminable discussions in the gardens of the Luxembourg, to which Paul Bourget, then little more than an adolescent, brought his fine analytical mind and his elegant curiosity.' Fifty years later, on the occasion of France's death, Bourget also looked back to that time and to 'the France with whom I so often discussed the problems of our *métier*, wandering to and fro on the terraces of Marie de Medici.'

In 1874 France set the seal on his position of authority within Parnasse by writing a treatise of poetic theory, in which he explained and expounded the Parnassian position – 'Since all the fictions of which the human spirit can dream were conceived in ancient times ... Since nothing is new under the intellectual sun, if art does not wish to immobilize itself by the use of worn-out symbols, it must give up meaning and concentrate exclusively on form.' – Of so little general interest that it had to be sent by Leconte de Lisle to his native Île Bourbon before a periodical could be found that would publish it, France's paper was nevertheless accepted by the Parnassians as their gospel. 'For a long time after that,' wrote Calmettes, 'we lived on the theory consecrated by the article of Anatole France.' Subsequently there was never any serious doubt that, as another of France's followers of this time, Robert de Bonnières, a literary journalist who had also been at school at Stanislas, put it, France was 'le premier après le maître'.

It was not, however, only in the salon of Leconte de Lisle that France was assertive of his new-found authority. As one of the selection committee of three – Coppée and Théodore de Banville were the other two – for the third and last volume of *le Parnasse contemporain*, France was a severe judge of contributions. It was he who was mainly responsible for the fact by which this otherwise unremarkable collection of verse is mainly remembered – that it excluded poems submitted by Verlaine and Mallarmé. Verlaine at this time was in prison at Brussels for having wounded Rimbaud and in deep disgrace for the desertion of his home and the damaging disclosures about his private life which had come out at the trial. It seems likely that his submissions

– several extracts from 'Sagesse' – were rejected more on moral than on literary grounds. Even so, while Coppée and Banville were non-committal, France put a decisive 'no' and added – 'The author is revolting and the verses are the worst we have seen.' Mallarmé sent his *l'Aprés-Midi d'un Faune*. Banville wished to accept it because of its 'rare harmonies and musical qualities', but France again put in a firm 'No – they would laugh at us,' and managed to persuade Coppée to support him, thus giving a majority for rejection.

In later years, in *La Vie Littéraire*, France sought to make amends to both poets, and so far as Verlaine was concerned, succeeded so well that Jules Renard noted in his *Journal* – 'It is France who has made Verlaine.' So many and much worse things had happened to the vagrant, vagabond poet who made a mess of everything except his poetry than this rejection, that he was quick to forgive and forget. But the gentle and sensitive Mallarmé was deeply and lastingly hurt. When, after France's death, Paul Valéry, in his early years Mallarmé's disciple, on succeeding to France's *fauteuil* in the Academy, paid, contrary to custom, a most tepid tribute to his predecessor, it seems likely that the underlying reason was a desire to settle this very old score.

France, also, on the purely personal grounds of his dislike of Charles Cros because of his behaviour over Nina, threatened to withdraw his own contribution if those of Cros were included, or even considered. He also sent back a poem submitted by Xavier de Ricard, who in 1873 had returned to Paris, but not to favour, with the curt and uncharitable suggestion that Ricard should 'clean' his poem, which was 'littered with incongruous filth'. But, after all, Ricard, even if he had sympathized with the Commune, which France in a letter to Charavay called 'the committee of Madness and Crime', had before the war been far his closest friend in Parnasse. France was under no obligation, because of their past friendship, to accept Ricard's poem, but because of it he could at least have tempered the tone of his rejection, particularly to someone so obviously down on his luck. His first taste of authority seemed in fact to have brought out a 'hard and bitter' side of France's nature; the existence of which, those who had not read Servien – as, of course, no one yet had – would never have suspected.

In retrospect, the course of France's career in these post-war years seems to show a direct and deliberate assault on the heights of Parnasse, with little thought or mercy for those alongside – yet this determination to succeed, the outward expression perhaps of some deeper dread stirred up by the events of the last year, may not have been calculated – nor even conscious. Certainly the gentler, vaguer, scholarly side of France's character was still much in evidence and it was this side that still impressed itself the most strongly on his friends. 'Chez lui, absolutely no haste to arrive,' wrote Bourget, 'Reads a lot, meditates a lot, looks about a lot, adjusts at his leisure his lovingly chiselled verses, revises his carefully-worked essays, waits in fact until the tree of his thought has grown so that he may pick its fruits in due season.' Bergerat, recovered from his period of hiding in Charavay's flat, even if neither the flat nor Mme. Charavay had as yet got over the shock of it, described France 'ambling about with the pottering pace, interrupted by sudden halts, by which one recognizes dreamers and collectors. He seems to have only a vague perception of the things and people of the street, but no shop window escapes him.' Verlaine pictured him always 'with some old book under his arm, the find of the incessant scholar that he is, just picked up on the *quais*.' Bonnières recalled that at this time, France had his mind 'set on archaeology and prehistory. I do not know what put this bee in his bonnet, but for some time he could think of nothing but mammoths . . . and megalithic monuments. It passed.' Bourget had the perception to notice a contrast of expression – 'a face at once simple and shrewd, open and subtle' – but not the profundity to see that this contrast fitted France's actions as well as his appearance.

So far as his work was concerned, France was mainly occupied over this period in writing the poetry to justify his position in Parnasse, and with his journalism. France worked hard at his rhythms and rhymes and produced enough to fill a volume of his own which Lemerre published in 1873 under the title *Poèmes Dorés*. At his best, notably in *Les Noces Corinthiennes*, a poetic drama published in 1876, France could attain a rolling classical grandeur –

> J'ai voyagé: j'ai vu la Force ausonienne
> Tibur, Neapolis, Paestum, Anconia
> Les arcs et les jardins que César dédia
> Les buissons genereux d'arbouses et de mures
> Les arbres des vergers rougis de pommes mures
> Et la plaine et ses blès et le raisin vermeil
> Qui boit en flanc des monts la liquer du soleil.

At his worst, notably in 'Le Bain', a poem inspired by the sight of the infant Pierre Calmettes in his bath, he could sink to a painful banality –

> Et voici que s'élève une clameur joyeuse
> Et la mère sourit, et se plaint à mi-voix
> Car le savon, trompant sa main industrieuse,
> Dans le vaisseau profond s'est echapée trois fois.

– surprising in so particular and critical a person. But at his best or his worst, France was clearly never at ease in the realm of poetry. Although he laboured hard at his poems, his labours were never those of love. Once he had outgrown Parnasse, he wrote no more poems. Asked in later years why he had written so much poetry at this time, but none afterwards, he replied, 'Heu. It was fashionable in my youth. I wrote poetry like everyone else. It gave pleasure to some of my friends – De Lisle, Prud'homme, Heredia. It gave none to me.' He once told Brousson – 'I am not a poet. A poet thinks in poetry. I think in prose.' It was also possibly significant that his favourite expression of contempt was 'bête comme un poète'.

But if France got little joy out of his poetry, it was, curiously, quite a different matter with the more ephemeral, matter-of-fact, matter-of-existence side of his writing – his journalism, with which must be included his work for Lemerre, of which during these years, his most important commission was a five-volume edition of Racine, published in 1874 and 1875. Despite his dislike of the pressure that journalism inevitably imposed with its datelines and directives, France could still write in *La Vie Littéraire*, thinking of his own experience, 'Journalism is not such a bad school of style as one might think. I do not think a true talent has ever been spoiled by it . . . One learns to keep away from the obscure and tendentious, into which pits fall often the most artistic writers when they compose far from the public. Journalism is like a bathe in the sea from which one emerges more alert and agile.' On another occasion, talking of Flaubert, France expressed his admiration, then qualified it by saying, 'And yet it would have done him good to have had to produce articles to order. It would have given him a suppleness he lacks.'

Over these years France continued to write regularly for *Le Bibliophil Illustré* (in 1873 Bachelin-Deflorenne switched his contributions and energies to a new periodical, *La Musée des Deux Mondes*); for Charavay's *l'Amateur d'Autographes*, and occasionally for other papers such as *La Rappel* and *La Vogue Parisienne*. Charavay also brought out briefly a *Revue des documents historiques*, which was a particular delight to France, as he recalled in a later article addressed to Charavay – 'You were running then, quite by yourself, *La Revue des documents historiques* which Molterez printed – also on his own in a *remise* of the rue Visconti, opposite the vine planted by Jean Racine. It had everything, that review – a learned text, excellent reproductions, good printing, and even a few readers. Why has it ceased to exist?'

In those days and in such journals, the demands of copyright were slight; the memories of both editors and readers short – and France often used his articles more than once. Thus an article on 'The library of Billaud-Varenne' first appeared in *La Gazette Bibliographique* of July 1868, then in *l'Amateur d'Autographes* of November 1868; finally in the *Almanach de la Revolution* of 1870. An article on Paris prisons during the Terror was first printed in *Le Bibliophil Illustré* of July 1870, reappeared in *La Vogue Parisienne* of August 1873 and again in *l'Amateur d'Autographes* of November 1873. In August 1870, an article on the 'Baron de Gleichen' was published simultaneously in *Le Bibliophil Illustré* and *La Vogue Parisienne*. Three years later it appeared in *l'Amateur d'Autographes* of September 1873. As well as re-writing whole articles, France sometimes incorporated passages and paragraphs from previous work. His faithful readers must often have experienced a feeling of familiarity, the sensation that they had been here before – which, of course, they had.

France's first really big journalistic opportunity came through his acquaintance with Charles Edmond, a Pole who had changed his name, originally Count Chojecki, with his nationality when he became naturalized French in 1861. In the course of an adventurous career, Charles Edmond had fought against the Russian domination of his native country; in the Turkish army; had been secretary to the Prince Napoléon, and written several plays which had been produced on the Parisian stage. He was also one of the founders of *Le Temps*, and now was head of the Bibliothèque du Sénat, a fact which was also to prove to be of considerable importance to France. Largely because of his friendship with Charles Edmond, France, in January 1875, had an article on 'Les femmes de Horace' published in *Le Temps*, and later that year was commissioned to write a series of articles on contemporary novelists, of which the first appeared in November. Thanks to his work for *l'Amateur d'Autographes, Le Bibliophil Illustré* and for Lemerre, France by now had found his form and formed his style as a critic. *Le Temps* provided a stage worthy of it. His critical articles, although they appeared only at intervals, brought him immediately to the notice of the discerning and the distinguished. 'Would you have the kindness to send me your article in *Le Temps* . . .' wrote Taine in a letter of 2nd February, 1876 – 'You will divine the use I wish to make of it – when a man has talent he must find his proper place.' Georges Sand, after reading an appreciative article on her work which appeared in April, 1876, wrote, not to France, but to Charles Edmond – 'France has a great deal of style, a fine simple form of writing, and is in the true tradition of our tongue – which is becoming jolly rare! Cultivate and encourage this young talent, you will not find many like it.'

However, as well as making many friends amongst the influential and illustrious by his articles in *Le Temps*, France also made the occasional enemy. This was the time when he crossed swords with Edmond de Goncourt over his review of *Manette Salamon*, the impressionistic novel of artistic life written by the two brothers and first brought out eight years before. To the success of the new edition – which Lemerre was publishing – Goncourt attached a particular importance, not only because of his supersensitivity to public opinion, but because he looked upon it as a monument to his now dead brother.

Goncourt took the trouble to visit not only *Le Temps*, who agreed to commission an article, but also France whom they asked to do it. Yet, to Goncourt's dismay and astonishment, the article, when it appeared, was not the favourable notice he had expected, but, in his own words, consisted of 'an absolute negation of the talents of the two brothers'. In his *Journal* he recorded his anger, irritation and surprise – 'The author of the article is the young France, the son of the bookseller. My brother and I were always charming to the young wretch . . . When he published for Lemerre several short but proper prefaces, I wrote him the most Hugolian letter of encouragement. In such circumstances, when I went to ask about the article for *Le Temps*, when I talked to him sincerely and honestly about the interest which Lemerre's new edition held for me – not for my own account but for the memory of my brother, I think he ought to have replied to me – "My dear sir, you are wrong. I have different ideals to yours. I do not like your work at all. Any article of mine would not benefit your books in any way. You had better approach someone else." He preferred to practise a deception, this young man. Was he put up to it by Leconte de Lisle, of whom he is the disciple? They tell me, "No," and assure me that he has simply followed his nature, which is that of a Jesuit republican, and has given himself the pleasure, and the credit with his friends, of executing us in the name of healthy literary doctrines and of revolutionary principles. The most curious part of the whole affair is that such an article should have been written by the employee of Lemerre, and that it should have been printed by the paper which serialized *Manette Salamon*.' After this contretemps, Goncourt went, not surprisingly, into a long huff, which only slightly thawed some twenty years later when France, who had just been given the Légion d'Honneur, told him he considered it a great honour to hold the same decoration that he did.

For the raw and resentful element in France's make-up, which Goncourt had unwittingly roused, the salve, of course, was success. He had his first real touch of this with his articles for *Le Temps*. He had also by now reached the top of Parnasse. Yet because of the conflict between the highly impersonal Parnassian theory and his highly personal talent, it was difficult to see where this particular pre-eminence could lead him. In fact, it led him to the Bibliothèque du Sénat.

A vacancy amongst the *commis-surveillants* occurred in the summer of 1876. With Charles Edmond as the head-librarian, and Leconte de Lisle, whose appointment in 1874 must have been some recompense for his lost pension, as well as Coppée, already on the staff, France's candidature stood a very different chance from when he had first applied in 1867 at the time of the sale of the bookshop. This time he was successful. His appointment in August, 1876, gave France 2,200 francs a year, the prospect of a pension, an official status, and very little extra work. Three months later, as if to complete the structure of a secure and successful life, he got married.

Chapter

4

—————◆—————

FOR SOMEONE who was to have so many *amours* in the later part of his life, France had remarkably few in his youth. During the short period he was clerking for the bookseller Nottet, after he left school, he is supposed to have formed an equally short attachment for Nottet's daughter. There were, of course, his obliging neighbours during the months he was in his garret in the rue du Pré-aux-Clercs. There was, also, his brief skirmish with Nina. But it all added up to little weight in the balance against the long period of his youth which ended with the outbreak of the Franco-Prussian war. France was probably thinking of his own relatively loveless existence when, in *Servien*, he described Jean looking out of a window, watching his father's apprentice kissing a shop-girl he happened to have met in the street – 'He kissed the girl without thought of the passers-by. The girl – unhealthy and pretty – admirably poised in her rags on her well-made shoes, held him to her while pretending to push him away . . . As Jean watched he felt jealous of his father's apprentice.' So, perhaps, did France, as he watched his less shy friends picking the spring flowers they found on their way.

The main reason why France was so backward in coming forward was probably his mother's deep but possessive love for her only son. Many years later, France was once to burst out to Brousson, who had been bemoaning his own neglected childhood – 'Voyez-vous, mon ami, there is something worse than indifference: it is love, love that has become tyrannical. You complain of your loveless childhood. You don't know what you are talking about. I myself had the most loving of mothers. She adored her only son, Anatole, as her masterpiece, her possession. I inherited all my good qualities from her. As for my faults, needless to say, it was my father who had given them to me. Poor man! she loved him well, also, but she scorned him more, and everything which their union had not achieved she now placed on my head. I was loved for two. It was a great deal, mon ami; it was a great deal too much. To be exact, she poisoned my life. She stupefied me, she confused me. She made me inconsistent and timid. We were both of us ridiculous. She still spoke of me, when for a long time I had had a beard on my chin, as if I was a child.

'... Of my youthful loves she had to know everything; the object, the intensity, the details, the price. She never provoked a confidence, but Vidocq on the track of a criminal was only a little boy in comparison with this good, Christian, bourgeois mother, spying out the modest loves of her son. A certain photograph that I had forgotten in an overcoat pocket I would find, spread out on my desk as if on an altar. I would find there, also, patiently pieced together, the mosaic of letters I had thrown into the wastepaper basket. And, in addition, there were the silent despairs, the eyes filled with tears, the sighs that would have turned wet windmills.'

'Until I was thirty-five, my mother never went to bed before she had seen me come in. At midnight, or at four in the morning, I would find her, silent and implacable, a candle in her hand. It became a sort of rite. Gently, silently, she handed me the candle, kissed me on both cheeks. Then she went to bed, sighing and groaning, to start all over again on the following day.' The memory of either France or Brousson can be faulted by the fact that France married at thirty-three, so this frightful nocturnal ritual can hardly have continued until he was thirty-five; yet in general, the picture has about it an air of grim, terrifying authenticity.

From this ridiculous and impossible situation, marriage offered the obvious and best means of escape. It was mainly for this reason, one would think, that France, after the war, made a series of unsuccessful attempts to get married. First, in 1873, there was Isabelle Combrouse, the daughter of a distinguished numismatist, one of Père France's most regular and valued customers. France dedicated his *Poèmes Dorés* to her. But she preferred a handle rather than a book to her name, and a M. de Launay. The same year, on holiday at Avranches in Normandy, France met Élise Rauline, to whom he also proposed. She chose, however, to go into a convent. On learning this, France wrote, and sent her, a distasteful poem in which he expressed his regret that she had chosen Christ rather than him.

The following year it was the turn of Marie Charavay, the younger of Étienne's two sisters. Étienne, to see to family affairs, had for a while to leave Paris. In his absence, France undertook to edit *l'Amateur d'Autographes*, and Marie helped him. In his inflammable state, their proximity could have only one result, and France duly paid his court to Marie. This was far the longest and the most serious of France's unavailing courtships, and the only one in which one senses he may possibly have fallen in love with the person as well as with the prospect of marriage. When Marie left Paris, France wrote to Mme. Charavay – 'Do not say so to Marie, but in her absence nothing is pleasant or gay. Paris seems to me . . . quite insupportable since your daughter is no longer there.'

For two years France paid court to Marie, yet in the end nothing came of this either. Even the Charavays, whose flat in his childhood and youth had been a second home to France, and who offered him always a warm welcome as a friend and godson, seem, because of his insecure position and uncertain prospects, to have been unwilling to welcome him so warmly as a son-in-law. Certainly Marie's aunt wrote in a letter at this time – 'They do not speak of marriage for Marie . . . What does not please me is to see M. Anatole France so attentive chez Mme. Charavay. He would be a nephew little to my liking.'

After he had abandoned hope of Marie Charavay, France became briefly interested in another Marie – Marie Rioux de Maillou, who subsequently married Louis Ménard, the ex-Parnassian. At some other, unspecified, time, France also made approaches to Élise, the daughter of a future colleague and friend at the Bibliothèque du Sénat, Louis Ratisbonne, who, however, at the time of France's proposal, thought his personality and prospects so dim that he refused even to consider him for his daughter.

So shattering a succession of reverses can have done little good to France's self-esteem. Yet the main reason under-lying these refusals was not really a personal one at all – as France may have had the sense to see. It was simply that as a penurious poet, a relatively ill-paid publisher's hack who could be turned off at a moment's notice, and as a promising, but little-known journalist who had not as yet found the ear of an influential editor or the eye of the public, France was simply not a marriageable proposition. How-ever, France's success on *Le Temps* and his appointment to the Bibliothèque du Sénat, changed things altogether. His articles gave clear and incontestable proof of his talent, as his poems never had done, and his appointment to the Bibliothèque du Sénat gave him security, which from a marriageable point of view was possibly an even more valuable asset. As a proved critic and as an official librarian, France was now a person of some standing. Hitherto, even his prominence in Parnasse had counted for little in the out-side world, but now as a *commis-surveillant*, France was a civil servant, and as such, a member of the most envied class in France. In a century of such uncertainty, stability and durability were highly valued, and civil servants were thought – rightly – to be as irremovable as the Seine itself.

Had France's critical success and appointment to the

Bibliothèque de Sénat come earlier, he might have married Marie Charavay, Élise Ratisbonne, Marie Rioux de Maillou. As it was he married Valérie Guérin de Sauville, a tall, shy girl of twenty with a beautiful skin, whom he had met only six months before. The only child of Jules Guérin de Sauville, a kindly, reasonably well-to-do senior official in the Ministère des Finances, now a widower, Valérie came of a distinguished artistic family, originating in Alsace, whose most celebrated member, Jean Guérin, had been court painter both to Marie Antoinette and to the Empress Josephine.

But if from a worldly point of view, France had good reason to be pleased with himself when on 28th April, 1877, he led Valérie down the steps of Saint-Sulpice and out into the adventure of married life, he also had a wife of whose appearance he could be very proud. The Comtesse de Martel, alias 'Gyp', who both as Society woman and as a highly successful novelist, was well qualified to judge points and standards of beauty, declared Valérie, a year or so after her marriage, to be absolutely 'ravissante. Her hands and her feet were marvels. She was a blonde of a very rare type.' Her soft skin and cool complexion caused France to murmur, rather fatuously, on the eve of his wedding – 'She has the air of a river of milk. Let's hope she will have its suavity.' Probably Valérie was one of those women whose beauty shows particularly when enhanced by the bloom of youth. Although she was to remain a good-looking woman, her face and her figure were to fill out and some bad teeth were to spoil the look of her mouth when she spoke. In those early years of his marriage, France undoubtedly skimmed the cream off his 'river of milk'.

At first the difference of age between them showed very markedly. France appeared old for his thirty-three years, Valérie young for her twenty. 'Gyp', when she saw them together for the first time, thought that Valérie had more the air and appearance of being France's daughter than his wife. In fact, France's approach and attitude to Valérie seems at this stage to have had something of the parental in it, for in a letter to Jules Breton he wrote – 'You will have noticed, perhaps, that she speaks little. It is because she is very timid. I am working to correct this. It is delightful to me to complete the education of the woman I love. The husband ought to be an educator so that he can adapt his companion to himself.' As a theorist France was not, however, to prove so successful in his own home as he had been in Parnasse. France was very proud of Valérie's artistic inheritance and in the same letter, he wrote – 'She is a Guérin; she has the taste of painting in her blood.'

At first, and for some years, marriage seems to have given France all that he had hoped for. A letter, of that autumn, to an importunate poet, excusing a delay in the return of a manuscript, breathes an air of complete content. France, who advised Charavay about the books his firm published, had told an underling called Malin to send back the manuscript. Then came France's marriage, 'happy and perfect', which had caused him to forget about the manuscript. Malin also forgot about it. France excused him on the grounds that he was a dreamer. 'While I was on my honeymoon, he was on I don't know what other moon. You must excuse both of us.'

On their return from their honeymoon, France and Valérie went to live at the flat – 90, rue de Rennes – to which France and his parents had moved two years before, but which the old couple now vacated, making the last move of their lives – out to Neuilly. The next year, 1878, France and Valérie followed them there, but for the time being went to live in the house of Valérie's father, in the rue Louis-Philippe. A shared household is not always an ideal arrangement for a young couple, but for France there was little difficulty in settling down with 'Papa Jules', a gentle, quiet man who sought – in so far as he could and he could very considerably – only to ease their financial burdens, and who was glad of their company. France's spontaneous affection for his father-in-law showed in a letter he wrote that year asking that he should be included in a wedding invitation – 'I send you this letter secretly because my excellent father-in-law, a very affectionate and simple man, was very hurt to be forgotten on a similar occasion some time ago. It is a question of giving pleasure to a most excellent man.' Two years later, France and Valérie bought, with Valérie's very substantial dowry, a charming house in the near-by rue Chalgrin. There the following spring, on the 1st March, 1881, Suzanne, their only child, was born, thus completing the framework for a full and happy family life.

It was a pointer to France's literary loyalties at the time of his marriage, that his two *témoins* were Lemerre and Charles Edmond. It was also possibly significant that Leconte de Lisle was not one of them. Parnasse, so far as France was concerned, had now served its purpose. He owed it a great deal – its current had caught him at a crucial time in his development and it had carried him far. But its hard doctrines were too antipathetic to the true bent of his talent, and the dominion demanded by its autocratic leader too exacting for it to be possible as a permanent home. As he found his feet, France found that increasingly they led him away from the flat in the boulevard de l'École-des-Mines which, since the end of the war, had been the summit of Parnasse.

With Lemerre, too, his relations were quickly to change. After his appointment to the Bibliothèque du Sénat, France ceased to be on Lemerre's payroll, but was paid by the piece – never, however, a great deal, never more than two to three hundred francs for the production of some edition of a classical author – a commission which generally included a lengthy preface and which often entailed some months' work. Nor was Lemerre at all prompt in his payments, which were often produced an incalculable time after the completion of the work. For France, as a married man with a wife and a home to support, such niggardly and dilatory payments were now not good enough. Lemerre's attitude of possession towards him he also, understandably, found irritating, for although France was no longer on his staff, Lemerre clearly considered that he still had absolute and unquestionable rights over everything he wrote and much that he did.

It was not, however, France's method, or his nature, to make an open and direct approach to Lemerre in an attempt to lance this abscess of ill-feeling. Instead, he let his discontent be known amongst his friends and in due course one of them put him in touch with Michel Lévy, the younger partner in the firm of Calmann Lévy, with whom France, in October, 1878, signed a contract giving them the rights over his next two works. The first of these was *Jocaste*, a *conte* which had already appeared earlier that year in *Le Temps*. Lemerre had assumed he would be publishing this, and had already put it in print when, to his astonishment and extreme anger, he received a curt note from France – 'I do not wish my *Jocaste* to be printed. Is that clear?' France followed this with a more courteous, conciliatory but none the less conclusive letter of explanation dated 8th November, 1878. In this, France told Lemerre that acting from thought of his career, and on the advice of all his friends, he had given *Jocaste* to Calmann Lévy. Perhaps unintentionally, perhaps not, France threw salt in the wounds he had already inflicted on Lemerre by pointing out that his only reason for doing this was so that he should get known 'a bit more and a bit better' – in other words, he wanted a better publisher. However, despite his contract with Calmann Lévy, France continued, he hoped to do other work for Lemerre since 'Your books honour my prefaces; and my prefaces honour your books . . . We are destined to collaborate.'

Lemerre's foretellable and furious reaction was to confront France with another contract, dated 16th November,

1878, in which he attempted to tie France so tightly to him that he would not be able to budge for the rest of his life. Two of the more outrageous points in an altogether appalling document were that France should give Lemerre the limitless right of republishing his works, and specifically the two works which he had already given to Calmann Lévy. Unable to withstand, any more than to make, a frontal attack, France duly signed this second contract within three weeks of signing the first. Yet although this duplication of his commitments was to be the cause of incessant wrangling for the next thirty years, terminating in 1911 in a law-suit won for France by the brilliance of his counsel, Poincaré, this second contract did not in any way alter or inhibit his intention that Calmann Lévy, not Lemerre, should in future be his publisher. All of France's many successes were to appear over Calmann Lévy's imprint. Despite the binding clauses of his contract, Lemerre was only, in fact, to get out of France *Servien*, which had clearly missed its moment, and a number of hack works, produced by forced and grudging labour and so, entirely lacking the sparkle that was to bring France much of his success. Some of these Lemerre did not even bother to print. Vague and impressionable though he might seem, France was not, in fact, an easy person to deflect from the direction in which he wanted to go. A close friend of this time, Henry Roujon, wrote that 'on the surface France appeared to submit easily to outside influences, but, in fact, he only permitted himself to be led where he wanted to go, and by so doing, he avoided the troubles of the journey.'

Under the entirely erroneous impression that he now had his rebellious and recalcitrant protégé firmly under lock and key, Lemerre allowed his fury to abate and so left France free, for the moment, to concentrate on his journalism, his main means of supplementing the secure but inadequate income that the Bibliothèque du Sénat provided. Needing the money, France had now to limit his contributions to those papers which paid better than could those of small, if select, circulation such as *l'Amateur d'Autographes*, for which France wrote his last piece in 1877. *Le Temps* took some thirty of France's articles between 1875 and 1879; *Le Globe* published fourteen in 1879; *La Jeune France* printed his contributions regularly from 1878 on.

It was through this journalism that France at last found his way to the writing of books; but the books which he wrote were at first recognizably extended and enlarged pieces of his journalism. *Jocaste* and *Le Chat Maigre*, another *conte* which Calmann Lévy included to make up the length of a book, were both essentially magazine pieces intended only to while a few hours for their readers. They showed France writing more elegantly and easily, but were entirely lightweight, to be forgotten as soon as they were put down.

Le Crime de Sylvestre Bonnard, the second of the works for which France had contracted with Calmann Lévy, was also written to please. It did and it still does. In it France expressed his affection for the *quais* and the Paris in which he had lived virtually the whole of his life, with a charm that showed for the first time in full flower. Like *Jocaste et le Chat Maigre*, *Bonnard* consisted of two separate *contes*, but sharing this time a central character, the benign, scholarly Bonnard, *membre de l'Institut*, the reincarnation of all those courteous, erudite old men who, in the days of France's childhood, used to frequent his father's bookshop. The first of these *contes*, 'La Buche' – the story of how a small act of charity, the gift of some logs to a pretty but penurious widow living in the garret above Bonnard's apartment, was repaid, several years and some eighty pages later, by the present of the manuscript for which Bonnard had been long and widely searching – appeared in *La Revue Alsacienne* of December, 1879 and January, 1880. Almost exactly a year later, the complete work, 'La Buche' joined by the longer *conte* which France first called 'La Fille de

Clémentine' – the account of his rescue of the orphaned daughter of Clémentine, Bonnard's early, only and essentially unattained love, from the hands of a grasping guardian and an ogress of a school-mistress – was serialized in *La Nouvelle Revue*. Some twenty years later, France changed the title of the second *conte* to 'Jeanne Alexandre', as the passage of time made it more appropriate that she should become 'la petite-fille de Clémentine'. This is one of several signs that France saw himself personally linked to, if not necessarily as, Bonnard.

Much of the scholarship with which France filled out the character of Bonnard, and weighted the story, so light it might otherwise have blown away altogether, had been acquired from his three archivist friends, Charavay, Calmettes and Pelletan, and during the time he spent waiting for them at the École de Chartes. He also took much of his material for a description of Sicily, where Bonnard chased the missing manuscript and which France had never visited, from Renan's *Vingt Jours en Sicile*. This did not deter him from discoursing at some length on the character of the Sicilians – 'They are still Greeks and as such their gaiety resists everything' – nor prevent him from painting a delightful picture of their country, if necessarily sketched in somewhat vague outline. But the charm, the style, the gently ironic attitude to life, the picture of the Paris of the *quais* and his childhood, were all very much his own.

On his two threads of thistledown, France hung not only his affection for Paris, but his love of books, even of booksellers – 'They are all my friends and I never pass by their stalls without finding some book I lacked until then without realizing my lack' – of collecting in general – the Prince and Princess Trepof only collected matchboxes, but 'even so they were collectors, they were of the brotherhood' – and a smiling, if slightly sad, scepticism. Treat life gently, said France through Bonnard, and it will probably treat you gently in return. Do not expect too much of it – 'life only seems short to us because we take its measure by our foolish hopes.' Avoid extremes. Aim at achieving an existence like that of Bonnard, which, 'exempt from great misfortunes and great joys, was happy'.

What pleased Parisians particularly about *Le Crime de Sylvestre Bonnard* was the reassurance it contained that their city, after all it had been through, was still not only one of the most beautiful, but one of the pleasantest places in which to live. If many of the pages of *Bonnard* were impregnated by the 'vague tristesse que distille la vie' they expressed also an obvious delight in life and pleasure in living, particularly in Paris – 'All that I see from my window, the horizon stretching away on my left to the hills of Chaillot, and on which the Arc de Triomphe stands up like a milestone, on my right the ancient and venerable Paris with its towers and its spires – all this is my life, myself, and I would be nothing without all these things which are reflected in a thousand variations of my thoughts, and which inspire and animate me. That is why I have for Paris an immense love.'

Le Crime de Sylvestre Bonnard was a mixture of simplicity and sophistication, of scholarship and sleight of hand, of wisdom and naïvety, of sentiment and sentimentality. It had something in it for almost everybody and almost everybody liked it. It was crowned by the Academy and brought France his first real success. France himself was subsequently to tire of the mixture, and to tell Brousson that it was the most tiresome and faded of his works: but he was one of the few people who did.

The birth of Suzanne in April, 1881 – some two months before Calmann Lévy produced *Bonnard* – seemed to complete the family frame within which France could hang the portrait of his happiness. Within his reach he appeared now to have all that he had wished and worked for – a wife, a child, a house of his own, a secure job, many friends, and a growing reputation as an erudite but entertaining critic. Paul Bourget was later to discern – somewhat disparagingly – in France 'a strong bourgeois side to his character'. If it is bourgeois to want a happy home, and the comfort and support it provides, then it was certainly this side of France that was foremost during the years that separated the birth of Suzanne and Bonnard in 1881, from that of his next book, *Le Livre de mon Ami* in 1885.

Over these years France seemed to be filling out to a figure that would fit the frame of domestic happiness. The image of the pertinacious Parnassian which had followed that of the raw, awkward youth who had first come to Lemerre's door, was in its turn followed by that of the benign family man, leading a quiet life on the edge of Paris, whose attitude was as tranquil as his surroundings. Robert de Bonnières wrote that at this time France 'does not like to show himself and makes every effort to stay in the shade. I do not know any man less suited to action. I do not know any man more suited to thought, or who is more eager, not only to learn about things, but to understand them ... His general detachment shows in his lazy and placid face, in his slightly effaced features, in the extreme slowness of his regard, which is amiable, distracted and gentle, and even in his speech which is hesitant and embarrassed – which is a pity for he would talk well without that.'

'His life,' continued Bonnières, 'is as calm and reasonable as his thoughts. One can see it in his habits and associations, in the quiet life that he leads at one end of Paris, where there are avenues and trees.' Virginie Bréton confirms this picture of a peaceful, contented family life, describing a visit to the rue Chalgrin, where she found France at his slippered ease, talking happily of his garden, his bees, his wife – in, it seems, that order.

Bonnières noted, with approval, that France's house did not reek 'too strongly of literature'. It may, however, at times reeked of the stables, for there was a riding school, the Manège Pellier, next door. No. 5, rue Chalgrin was a charming small house – not, in fact, so small as all that, for it had two upstairs floors as well as a basement below – which France's friends, amongst them Henry Roujon, entered 'through a narrow door, painted a browny-red, which opened on to a short flight of stairs; the ante-chamber, the dining and the drawing-rooms filled the ground-floor that was slightly above ground level; in the large kitchen in the basement lived Virgil, the servant with the enigmatic face, Adéline, the maid with the long nose, and Pascal the cat. The staircase, that led to the first and second floors, was hung with prints. The *décor* was modest, but France had managed to collect a few pieces of antique furniture to give both charm and originality to the house. His young wife, grand-daughter of the painter Jean Guérin, had taste and grace . . . From the drawing-room, through French windows, one went out into a tiny garden, half-covered with flowers.'

This was the first time in his life that France had lived out of the vicinity of his beloved *quais*. But even he can have little regretted the change. For Neuilly was a delightful district in which to live. It still is – even if the lava of an erupting city life has now spread over most of what France knew simply as space. Not too far away the trees of the Bois still poke their heads over the roofs of the smaller houses, and the whole district has retained a pleasantly countrified character and an independent air. Neuilly is now the 17th arrondissement of Paris, yet one feels that its inhabitants have retained something of Villon's splendidly self-centred attitude, and basically look upon Paris as 'a little parish' – near, not Pontoise, but Neuilly.

Pleasant though it still is, how much more delightful must it have been when France and Valérie went to live there. At that time an inhabitant of Neuilly had the best of both worlds. On one side the Place de la Concorde was only half-an-hour's walk away; while on the other, he could be in the Bois or in fields in a matter of minutes. The peace of the countryside and the convenience of the city were thus both his at the same time. The amenities as well as the atmosphere of Neuilly were also still charmingly countrified, or painfully parochial, depending on one's point of view. The rue Chalgrin, for example, was not yet paved and so little used that 'the passage of a carriage or a stranger was an event'.

But it was not only in the geographical sense that France, out at Neuilly, was able to enjoy the best of two worlds. Socially, too, he was able to combine assiduous attendance at the various literary functions which came his way, and of which the frequency was increasing in pace with his reputation, with enjoyment of a restful family life in the rue Chalgrin, whose peripheral position allowed the pleasurable feeling of a country retreat. On the one hand over these years he impressively enlarged the range of his friendship to include famous literary figures, as the younger Dumas, Taine, Ludovic Halévy, Alphonse Daudet. On the other, he and Valérie gathered round themselves out at Neuilly a closer circle of younger, more intimate, less famous friends who would often drop in of an evening, with or without an invitation, just as in the days of France's youth, his father's friends used to foregather in the bookshop. These included old friends such as Charavay, Calmettes, Pelletan, Plessis, Bonnières, Pierre de Nolhac, Henry Roujon, but also a sprinkling of new ones – Charles Grandjean, a colleague at the Bibliothèque du Sénat, Gilbert-Augustin Thierry, the nephew of the historian, Soldi, a sculptor, Camille Benoît, the musician; and in 1882, almost as soon as he came to Paris, the youthful Maurice Barrès.

Two of the most frequent and faithful visitors to the rue Chalgrin were a newly-married couple, Jean and Noemi Psichari. Noemi, the daughter of Renan, has described how many evenings she and her husband would join other young people like themselves – 'all poor or very poor, full of enthusiasm for the oppressed, writing verses without cease. We amused ourselves greatly.' In this happy friendly company, France seems to have lost his hesitant manner. At such times, remembered Mme. Psichari, he was 'not at all awkward and timid . . . on the contrary he gave an immediate impression of superiority and ease.'

It was through the Psicharis that France made what was to prove far the most important of these new friendships. Sometime in 1883 or 1884, Jean Psichari introduced him to his father-in-law, Ernest Renan. The *rapport* between the two men was immediate. 'No need of initiation,' wrote Mme. Psichari, 'their spirits met: the two men became friends.' At the time of the meeting, Renan was Principal of the College de France, and France became a frequent visitor to the receptions held most Friday evenings in the great green-carpeted salon of the college. To Renan the friendship meant a great deal, so much so that in 1892 when close to death, he was to tell France, 'Your sympathy has been one of the sweetest things of my life.' But to France it was to mean even more. The effect of Renan's influence on him can be seen in many of his works, particularly *Thaïs*. In *La Vie Littéraire*, France was often to voice his admiration, most notably in a review of Renan's *l'Histoire d'Israel* of 1887. To produce such a work, France wrote, one needed to possess 'a critical sense always on the alert, a scientific scepticism capable of seeing through all the ruses of believers . . . at the same time a strong feeling for the divine, an instinctive understanding of the needs of the human soul, an objective piety. This dual nature combines in M. Renan with extraordinary richness. Born an artist, he has made himself a savant.' The interaction on each other of these two very similar, very different minds, was happy and fruitful. Of the two, Renan was probably the greater savant, France the better artist. The influence of Renan's humane but slightly academic scepticism deepened France's understanding of life; but on its way through France's prismatic personality, it was split into cleaner, more appreciable colours than Renan himself could ever have achieved.

The group of friends who gathered in the rue Chalgrin not only gave France much happy company and a pleasant feeling of personal support, they also at times provided an appreciative but still usefully critical audience on whom he could try any piece of work he happened to have ready. They were thus the first to hear 'Abeille', printed by Chara-vay in 1883, a long fairy story, the first France had written for children, although he had, of course, in *Bonnard*, al-ready written one for grown-ups; 'Les Autels de la Peur', printed in the *Journal des Debats* of 18th March, 1884, a *conte* set in the Terror, and the first time France drew on the immense fund of Revolutionary knowledge he had accumu-lated in his father's bookshop; and many of the scenes of family life that were ultimately to be incorporated in *Le Livre de mon Ami*.

But if France's friends meant much to him at Paris, they still mattered greatly to him when he was away. On holiday he took considerable pains to keep closely in touch with them. Thus Henry Roujon received a series of letters and postcards from Alsace, where in August, 1882, France took Valérie and Suzanne. The placid, profound beauty of the Vosges delighted France. 'You know my Hohwald,' he wrote to Roujon at the beginning of August, '*eh bien*, it is always beautiful, with its bluish-green firs, its fine clear valleys, its clouds moving in flocks along the flanks of its mountains.' On the 15th August he wrote again, 'We are on a plateau in the middle of fir-covered hills and of valleys through which run fresh, singing streams. Nature here has an air grave and good . . . What a country we have lost here!' A few days later he added on a postcard – 'Valérie adores the mountains but wishes they were flat. Suzanne understands nature much better than Lamartine.' The next year they went again to Alsace, and from it France wrote to

Roujon – 'We are staying at the Sign of the Great Lake, beneath a holly branch. Our room looks on to a beautiful garden, and from it we can see the edge of the forest. We are happy . . .' There can be no doubt that at this time, either in Paris or on holiday, they were.

Yet every silver lining has its cloud, and the particular one which cast its shadow over France's happiness at this moment had the formidable shape, and threatening appearance of Lemerre. The success of *Bonnard* had hit Lemerre where it hurt most – in the pocket. It was not that through it he had lost financially, but a *manque de gain* is sometimes the most difficult loss of all to bear. Now he came for his revenge, brandishing the contract which France had been unwise enough to sign two years before. On it, as well as tying, or attempting to tie, France to him in general terms for the rest of his life, he had itemized several particular tasks he wanted out of him. These included a *Histoire de France*, a Greek anthology, an abridged version of the *Dictionnaire de Cuisine*, the editing of another volume of Molière, prefaces for Benjamin Constant, Sainte-Beuve, Glatigny. Once the contract had been signed, Lemerre had not then seemed particularly concerned to exact delivery of any of them and had, in fact, commissioned from France, outside the contract, two anthologies – one of classic, one of contemporary, poetry. These France delivered, more or less on time and imagined, in consequence, that he was now clear of his commitments.

Now, however, Lemerre demanded immediate or early delivery of all the items he had detailed. When the distraught France demurred that this was more than was humanly possible, Lemerre retorted by sending him a series of solicitor's letters. So, dolefully, France had to settle down to do the best he could. The yellowing pages of *Jean Servien* were dragged out of a drawer, revised and sent in as the first of two original works for which France had specifically contracted (France was not to deliver the second until 1896 when at Lemerre's demand, he was to scratch together some childhood sketches to produce *Pierre Nozière*, the forerunner of the more finished and famous *Le Petit Pierre*). Lemerre published *Les Désirs de Jean Servien* in October, 1882, which, as any but an enraged publisher could have seen, was quite the wrong moment for its appearance since the trend of the times was entirely against an interrogative, introspective work of its sort. '*Les Désirs de Jean Servien*', wrote Robert de Bonnières, 'which was written before *Le Crime de Sylvestre Bonnard*, had the misfortune to be published after it. The general public was not at all grateful to the sage-like author of a consolatory book that he should have turned then to tell the troubles of a little apprentice, in love with an actress.' France also managed to produce the Greek anthology and the preface for Benjamin Constant by the autumn of 1882. His real headache, however, was the *Histoire de France*. For some time he had been spasmodically and not very successfully, struggling with this. Now he had to finish it off in a matter of months. The winter of 1882–83 thus became for France a frantic rush through several centuries of French history. By the end of February, and through the intermediacy of the bailiffs whom Lemerre set upon France, the final instalments were in the Passage Choiseul. There, however, they remained, Lemerre making no attempt to publish them for nearly thirty years, thus showing beyond any possible doubt that his bullying of France was directed more by pique than by any practical plan for publication. Having now exacted his several pounds of pulp, Lemerre's anger subsided; but for France, although for fear of further retaliations he was to remain on terms of formal politeness, it was virtually the end of his relationship with Lemerre. He never again went to the shop in the Passage Choiseul, up whose spiral staircase he had climbed into Parnasse, and thence to fame.

France had now thrown in his lot with Calmann Lévy, and in return, Calmann Lévy threw a lot in his way. In the summer of 1883, France became a regular columnist for *l'Univers Illustré*, a weekly published by Calmann Lévy, which carried always on its front page, an article of topical comment under the pseudonym of 'Gérôme'. France now became one half of 'Gérôme', writing on alternate weeks – mainly on literary affairs – while a journalist who wrote as 'Richard O'Monroy', thereby concealing the even more implausible-sounding real name of Jean Edward de l'Isle de Falcon de Saint-Geniès, filled in on the other weeks, dealing principally with political matters.

The secret of 'Gérôme's' identity was at first well-kept, and France used it to give an occasional puff to his own work. Thus, on the 1st November, 1884, 'Gérôme' mentioned a forthcoming book (*Le Livre de Mon Ami*) by 'the author of *Le Crime de Sylvestre Bonnard*, of which we have already described the merit and the success'. When, two months later, in January, 1885, France became a Chevalier of the Légion d'Honneur, 'Gérôme' commented – 'The Minister has been well inspired to give this distinction to M. Anatole France, whose writing has so much charm, and to whom one owes that marvel of grace and good-fellow-ship, of finesse and feeling, *Le Crime de Sylvestre Bonnard*.' Nor did France forget his friends. Taine, the younger Dumas, 'Gyp', Coppée and an important new friend, Jules Lemaître, an ex-school-teacher, some seven or eight years younger than France, who had made his name and his mark as dramatic critic for *Le Journal des Debats*, were amongst the many to whom France, or rather 'Gérôme', now gave a helping hand.

As the years passed, however, the disguise began to wear thin, and finally in 1890 France dropped it altogether. By his account this was because of a quotation which he had stuck on to his proof the wrong way round. In future, he was told, or so he said, he would have to bear the responsibility for his mistakes. The real reason for the change, how-ever, was of course, that by then it was much more of an advantage for a paper to have 'Anatole France' writing for it than 'Gérôme'.

By now most Parisian papers and periodicals were open to France, and he contributed to many of them. Thus, pieces of *Le Livre de mon Ami* appeared in *La Revue Bleue*, *Le Magasin Pittoresque*, *La Nouvelle Revue* and *La Jeune France* before being published in book form by Calmann Lévy in 1885. With *Le Livre de mon Ami*, France repeated the formula and much of the success of *Sylvestre Bonnard*. Here again were his beautiful, beloved *quais*, the enchanted environment of his childhood; here the great, gay courtyard of 19 quai Malaquais; here the old Paris of his youth, sophisticated yet countrified, sure that it was the capital, not only of France, but of the world, and still close to the land on which it was built.

On top of this, France imposed the image of a happy family life, clearly drawn, one would have thought, from his own. A passage of the preface shows how well France could capture the quiet glow of family happiness as well as those still shadowy moments of solitude when the room is empty but the mind full – 'It is sweet to remember. The silence of the night invites it. Its calm tames the phantoms, which are timid and fugitive by nature, and need shadow as well as solitude in order to come and speak into the ears of their living friends. The curtains of the windows are drawn, those of the door hang in heavy folds on the carpet. Only one door is ajar, there, in the direction in which my eyes instinctively turn. From it steals out an opalescent light; from it comes the sound of even and gentle breathing, in which even I cannot distinguish that of the mother from that of the children. *Dormez, chéris, dormez*.

Le Livre de Mon Ami was more obviously contrived and less carefully stitched together than *Sylvestre Bonnard*, and so lacked something of its charm and its craftsmanship. On the personal side, too, a shadow of doubt hung, despite all France's efforts to dispel it, over his fireside scene of domestic content. In spite of life having given him 'treasures ... by comparison with which all that I desired seems cinders and smoke', he could not, he wrote, say '*A demain*, without experiencing a sensation of sadness and anxiety.' Yet if today had really been as pleasant and perfect as France had taken such pains to make out, what need had he to fear the morrow?

━━━━━━━◆◆◆━━━━━━━

THREE DOORS of the many that the success of *Sylvestre
Bonnard* opened to France were to prove of particular importance. They were those of the Comtesse de Loynes in
the Champs-Élysées, of Mme. Aubernon in the rue d'Astorg,
and of Mme. Arman de Caillavet at No. 12, in what was then
the avenue de la Reine Hortense, but was shortly to become,
and to remain, the avenue Hoche. Between them, these
three women showed how different could be the qualities
that combined in the make-up of a successful hostess; and
how diverse the paths that led to the establishment of a
successful salon. Beauty, brains, birth – one or other of
these seemed to suffice – provided that it was linked to the
two essential, not all that common, denominators – personality and money.

Mme. de Loynes, although on the wrong side of forty
when France first met her, undoubtedly had, or had had, the
beauty. When, as Jeanne de Tourbay, she had first come to
Paris from an obscure home in Reims, at the age of nineteen, she had had an immediate and prodigious success.
She had a cool as well as a beautiful head and played her cards
well. In due course she had become, not only the mistress,
but the protegée of the Prince Napoléon, who had eased the
way for the creation of a salon around her which included
such eminent figures as Sainte-Beuve, Gautier, Renan,
Flaubert, Taine. With the reign of the Second Empire, and
possibly also of her beauty, coming to an end, Jeanne de
Tourbay had sought to secure her position, and had become

engaged to Ernest Baroche, the son of the Minister of Justice. Before they could be married, however, he was killed in the Franco-Prussian war, leaving his fiancée his immense fortune. Almost immediately, she married the good-looking Comte de Loynes, from whom, to no one's great surprise, she soon separated. Now, with the means – money and a name – to be independent, she had restarted her salon, which from then until the turn of the century remained amongst the most influential in Paris. Jeanne de Tourbay, Comtesse de Loynes, was an outstanding example of the beautiful adventuress with a feeling for culture, of whom Laure Hayman, Proust's friend, who corrected her crowned lovers for faults of spelling and demeanour, was another.

France, taken to Mme. de Loynes' salon by Jules Lemaître – ultimately, but not yet, its star – was a regular attendant over a number of years, but never seems to have been as assiduous in his attentions to his hostess in the Champs-Élysées, as he was either in the rue d'Astorg or the avenue Hoche. The ambitions and concerns of Mme. de Loynes were entirely centred on her beautiful person, whereas both Mme. Aubernon and Mme. Arman were, in their different ways, striving to create something that had a life and a use of its own. It may have been this that put France off.

Mme. Aubernon had the birth, but not the brains or the beauty, although she once alarmed one of her guests by declaring roundly and loudly, 'I have a magnificent body', never being one to understate her case. In her own way and home, she was a strict disciplinarian, and conversations at her dinner parties were regulated by the ringing of a bell. This practice and the dictatorial temperament which prompted it, made her prone to ridicule. There was the occasion when she shut up a guest, whom she thought to be trying to intervene in the conversation, only to find, when she eventually silenced the company to hear what he did have to say, that he only wanted to ask for some more potatoes. There was another when she went to a fancy dress ball decked out as 'the Glory of Dumas' – who for a long time was the star of her salon – with a bust of Dumas on her head, and ribbons, bearing the names of his various works, draped around her voluminous figure. 'I shall need a strong back to bear the weight of such ridicule,' said Dumas in horror when he saw this apparition of his achievement. Yet lodged in Mme. Aubernon's ample bosom was a genuine desire to give a helping hand to those who needed and sought it, whether young writers, aspiring artists, or simply those who wished to improve their social position. She had a particular and keen interest in the theatre, and many worthwhile plays, which might otherwise never have had their chance, made their first appearance on one of her theatrical evenings. It was in Mme. Aubernon's salon that France seemed at first to be making the most progress, and by 1894 he was already sufficiently in favour to read a fragment from a forthcoming work (presumably *Le Livre de mon Ami*) to her assembled guests.

Mme. Arman de Caillavet, although pretty and vivacious, had not beauty in the sense that Mme. de Loynes gave to the word; nor had she the advantage of Mme. d'Aubernon's aristocratic birth, for her parents, although wealthy, cultured, and, on her mother's side, titled, came from Jewish families. But she had brains – to the extent that she was not simply intelligent, she had an intellect. This implied a difference in her motives for establishing a salon. Whereas, for Mme. de Loynes, her salon was a habit, a means of holding the conquests and company she had first subjugated by her beauty; and for Mme. d'Aubernon it was the means by which a normally gregarious, socially-minded person made use of her talents and let off steam generally; for Mme. Arman it was a means of creative expression, a means through which she sought fulfilment for her considerable intellectual ability. This difference characterized her salon throughout the twenty-five years of its existence. It had always a quality of intellectual intensity, which distinguished it from other more social gatherings. Mme. Arman was not simply providing the setting for a few moments of social chit-chat, or the means of making useful contacts. Her receptions and dinners were serious occasions at which serious people had serious thoughts.

Mme. Arman's character had been conditioned by her upbringing, which, for an age when social attributes were thought to be of paramount importance, had been exceptionally cultured. As Léontine Lippmann, she belonged to a family of financiers, whose interests and outlook ranged far beyond France. From an early age she had travelled extensively, and in the course of her travels had been taken to many of the noteworthy museums, churches and galleries throughout Europe. She had learnt to speak fluent German and Italian, and had also studied philosophy, literature and the fine arts. From all of this she had acquired a wide, cosmopolitan, cultural background, and a particular respect for things of the mind, in which was set a strong desire to make something of her own. Her parents had finally capped this admirably conscientious and comprehensive education by arranging her marriage to a man without any intellectual or cultural interests whatever. M. Arman – he tacked on the de Caillavet from the name of a wine-growing property in the Gironde – was the extravagant, extrovert son of a Bordeaux ship-owner. His father had been the close friend, and as it turned out, the dupe, of the Emperor Napoleon III. He had been nearly ruined when, on the Emperor's suggestion, he started to build seven warships, only to find the order was never ratified, the warships having to be sold, at a considerable loss, to America.

The marriage of Albert Arman to Léontine Lippmann was very much an Imperial alliance – for the Lippmanns and Koenigswaters (Mme. Arman's maternal family) had been useful financial friends to the Emperor. It took place in the Tuileries in 1868 in the presence of the Emperor and Empress. Yet in spite of so splendid a start, the marriage quickly came to grief, due to the obvious incompatibility of the two partners. Had not a son, Gaston, been born in 1870, had not Mme. Arman liked the social security which a husband, however tiresome, provided, had not M. Arman needed money badly, they would probably have soon separated. As it was they contrived to lead separate lives under the same roof, and were still in this way together but apart, when France, some time in 1883, first visited their house. From their first meeting, France seems to have felt a great personal attraction towards Mme. Arman; and from then on, it was on her that his ambitions, social or otherwise, seem to have centred. Yet at first he was rowing against an adverse tide. As late as 1885 Mme. Arman told Jules Lemaître that she liked France's 'style and wit but not his character or his manners'.

The Comtesse de Loynes, Mme. Aubernon, and Mme. Arman, different though they were in character, and different though the character of the salons they created, had at this time one thing at least in common – they all were in need of a centre-piece, of a figure round which they could mould their salons to the shapes they wanted. This was not only because it was fashionable at this time for a successful salon to have its resident star, but because they were all sufficiently feminine to prefer working behind, and ostensibly for, someone else rather than openly on their own.

This need of a figure-head was particularly strongly felt by Mme. Arman, for her salon was much the most recently established. She had, in fact, served an apprenticeship of several years in the rue d'Astorg, where she had learnt much but had had to endure much – typical of Mme. Aubernon's patronizing attitude being her reply to anyone who complimented her on the charm, capability or intelligence of Mme. Arman, whom she looked upon as her protegée without realizing she was really her rival – 'Yes, I invented her myself.' But gradually Mme. Arman had

gathered round her a group of particular friends from which
to form the nucleus of her own salon, and whose unity and
loyalty she cemented by a series of excellent dinner-parties.
Unlike Mme. Aubernon, at whose house the food, by
general repute, was bad, Mme Arman had a superlative
chef, and his sauces were probably an essential ingredient
of her early social success. Out of this group, the choice of
a centre-piece seemed gradually to be narrowing to one of
two – either Victor Brochard, an eminent scholar and the
author of an excellent book on *Les Sceptiques Grecs*, but
a man who knew his way quite as well round the contemporary as the classical world – or the Commandant
Rivière.

The Commandant Rivière was an artist-adventurer, an
intelligent man of action, of whose type Saint-Éxupèry and
Malraux have been more recent examples. At the centre of
his character there seems to have been something unresolved,
perhaps unhappy. When in Paris, he seems always to have
been thinking of his voyages, but when on them, he was
often dreaming of an armchair in the Academy and of the
novels he would need to write to get there. In 1881, after
several exciting voyages of discovery in the South Seas,
Rivière was sent out to Saigon. At this time France, eager
to increase her influence in the Far East, had designs on the
vast territory of Annam, then subject to Imperial China.
Rivière was the man to suit a mood and moment of imperial expansion, into which his own ambitions conveniently
dovetailed, and in 1882 he started the Second Tonkinese
war by the extremely gallant capture of Hanoi. In a letter
to Mme. Arman, however, he referred to this daring conquest – his forces had been greatly outnumbered – as if it
was simply something in the nature of a distraction, something to ease the monotony of life in a hot climate. In this
and other letters he wrote to Mme. Arman from Hanoi,
there were signs that he was seeking a closer, more intimate
relationship. He believed in God, he wrote Mme. Arman,

but as God was a long way off, it was wise, he thought, to believe also in someone, something closer at hand – in a man, or a woman, in friendship, or in love. The sort of love he wanted was quiet and understanding, an amused affection which believed in pleasure rather than in love.

By inference, there were signs, too, that the desire for a closer relationship came not only from his side. His attitude to women, he wrote indignantly to Mme. Arman, was not at all what she thought it was. He was not so much of a Turk as she believed. Yet no woman taxes a man about his attitude to women in general, as Mme. Arman had evidently been doing, unless she is concerned about his attitude to one woman in particular.

His relationship with Mme. Arman was not the only one of Rivière's ambitions which seemed in 1883 to be on the brink of fulfilment. In a letter written in May to Mme. Arman from Hanoi, he added a postscript, mentioning that Dumas, who was a close friend, had written suggesting that he should arrange to be put up for the Academy. However, he thought, wrote Rivière, that this might be a bit premature, that it would be wiser, before doing so, to 'write another book and take another town'. What did Mme. Arman think? He never had the chance to find out. Eight days later, in the process of taking this other town, Rivière was ambushed, captured by the Chinese, tortured and put to death. Had Rivière lived to take his town and write his book, there can be little doubt that he would have gained, not only his arm-chair in the Academy, but the place of honour in Mme. Arman's salon.

France first came into Mme. Arman's house in the year of Rivière's death, but not for at least three years after that did he come into her plans. During these years, as in the circumstances was only to be expected, it was round the figure of Brochard that Mme. Arman's salon seemed to be grouping. Yet for one reason or another, Brochard does not seem to have made an entirely satisfactory centre-piece, and

Mme. Arman was quick to respond to the advances of Jules Lemaître, who was introduced to her about the same time as France, but made much quicker headway in her consideration. Lemaître was soon sending her his work to be criticized, a sure way to Mme. Arman's heart, but making doubly sure by the warmth of his accompanying notes. He did not really know, he wrote in one, why he sent her these 'bagatelles'. Perhaps it was simply because it gave him pleasure – which perhaps was as much as saying that he loved her very much. He hastened to correct anything 'improper' in this declaration by adding his most 'proper respects'.

France and Lemaître seem at this time to have been hunting as a couple and there were no signs or sense of any rivalry between them. France, who was considerably handicapped in his social life by his vagueness about times, dates, engagements, would refer to Lemaître to get him out of his difficulties. Thus he wrote to Lemaître in June, 1885 – 'Can you help me out of an embarrassing situation? I cannot remember on which day Mme. Aubernon has invited me to dine. I only know it is a Thursday and that it is with the Comtesse Potocka. Thus if you know when the Comtesse dines, you will know when I dine . . .' When Lemaître, writing to Mme. Arman, expressed his disappointment that she had not been at a dinner-party at which he and France had been guests, he joined France to him in his regrets – 'We lamented your absence between ourselves, France and I.'

Gradually there were some signs of a thaw in Mme. Arman's attitude towards France, but it was a slow process. Early in 1886, France and Valérie were invited to dinner, but in a letter to her son Gaston telling him of their coming – it was for an evening in Lent – Mme. Arman implied by her tone that the invitation was part of her Lenten penance. That autumn she invited both of them to Capian, a delightful, cool country house in the Gironde, to which, accompanied by her family and by her chef, she retired in the late summer to recover from her hectic social season. But it was a very half-hearted invitation. In a letter to Gaston telling him that M. Arman had written to ask France and his family to stay, Mme. Arman avowed that it would bore her so much if France accepted 'en bloc' that she would find some excuse to put them off. But if, she continued significantly, France came by himself, that would be quite a different matter. France evidently did accept 'en bloc', for he and Valérie did not go to Capian that year.

Mme. Arman was clearly not enamoured of Valérie, but two things during the winter of 1886–87 warmed her feelings considerably for France. The long-foreseeable split between Mme. Aubernon and Mme. Arman finally occurred, ostensibly because of the secession of Dumas, whose daughter had married Mme. Arman's brother, from the rue d'Astorg to the avenue Hoche, but really because the same salon was now not big enough to contain the two women. Most of those who were habitués of both salons continued to visit both, but France was one of the few who made a clear choice between them. He never again returned to the rue d'Astorg. This open avowal of his loyalties both pleased and flattered Mme. Arman.

Also, during this, as it was to turn out, fateful year for France, he became the chief literary critic for *Le Temps*. In March, 1886 he had been appointed by Adrien Hébrard, the editor, to write a weekly column under the title 'La Vie à Paris', which, during his temporary absence from Paris on holiday, became 'La Vie hors de Paris'. In the autumn Hébrard narrowed France's attention and activities to *La Vie Littéraire*, but in so doing, he increased his stature, for France's predecessor, Edmond Scherer, who had written for *Le Temps* since 1861, had made his column into one of the most important literary tribunes in Paris. France was to push its reputation even higher. The three hundred odd articles he was to write for *Le Temps* over the next seven years gave him the opportunity to show himself as one of the most creative of critics as well as the most delightful of essayists. *La Vie Littéraire* was to prove the perfect medium for his particular mixture of knowledge, charm and style; and was to provide, when collected and selected into book form, five of the most evergreen volumes in French criticism.

In retrospect, France's work as the critic of *Le Temps*, shows clearly as the culmination of all the assorted criticism he had done over the previous twenty years, but if it owed a great deal to the past, it also owed much to the present, and to the happy chance which put him in harness with Hébrard, an energetic, incisive editor who kept France up to the mark and saw to it that it was the highest of which he was capable. Until the last period of his life, France was always to need pushing to get his best work out of him. For many years Lemerre had supplied the pressure, but Calmann Lévy, excellent though he was in every other way as a publisher, was too courteous, considerate and nice a man to be willing, or possibly able, to do so. Hébrard, however, provided just the brusque, outspoken, appreciative yet critical personality needed to put, and to keep, a fine edge on France's talent. With a great deal of truth, France wrote in the preface with which he dedicated the first volume of *La Vie Littéraire* to Hébrard – 'Permit me to offer you this little book; you are due it, since certainly it would not exist without you . . .'

France was himself that year to have a brief experience of being an editor. At the end of 1885 he had been put in charge of a sumptuous cultural monthly, *Les Arts et les Lettres*, in the production of which no expense had been spared. Beautifully printed on fine vellum, excellently illustrated, it could but sell for an absurd price, costing 30 francs, approximately £3, a number. France, astonished by his appointment – 'I will perhaps amaze you,' he wrote in a letter of August, 1885, 'by telling you that I have been made editor of a review, but you cannot be more surprised than I am' – managed during the few months he was in charge, to assemble a collection of distinguished contributors who inevitably included many of his own friends – Leconte de Lisle, Pailleron, Pierre de Nolhac, Camille Benoît, Heredia, the younger Dumas, Coppée, Henry Roujon, Lemaître, Barrès amongst them. When, however, France was appointed to *Le Temps*, he had neither the time nor the need to continue with a task for which, probably, he had little true talent or taste. In the autumn of 1886 he resigned from *Les Arts et les Lettres*, which, somewhat surprisingly, survived for a further three years.

If, in more than one way, 1886 was a critical year for France, it was also a sad one, for in June his mother died. The removal of this sheet anchor may well have had an important effect on the general loosening of his domestic ties which seems to have taken place at this time. France's mother, once she had overcome her possessive inclinations towards her son, had become devoted to his family and was staunch in their support and her belief that they provided the best safeguard of his happiness. France, stricken with grief, the more since he considered that his mother's death might have been prevented had his father brought her under medical attention earlier, did not, however, allow the pace of his work to falter. In a letter to one of his editors, announcing his mother's death, he wrote – '*Mon cher ami*, I have some very sad news to tell you. I have lost my poor mother. She passed away on Thursday . . . Don't worry about the article. You will have it on time.' It was not only for his talents that his editors appreciated France. They could be certain that whatever calamities befell France, so long as he was still able to work, they would get their copy.

France was not long in getting into his stride as literary critic for *Le Temps*, but his appointment by itself probably raised him considerably in Mme. Arman's estimation. Certainly during the course of the following year he went much more often to her house, and each visit seems to have increased her importance in his eyes. When in August, 1887 he and Valérie went on holiday, he tried to bridge the distance between them by a series of letters of which the tone was urgent, at times imploring – 'Why do you not reply by a single word?'; 'Where are you . . . I cannot resign myself to not knowing, chère Madame, where you are'; 'We will be back on the second, and come to see you on that day, after a separation which has seemed long to me'; 'I am well content that my article satisfied you. I fear nothing more than to displease you as I desire nothing more than to see you again.'

That year, in September, France and Valérie went to stay at Capian. Poor Valérie, one can not but sympathize with her at having to brave what must already have appeared to her as the lioness's den, but a difficult situation clearly made her as difficult as possible. In a letter to Gaston, on the eve of her departure for Capian, Mme. Arman wrote that she had just seen France and Valérie – 'he was trembling and stammering before his imperious spouse'. France, apparently, had put forward a scheme for their journey to Capian, which Valérie had 'immediately demolished'. At Capian, things went little, if at all, better. 'Les Frances,' Mme. Arman wrote to Gaston who had wisely gone off on a holiday in Spain, had arrived on Monday evening – 'she very forbidding, he very preoccupied with two articles that he had promised for this week, so much so that, so far, the pleasure of their visit has been slight.' They were short of horses, but Mme. Arman's father sent some of his over to Capian. As a result, went on Mme. Arman, they would soon be able to take Valérie for drives round the countryside, but they missed Gaston badly to put 'this conqueress' in her place. 'I hope you will be returning soon,' concluded Mme. Arman, 'Valérie badly needs to be brought to heel.'

Yet, of course, far from being the 'conqueress', Valérie

was the almost inevitable 'loser' in this contest, and, as is quite clear from her conduct, already realized it. Disagreeable though it seems to have been for everyone concerned, this stay at Capian was probably decisive in settling the future shape of the relationship between France and Mme. Arman. Before it, France was only one of several contenders for the place of honour in Mme. Arman's salon and her life. After it, there was clearly no question or possibility of anyone else. With Valérie in attendance, and in so forbidding and suspicious a mood, it is unlikely that it was anything that France actually said or did during their stay that caused the change in Mme. Arman's attitude. More probably it was simply the realization by Mme. Arman, who was no marriage-breaker, that France's marriage was, in fact, already broken.

'Gyp', the Comtesse de Martel, was to describe France at this time as 'athirst for social success', and to assert that it was this that primarily drew him to Mme. Arman. Admittedly, France's upbringing, in particular the period of his schooling at Stanislas had left him with a sense of social inferiority of which he was to be long in ridding himself. 'Gyp' was also to declare that the social success which France was to attain through Mme. Arman was the making of him as a writer, and that without it, he would never have become an Academician. But France does not at first seem to have found any great pleasure in the extension of the social round which the success of Bonnard brought him. Émile Hovelaque, meeting him now for the first time, described the impression France made on him – 'a long and heavy equine face, twisted as if by a slight pain . . . a long nose, coarse-grained and grey; only the black eyes very bright, magnificent with vitality and intelligence, lit up this rather disquieting physiognomy, in which there was something of the seminarist, of the Bonapartist, and of the faun. He spoke and spoke badly. His voice was grave, and rather unctuous, hesitant and at times nasal; his tongue tied . . .

This first meeting deceived me.' The picture is hardly that of a man at his ease, enjoying himself. In *Le Livre de mon Ami*, France wrote pointedly, 'I am of the opinion of Lord Palmerston who said that life would be bearable if it were not for its pleasures.' But would France have endured what was clearly a painful experience simply for the sake of further social advancement, particularly since the loyal group of friends who came to the rue Chalgrin must surely have given him much of the social assurance he needed. Hovelaque's description contrasts noticeably with Noemi Psichari's portrait of France in the rue Chalgrin, – assured, forthcoming, talking very nearly as well as he wrote. Surely France could have been well content with the social support his friends provided and – if this was all he was after – had no need to look elsewhere.

Nor was it true that Mme. Arman made France as a writer. She influenced, developed, changed him certainly. But his reputation was well established before he played any significant part in her salon, or she in his life. *Bonnard, Le Livre de mon Ami*, his – as yet occasional – articles for *Le Temps* and other papers, had seen to that. His reputation was further secured and consolidated when he became literary critic to *Le Temps* – an appointment in no way due to social influence, save that Hébrard, a senator, may have got to know France better by seeing him constantly in the Bibliothèque du Sénat, than he would had he known him only as an occasional visitor to his office.

But if France's household in the rue Chalgrin had, over the years 1880–84, attained a state of happy sociable domesticity – or so it seemed from its reflection in *Le Livre de mon Ami*, and from the descriptions of his friends – the whole structure rested, as in any marriage, on his relationship with his wife. If that failed, all the rest fell apart. At this time something seems to have come between France and Valérie. What it was one does not know. The details of such intimate processes are rarely revealed. Both France and

Valérie were subsequently to produce varying reasons for the failure of their marriage. On his side, France was to allege that Valérie considered she had married beneath her, and that she took little interest in his work – but at first he had been proud enough to be married to a Guérin, and Valérie certainly helped him with *Bonnard:* Valérie on hers, that France spent much of what should have been the housekeeping money, on buying books and other items for his collections. Yet such differences are not the stuff of which divorces are made. They seem rather the outward expression of some physical or psychological difference that at this time split their relationship. France's pursuit of Mme. Arman only makes sense if one considers that he was seeking, rather than social success or literary advancement, a personal support and satisfaction he could no longer find in his marriage.

Like most love-affairs, that between France and Mme. Arman is not well-documented. As France had written in *Bonnard*, 'Lovers, when they love well, do not write about their happiness.' Seeing each other most days, what need had France and Mme. Arman when in Paris to correspond? It is, thus, only their absences that are chronicled. Some time during the winter or spring following the stay at Capian, France declared his love to Mme. Arman and found that it was answered, but it was only at the end of July, 1888, when Mme. Arman went on her annual cure to Saint-Gervais, that he put it on paper – and on record. 'At last I can cry it; my beloved, my all, I love you. I love you infinitely, and that is why I am happy in my sadness, that is why I am happy in my sufferings, and I bless my sufferings and my sadness because they have the same source as my joy and because everything that comes from you is blessed.' He received a no less ardent answer. 'I only live for you and I torture you,' wrote Mme. Arman on the 2nd August, 'And you, you think that I do not love you so much;

it is only that I love you badly, I love you without thought of sacrifice, without resignation. I love you ferociously, for myself. Forgive me I beg you, I ask it on my knees: I would like to have long years of youth left to give you but the little that remains belongs to you, to you.' France wrote again on the 7th August – 'I see you ceaselessly, the head thrown back, on your lips the profound and beautiful smile which precedes oblivion.'

But if France could cry his love to Mme. Arman, he could not yet cry it from the housetops. 'Mon Dieu,' wrote Mme. Arman on the 12th October from Capian, 'if we could only escape, the two of us . . . but, alas, we are labelled, classified. Society is a house of detention which does not release its prisoners. At least we have hasty and furtive joys such as prisoners cannot know. Let us try to be content with them, for they have a supreme ecstasy.' Unless they chose to break with convention and society – and Mme. Arman was certainly unwilling to do this – theirs had to be a secret love. In the spring of 1889, France took a furnished room in the rue Washington – close to the Champs Élysées – in the name of 'Monsieur Jourdain'. It was there he and Mme. Arman met when they wanted to be on their own. France never directly described this hide-out in the rue Washington, but in *Le Lys Rouge*, the novel written some years later, at Mme. Arman's behest, to express and en- shrine their love, his lovers met in the rue Spontini, also in a rented room – 'silent, stuffed with cushions, curtains, carpets, bronzes, hanging on walls covered with cretonne, shone with the glow of revived embers . . . everywhere gleams of light quivered in the warm shadow.' – and per- haps, when describing the room in the rue Spontini, France had in his mind the room in the rue Washington.

Situated as they were on the exposed slopes of public life, France and Mme. Arman had to evolve an elaborate plan and pattern of deception, which entailed not only a double life, but a double correspondence. On her side, Mme.

Arman did her best to cover the cracks which might lead a peering and perceptive eye to suspect the truth, to conceal her intimacy with France beneath an appearance of family friendship. This, in particular, meant muzzling the frank, not over-discreet Gaston, who at first, very naturally, looked upon France as an intruder. In consequence, wrote Mme. Arman to France, she had undertaken on Gaston 'a civilizing process'. Already he had admitted he found France 'charming'.

France, on his side, when Mme. Arman was away from Paris, covered his love letters with the camouflage of a more formal correspondence, presumably intended to satisfy prying eyes, which Mme. Arman could flourish as the proof of their friendly but entirely platonic relationship. In these France wrote as if he and Mme. Arman were still on the basis of the exchange of ideas, of gossip, of news that they had been the year before, as if they were friends but nothing more – and nothing less, for a sudden reversion to a purely impersonal style of writing would have been equally suspicious. 'Do you know, Madame,' wrote France on the 7th August, 'that your letters are marvels of taste and good sense . . . I have a very fine one on Venice, that about the firs is even more evocative . . .' But on the same day he had also sent off to Mme. Arman the letter in which he had described her as he saw her in his dreams – 'head thrown back, eyelids closed . . .'

France's less formal letters seem to show that he was now deeply in love – probably for the first time in his life. But the experience seems to have brought him pain as well as pleasure. From the start France was extremely jealous of all the other people, all the other activities that shared Mme. Arman's life. 'Far from you,' he wrote on the 17th August, 1888, 'everything wounds and irritates me. Yesterday I went for a walk in the Bois . . . No one passed by. What I suffered is unspeakable . . . Ma chérie, I am desperate. I feel I no longer have the right to desire you. What am I to you? An hour of your life. And the other hours? . . . I am jealous as I did not believe one could be . . . Oh, yes, I hate you. Forgive me.' Nor was this a quick passing mood. A year later, on the 24th August, 1889, when they were again separated by their holidays, he was still writing on the same plaintive note – 'Forgive me and pity me. What I suffer is unimaginable'; and a month later – 'Forgive my injustice. It is made of love. Excuse my suspicions. I am suffering. You cannot deliver me from the poison you have put in my veins.'

In the circumstances it was hardly surprising that France should have felt as he did. In their vertiginous fall into love, Mme. Arman undoubtedly kept her head better than France, which is not saying that she did not fall as far or as fast, but simply that she had a better head for depths. In *Le Lys Rouge*, France was to make his heroine, Thérèse, tell her lover, 'I intend that love should remain a pleasure,' and by repute, this is what Mme. Arman also told France. Love was to remain a pleasure, in its place. That place no doubt was far larger and more important than she had at first envisaged, but it had to remain such that it would not disturb the outward appearance and order of her life. Yet no man likes to share his love, with an ambition any more than with a person, and Mme. Arman's refusal to give France pride of place in her life, even if from now on she determinedly and devotedly gave him pride of place in her salon, undoubtedly accounted for the jealousy which at this time distinguished many of France's letters to her. From them it is clear that the one thing that at this time France wanted more than anything else was to have Mme. Arman to himself, and this was the one thing she would not allow him.

It was mainly, one would think, Mme. Arman's fear of social exposure that determined France to continue the travesty of his marriage – perhaps the cruellest and least forgivable of his actions. A clean and a quick cut would have

been much easier to bear – and much swifter to heal. Yet
France continued to live with Valérie in the rue Chalgrin
for nearly four years after it was plain that their relationship
was beyond help or hope. Inevitably they were years of
increasing animosity, increasing bitterness, increasing tension. The final judgement for divorce reveals something of
this painfully prolonged process of separation. After the
winter of 1888, 'Thibault, the so-called Anatole France,
little by little deserted his home. During the succeeding
years his absences became more and more frequent, sometimes lasting for several days.' Contact and conversation
between husband and wife gradually diminished to the
point where France would not speak to Valérie, and would
communicate with her only 'by notes passed by the servant'.

Valérie must have found these years of desertion and dis-
integration the more difficult to bear, because of the speed
with which France was now shooting to the front of the
literary scene. This was partly due to the increased interest
and attention which now attached to him as the acknowledged star of Mme. Arman's salon, but mainly because of his
success as literary critic for *Le Temps*. France had his own
ideas of what criticism should be. 'Such as I understand it,
criticism is . . . a sort of novel for the use of clever and
critical minds, and every novel, if one understands it right,
is an autobiography. A good critic is he who recounts the
adventures of his soul among masterpieces.' France was
a very subjective critic – he did not believe there was
any other sort – 'To be frank, the critic ought to say –
"Messieurs, I am going to talk of myself *à propos* of Shakespeare, *à propos* of Racine, or of Pascal . . ." 'And so once
a week France talked of himself *à propos* of Baudelaire and
Bismarck, of Georges Sand and Shakespeare, of Maupassant,
Merimée and Mallarmé: of the classic French writers and of
those of his contemporaries who might, or might not, prove
in their turn to be classics also; of anyone, in fact, who came

to his notice because they had written a good or interesting book, or had had one written about them.

It was not only, or usually, the famous whose company France sought. His inclination, as always, was to explore the side roads as much as the highways – and in these he found characters such as Becq de Fouquieres, the editor of André Chenier – 'the man of a single book'; Charles Mouselet, the most industrious idle man France had ever met; the romantic but cowardly Chevalier de Florian, too frightened even to get married; Marie Bashkirtseff, 'in whose short life', France found, 'something so acrid and desperate that it contracts the heart'.

But in talking about himself France was also talking about life. The key to his criticism lies in the title under which it appeared – *La Vie Littéraire*. France was writing about literature, but always also about life. He brought his criticism out of the shelter and seclusion of his study, into the wind and rain and sun of ordinary life. Like the weather it was subject to moods. France was not the most reliable or infallible of critics, but there have been few more human, more invigorating, more enchanting in a sunny spell, more melancholy in a sad one, and always he kept not only his sense of style, but his sense of perspective. It is always clear to his readers that literature is a part of life, and not life of literature. The Parisian public quickly took him to their hearts and he rapidly became the most read, respected and relished critic in Paris.

With the responsibility of producing an article of some 2–3,000 words every week for *Le Temps*, and another of 1,500 every week for *l'Univers*, it is hard to think that France can have had much time for anything else. Yet in an early letter to Mme. Arman France referred to 'our secret', and this was in fact *Thaïs* about which France had early consulted Mme. Arman. At this stage it was called *Paphnuce*, until Calmann Lévy, with the eye of a good publisher for a bad title, changed it. From the first Mme. Arman was enthusiastic – it must have been a great satisfaction to her to have her part in a creative work of this sort – and it was she who arranged its serialization in 1889 with Fernand Brunetière, the touchy editor of *La Revue des Deux Mondes*. Brunetière disliked France, or perhaps disliked rather the speed with which France's star was rising, and had recently refused one of his short stories. But he was too shrewd an editor to let something as good as *Thaïs* pass into other hands. In the end Brunetière managed to have it both ways, for while publishing *Thaïs*, he contrived also to insult and infuriate France by the capricious cuts he made in the text.

Thaïs appeared in *La Revue des Deux Mondes* in 1889, and was published by Calmann Lévy in August, 1890. In both its serial and book form it had an immense success, augmented when Massenet drew from it the theme of one of his most successful operas. Mme. Arman, a perceptive critic of France's work as well as his ardent admirer, once wrote to France that his particular genius lay in the way he infused into a classical style, contemporary problems and passions – 'You join to the adorable purity of antiquity, the expressions and emotions of our own time.' It was the combination in *Thaïs* of a classical style in a classical setting with the expression and exploration of a contemporary mood of doubt so deep that it was inclined to doubt even doubt itself, that particularly appealed to the Parisian public. Like most works that throw their anchor into a particular mood and moment of time, *Thaïs* has remained with it, and has now a larger place in French literary history than in French literature. Yet if one can make the leap back to that disturbed decade, seventy-five years ago, it requires little more effort to jump the further fifteen centuries that separate it from the time of *Thaïs*.

France had long had the legend of the converted courtesan at the back of his mind. It had been the subject of the interminable poem with which, in 1867, he had overloaded the last issue of *Le Chasseur Bibliographique* –

> En ce temps-la vivait une femme au pays
> Des Egyptiens, belle and qu'on nommait Thaïs.

But it had needed the warmth of Mme. Arman's encourage-ment and enthusiasm to make the seed germinate. France started work on this, his first full-scale novel since *Servien*, in August, 1888. A month later he sent a progress report to Mme. Arman, in which he told her he was beginning to amuse himself with the abbé Paphnuce, 'the creation of our conversations'.

For *Thaïs* France took his background material from many sources, including Brochard's book on *Les Sceptiques Grecs*. France was obviously delighted at stealing not only Brochard's place in the avenue Hoche, but also one of his characters, for he wrote maliciously to Mme. Arman that he thought Brochard might not like the theft since he seemed to think that 'all sceptics belonged to him'. Somewhat guiltily France was to make some amends and acknow-ledgement to Brochard in an article 'Sur la scepticisme' of *La Vie Littéraire* – 'In the little novel of mine which is appearing in *La Revue des Deux Mondes*, there are a dozen pages which I could never have written if I had not read the book of M. Brochard.' In fact, Brochard took the theft and also his supersession in the avenue Hoche very well. There as soon as he had seen how the land lay, he had quickly and quietly disengaged himself, turning his atten-tions to the rue d'Astorg, where in his turn, he had sup-planted Henri Becque, the dramatist, who for a while had filled the place left vacant after the disappearance of Dumas. Since Lemaître was soon to be adopted by Mme. de Loynes, neither of the other two principal contenders in this game of Society musical chairs was in the end left without a seat.

It was not only by giving him advice that Mme. Arman now helped France in his work. She aided him in other, humbler ways. She looked up and checked references, she searched foreign newspapers – to which her languages gave her the key – for items of information that could be useful for his articles; she noted down some of the thoughts which came quickly into his mind, and were as quickly gone, in case they should prove the starting points of future inspiration. Yet of her many services to France, her greatest was the simple gift of her admiration. For her, now, there was no greater writer in the whole of French literature. From St. Gervais in 1889, she wrote France that she had been reading him all day 'passing from enchantment to enchantment'. He was, she told him, 'so marvellous' that at times she wondered if he could really exist. Fifteen years later it was part of the ritual of her evening stroll to pause on the Pont des Arts in order to point out and ponder the house on the quai Malaquais where 'the greatest of French writers' was born. In other ways Mme. Arman may not have given France all that he wanted, but she gave him her admiration, utterly, absolutely and for ever.

On occasion, Mme. Arman also did some of France's articles for him, passages of his 'Gérôme' column, a preface for Benjamin Constant's *Adolphe*, part of a preface to a luxurious edition of *La Princesse de Cleves*. In the autumn of 1888, France complimented Mme. Arman – and himself – 'Hébrard, whom I saw this morning, said that the Gironde and its vines had inspired me. There is reason also to congratulate ourselves on our columns for *l'Univers*. I send you a paper which has quoted you, a great honour.'

Sometimes France played fair about Mme. Arman's part in his work. In the preface to *La Princesse de Cleves*, he introduced her contribution with the preamble – ' "What do you think about it?" I asked a woman, whose perceptive and penetrating mind I admire. This is what she had the kindness to answer . . .' Then followed two long paragraphs of what Mme. Arman thought about it in a style quite different from that of France – more abrupt, forthright, interestingly and intelligently written, but lacking the charm and expertise of France's subtle and sinuous prose.

More often Mme. Arman's contributions appeared without explanation or excuse under France's signature – 'These last few days,' wrote Mme. Arman in 1889, 'I have been amusing myself by doing a bit of a preface for *Adolphe* by Benjamin Constant. It will appear under the signature of Anatole from whom it has been commissioned.'

While, in doing such work, Mme. Arman's main concerns were undoubtedly to further France's career and to ease some of the weight of work off his back, yet she was not only thinking of France when she wrote for him, as she showed, in the continuation of the letter concerned with her preface for *Adolphe* – 'It will appear under the signature of Anatole . . . I wish to allow my talent to ripen before risking it under a pseudonym.'

This, for France was a period of extremes. If, on the one hand, he seemed to have found in his relationship with Mme. Arman a satisfaction and a delight he had never known before, he was, on the other, involved in a series of humiliating and bitter rows. The first of these was with the authorities of the Bibliothèque du Sénat where France was still officially a *commis-surveillant*. Since 1882, France's attendance had been occasional to say the least. However, as the job was deliberately meant to be a sinecure, and as over these years, France was producing plenty of evidence of his literary labours, this lack of attendance and lack of enthusiasm could well have been passed over, had he not fallen out with Charles Edmond who had largely been responsible for France's appointment.

For some time now their friendship had been noticeably cooling. France had originally dedicated *Jocaste* to Charles Edmond as 'a slight sign of gratitude and affection'. From a revised edition of 1885, however, the dedication was missing. In 1888 Charles Edmond appointed over France's head to the position of '*commis-principal*, a young man of twenty-six, who had only six years of service against France's twelve. In protest, France mounted his highest horse and rode it to the governing body of the Senate – 'The order which appointed M. Samuel to a post which was my due constitutes an act without precedent in the history of the French Civil Service.' The Quaestors of the Senate requested a report from Charles Edmond, in which he summed up France's contributions over the preceding six years in the one word, 'nil'. He revealed, however, the personal pique which underlay his actions, by writing that the Légion d'Honneur which France had recently been awarded, had been given him 'thanks to his personal relations'.

This time the worried senators managed to smooth over the quarrel, but it could not be damped down for long. Early in 1890, on receipt of a particularly barbed letter of reproach, France bowed to the inevitable and sent a letter to the authorities in which he wrote that he wished to resign in order not to continue a conflict which had already lasted 'too long'. It certainly had. Charles Edmond's charges against France were undoubtedly based on envy of his success. But why had France held on so hard to an appointment that for several years had been quite out of keeping with his position and with his needs? Was it some lingering trace of insecurity that made him loath to part with a government job that had a pension at the end of it? Or was it simply that France was incapable of cutting cleanly, competently and quickly away from anything or anyone?

Charles Edmond was not the only person on the staff of the Bibliothèque du Sénat with whom France, during the last years of his service there, was at war. Leconte de Lisle had watched France's progress with much the same mixture of rancour and envy as Charles Edmond. With age, the touchy temper of the Parnassian poet had not ameliorated. He had found some recognition – he was elected to the Academy in 1887 – but little real success, and considered the world to be still very much in his debt. Rigid in his views, autocratic in his attitude, he could not understand at all a character such as France, for whom the fact of change was a fundamental rule of life and one of its few certainties. Nor did he make any effort to do so. Determined at all costs to remain 'Maître' he was not an enlightened master who could accept easily, or really at all, the emancipation of his one-time slaves.

France's literary and social success rubbed salt into the wound of what Leconte de Lisle chose to look upon as his desertion. Seeking a general pretext for a quarrel that would enable him to air his resentment, Leconte de Lisle found it in the support which France gave in *La Vie Littéraire* to the Symbolists, whose poetic theory and practice was very different from that of the Parnassians. Leconte de Lisle's bitterness by now almost amounted to persecution mania, and he liked to think, or at least to suggest, that France had invented the Symbolists for the purpose of paining the Parnassians, in particular himself. In the spring of 1891, his neurotic rancour broke out in an interview, one of several arranged by an enterprising journalist, Jules Huret, to enquire into current literary trends.

Leconte de Lisle left Huret and his readers in no doubt as to his feelings. Symbolism was 'delirium' and 'cacophony'; naturalism 'a heap of garbage'. He then went on – 'there is also a man of whom I will not talk to you' – and promptly proceeded to do so – 'to whom, in former times, I gave in every way proofs of my friendship, but who has since odiously offended me. He is M. Anatole France. I acknowledge his talent, which is delicate and subtle, but I little esteem his character. He has invented Symbolism, without believing in it, in the hope of doing a bad turn to his friend Heredia and to myself.' It emphasized the personal disorder of Leconte de Lisle's mind that in the same series of articles, Heredia referred warmly to France as 'one of the most perfect writers of our time'.

Obviously a reply was expected, and France sent it in

the form of an open letter to Huret – 'In his zeal to combat those who, while admiring his poetry in general, do not altogether admire him, M. Leconte de Lisle has declared that "he little esteems my character". He must be referring to the character of my writing. For he has no right to refer to anything in my private life, and I strongly forbid him to do so . . .'

At this pert, but pertinent reply, all Leconte de Lisle's rancour and resentment rose to the boil. At last he saw the opportunity to throw down the glove he had long held in readiness – 'The private life of M. France in no way concerns or interests me. On the other hand, in spite of my age and the disparity between us, I am ready to give him the honour of a meeting. Two of my friends will await his seconds, *chez moi*, 64 boulevard St. Michel, Sunday, 3rd May, at two o'clock in the afternoon.'

This clearly put France on the spot, and one that could have proved perilous, for Leconte de Lisle with his honour at stake, could be counted on to see rather clearer in the dawn air of a duelling ground than he did at other times. Fortunately, France had a strong enough sense of the ridiculous to refuse the challenge, even if it meant some back-pedalling and some lip service to Leconte de Lisle. France excused himself from the contest on the grounds that he could not possibly fight anyone of such an age, that 'if he (Leconte de Lisle) generously forgets in my favour the fact that he was born in 1820, it is my duty not to forget it. Must I then make him realize he is one of the glories one does not touch?' Feeling that he had won his victory, even if not on a duelling ground, Leconte de Lisle did not push the quarrel any further.

If France had been briefly on the verge of a duel with Leconte de Lisle, for some time past he had been crossing swords vigorously with Brunetière. This time it was France, who never forgave Brunetière his cavalier treatment of the text of *Thaïs*, who was the attacker on the pretext of a

provocative review of Bourget's *Le Disciple* which Brunetière had written and printed in the same issue that contained
the first chapter of *Thaïs*. France printed his attack in *Le
Temps*, Brunetière replied in *La Revue des Deux Mondes*,
France riposted in *Le Temps*, Brunetière answered in *La
Revue des Deux Mondes* – and so it went on year after
year. Long after Bourget's *Le Disciple* was forgotten, its
critics were still quarrelling, in increasingly personal and
bitter terms. France never came as close to a duel with
Brunetière as he had with Leconte de Lisle, but the feeling
between them was no less strong. Long after Brunetière's
death, France could find nothing more charitable to say of
him than that he was a 'horribly fanatical, loquacious and
argumentative little man, hard in character, with a bitter
mind that cut like a paper knife'.

Yet, of all the battles in which France was involved during
this bellicose period of his life, the most bitterly fought was
in his own home. Although France and Valérie were now
the two poles of a cold war, this did not prevent, or preclude,
blazing rows between them. There is record of one such in
the summer of 1891. France had been given a Genoan
tapestry by Mme. Arman who could not find room for it in
her own house. France wanted to hang it in the drawing-
room of their home. Valérie, not unnaturally, objected, on
the grounds that any present from such a source was a
personal insult to herself. However, against her wishes,
France summoned a carpenter. When he came, Valérie, in
fury, stormed out of her room and the house. Having done
so, she locked the door of the room behind her. When she
returned some hours later, after a long visit, which included
lunch, to 'Gyp', she found a small crowd collected outside
the house, to whom the carpenter was appealing to break
down the door and let him out. When Valérie unlocked the
door, let out the carpenter and went in, she found her husband quietly writing at a desk. He did not lift his head at
her entrance.

A year later, after another row, France left his home for good. This is Valérie's version of France's departure as recounted by 'Gyp' – 'He was writing an article. I interrupted him. He replied. I finished by calling him a "——".' (Another source suggests that the word left out in 'Gyp's' account, was in fact *maquereau*, an expression signifying someone between a pimp and a gigolo, combining the worst of both words). 'Then he got up from his desk, and thinking he was only going out of the room, I also went out. A moment later I heard the street door shut ... I thought, "He cannot possibly have had time to dress himself ..." I ran to the window, and I just saw him shutting the gate. He was still in his dressing-gown, with his night cap on his head! The ends of his dressing-gown cords were dragging in the street behind him ... and on a tray he carried his inkstand and the article he had started ... an hour later he sent someone from the Hôtel Carnot for his linen with a note' – in which France told Valérie he would never again be returning to the house in the rue Chalgrin, or to her.

A few days later, France sent Valérie a letter deliberately intended to supply her with evidence of his desertion so that she could proceed to a divorce.

By the time you receive this letter I will have left our conjugal home, never to return. Your state of open revolt, your incessant quarrels, your insulting suggestions, the infamous calumnies which you spread every day against me, without regard for your daughter and yourself, all your conduct through which one could at last see the state of your soul, make it my right and my duty to leave you. I leave a house in which all work, as all repose, has become impossible for me. At the same time, it is infinitely painful for me to leave my beloved daughter. I hope you will be less odious to her than you have been to me. I am going to try to reestablish by my work my affairs which your disorder has compromised. I will have the indulgence to forget you. I only ask you never to speak to me again.

Anatole France

Even allowing that this was a letter written for the specific purpose of divorce, it makes sad reading – sad remembering, too, when one recalls that France, not so many years before, had written so fondly of those whom, in his mind's eye, he undoubtedly saw as his family, murmuring affectionately as he peered in at their sleeping forms – 'Dormez, chèris, dormez.'

6

———◆◆———

WHEN France stalked out of his home in dressing-gown and slippers, bearing his insignia – inkstand, quill pen and the papers on which he had been working – before him, he was striking out on his own for the first time since those abortive months in his youth and the rue du Pré-aux-Clercs when he had tried to stand on his own feet, only to find they were quite incapable of carrying him. Then he had been quite alone. Now he had Mme. Arman to comfort and console him. Inevitably his divorce took some time to come through, and during this period France rented a flat in the rue de Sontay which runs out of the Place Victor-Hugo. This was within easy walking distance of Mme. Arman's house, where from now on, for most intents and purposes, France really lived. There his place was now automatically laid at table; and a room on the second floor, between Mme. Arman's bedroom and the laundry, was fitted out for his use as a study.

But however convenient an arrangement, it was not the same thing as having a home and a house of his own. Mme. Arman may have been the *maîtresse de maison* as well as his mistress, but France was not the master of the house. However distinguished his place now in the literary world, and however much he was honoured in Mme. Arman's salon as its acknowledged centrepiece, the fact remained that in the Caillavet household his position was really that of 'the lodger'.

France's arrival at No. 12 avenue Hoche, was bound to

pose a problem for the two other people, beside Mme. Arman, who lived there – M. Arman, the titular head of the household, and Gaston, their son. Gaston, now grown up, was living at home, leading a pleasantly social existence, in the margin of which he was developing a considerable dramatic talent – he was later, working in conjunction with Robert de Flers, to become one of the most successful writers of farce for the Parisian theatre. Already he had written a revue that was acted by his friends in the winter of 1890, in which Jeanne Pouquet, his fiancée, appeared as Cleopatra, and of which Proust, who had rapidly become a close friend of Gaston's after their meeting at his mother's salon only the year before, was the prompter.

It was probably for the purpose of meeting France that Proust had first come to Mme. Arman's salon some time in 1889. All his youth, Proust had been a great admirer of France's writing. As a boy he had once set himself a questionnaire in which he asked himself, 'Who are your favourite authors?' His answer had been, 'France and Loti' and his admiration for France had grown as he did. But his first meeting with France had been something of a disappointment. He had expected, from the style of France's writing, 'a sweet singer with silvery locks', and he could not at first reconcile this image which he had fashioned 'drop by drop like a stalactite through the transparent beauty of his books', with the man he saw before him who had, then, a small black beard, who stuttered, and whose nose, Proust thought, looked 'like a snail's shell'. So far as France's nose was concerned, Proust's eye must have been out, for although his nose was aslant to the line of France's face – a fact which he later corrected by careful asymmetrical trimming of his beard – it was never anything like a snail's shell. However, on the ruins of this first, false image of France, Proust was to build a more accurate representation that retained his respect, and, over the years, gathered his affection also. This was the impressionable, acquisitive period of Proust's life when he was subconsciously gathering the material ultimately to be formed into *À la Recherche*. Much of France was to go into Bergotte, a part of Gaston into Saint-Loup; and something of Jeanne – over whom Proust was to be extremely tiresome with his protestations of passionate longings, and far too assiduous attentions, which fortunately neither Jeanne nor Gaston took too seriously – into Gilberte.

When France had first emerged as the pivot of Mme. Arman's salon, Gaston, not unnaturally, had been very much on the defensive towards him. But gradually, by his consideration and friendliness, also possibly by his literary advice, France had worn down Gaston's resistance and captured at least the greater part of his goodwill. Now Gaston made little objection to France's presence and position in his home, perhaps feeling that as France was already so frequent a visitor to their house, it made little difference that he should eat and work there as well.

With M. Arman, however, the process of thaw was, naturally, a slower one. From the start, France seems genuinely to have liked M. Arman – and there was clearly much to like about him. He was a large, generally laughing man with a loud voice, who wore a peculiar sort of cravat with trailing ends and a turned-up collar that made him conspicuous and known throughout Paris. He was a great *raconteur* of stories, both tall and low, and delighted particularly in walking the tightrope between those that amused and those that shocked. The real point, in fact, of many of his anecdotes was to see the apprehension growing on the faces of the more fastidious of his audience as they imagined the terrible climax that was coming, but which, of course, never did. He was a great friend of the younger Dumas – and this, in itself, was a considerable commendation, for Dumas was a discerning judge of character and did not choose his friends without reason. Perhaps M. Arman's most likeable quality was that if, for no particular reason, he saw life as something of a joke, he also saw himself as one at which he had no difficulty in laughing. For the moment, however, he was not greatly amused by France's presence in his home and he was delighted when circumstances contrived to show France the limitations of his position in the Caillavet household. This occurred on the magnificent steam-yacht, the *Cymbeline*, which M. Arman had bought only the year before.

Boats and his vines were now M. Arman's main interests in life. But although a knowledgeable enough sailor to be yachting correspondent for *Le Figaro*, where he wrote his column under the curious pseudonym of 'Djeb Topsail', it was really the social side of sailing that he liked most. He was at his happiest pottering around in port, chatting with crew and cronies. However, at the end of July, 1892, some six weeks after France had left Valérie, the *Cymbeline* did raise steam, put out from harbour and sailed across the Channel for the regatta at Cowes, with France as one of the party on board.

In more than one way, France now found himself at sea. It was not so much that this was the first time in his life that he had left the shores of France – for someone of his eminence and age, his experience had been remarkably parochial although the fact that that parish had been Paris offset much of the disadvantage; nor only that France felt ill-at-ease and at a loss in the smart, sporting world in which he now found himself – but mainly that just at a time when he particularly needed the solace of Mme. Arman's support, he had to treat, and be treated by her, as if he was simply one of the several guests she had on board. For M. Arman it must have been a considerable satisfaction to see France in this way reduced to the ranks. But it was altogether more than France could stand and he left the *Cymbeline* abruptly, long before he was expected to, in such deep dudgeon and obvious distress that Mme. Arman sent after him a worried letter, in which she wrote that she had not been the only one to notice that his departure had been for him 'a relief and almost a joy'. But what else, she queried, could she do except to leave him to sort things out for himself? She was not 'pitiless', and when he needed her she was always there. Her only regret, she told him, was that he did not need her more often.

Yet when she wrote this, was Mme. Arman being entirely honest with herself or with France? For surely she must have seen that at that time France needed her desperately – more possibly than at any other time in his life – needing, not so much the companionship of her presence in public, as the comfort and consolation which she could only give in private. Even if, at the end, there had been little left of any worth in France's marriage, the habits of fourteen years are not easily broken. France was the deserter, yet probably at no time in his life did he feel more deserted than now. He had not even the consolation of his books, for he had had to leave in the rue Chalgrin his *cité des livres* which, since he had married Valérie under the law of communal property, had to remain there until the terms of the divorce were settled. Yet Mme. Arman did not cut short even by a few days, her stay in the *Cymbeline* which, once the regatta at Cowes was over, set off on a cruise round the British Isles. If now, painfully, France had, for the first time in his life, to learn to stand on his own feet, was it altogether surprising that, having found he could do so, he should in later years have taken considerable delight in treading on Mme. Arman's toes?

On his return from Cowes, France took Suzanne, who from now on generally spent part of her holidays with him, to stay at an old priory which belonged to a friend of his at St. Thomas in the Aisne. He was, when he went there, or so he wrote to his secretary, 'so full of care, so weary and discouraged', that he forgot to take with him the books and papers that he needed to write his articles for *Le Temps*. So he had to 'invent' a Vie Littéraire. But as can often happen, the article quickly extemporized under the pressure of circumstance, proved to be one of his best.

Caught on the raw, in an emotional moment, with his sensibility stretched taut as a bowstring, France sent an arrow straight to the heart of the target. Under the heading 'Le Prieuré', France imagined a dialogue between himself and a friend Jean, a recluse who had retired into just such a delightful rustic retreat as that in which France was writing his article. Jean had done so since he believed that all action led in one way or another to harm, and so he was putting himself as far as possible out of harm's way. Jean, of course, was not so much a friend, as France's retiring and reflective self – the self who had always been inclined, if he had had the means, to follow the quiet path which M. Dubois had pointed out to him as a boy. Why bother to create, why not rather collect other people's creations, M. Dubois had said then. 'Now,' said Jean, 'I pass my time looking at the clouds and the sky . . . When the night is fine I watch the stars (at which I take pleasure in looking ever since I have forgotten their names) . . . I receive nobody, I think of nothing, I have not troubled either to attract you into my retreat or to keep you out of it.'

Jean was a caricature of the France who had been happy with his books, his bees, his friends and his family in a quiet corner of Neuilly where there were 'avenues and trees'. But now he was answered by another of France's several selves – a more realistic, more experienced self, who told him that such an outlook simply would not, could not, work. For it was impossible to do anything, or to do nothing, and be certain that this action or inaction would not have consequences quite unforeseeable and quite unpreventable in the outside world. 'To live is to act,' France told Jean sternly. One had to take part, and since even by doing nothing one was doing something, it was better to do something of one's choice than leave the choice to circumstance. In a small way, 'Le Prieuré' showed a large change of attitude, and it heralded an even greater change of action. For France, the quiet, retiring scholar, the mildly melancholy sceptic who seemed to value his privacy more than anything else in the world, was to come out of his priory, out of his shell, to become one of the most controversial characters, and prominent public and publicized figures of his time.

It was not so much Mme. Arman who affected the change as the type of life she caused him to lead. For one could not go on mixing week after week with the most eminent political as well as literary figures of the day, as France did in Mme. Arman's salon, without becoming interested in the problems in which they were interested and so to some extent being drawn into public life. As the guest of honour, France was, inevitably, asked for his opinions on contemporary issues. He therefore had to have some.

The effect of this evolutionary process on France's work showed in the spring of 1893. At the end of April, France gave up *La Vie Littéraire*. His main reason for doing this was that the previous month he had started in *L'Écho de Paris* what was really a column of social criticism which appeared throughout the following spring and summer in fortnightly instalments under the title of *Les Opinions de M. Jérôme Coignard*. In these France used the figure of the imaginary eighteenth century abbé as his stalking horse to creep up on contemporary problems, but Coignard was in fact the product of his previous work on which France had been labouring spasmodically and not all that successfully for years, *La Rôtisserie de la Reine Pédauque*, finally published by Calmann Lévy in March, 1893.

France had taken a great deal of trouble as well as time over *La Rôtisserie*, whereas *Les Opionions de M. Jérôme Coignard* were written quickly as they were needed. Yet by an irony which France himself would have appreciated, *La Rôtisserie*, over which he laboured so long, is now mainly interesting as the precursor of the second work which he threw off in a matter of weeks. When he started *La Rôtis-serie*, France seems to have been out to repeat the process which produces *Thaïs*, to transpose a mood of his own time into an historical setting – the mood, the free-thinking out-look of a society that felt it had been liberated by scientific and philosophical progress from many of the shackles of the past; the setting, an early eighteenth-century world of pot-houses and châteaux, a mixture of Hogarth and The Three Musketeers.

Unlike *Thaïs*, which France seems to have enjoyed writing, *La Rôtisserie* did not come at all easily. His letters to Mme. Arman over the period he was working on it are full of groans at the effort it was costing him and at the seem-ing lack of result. Even on the eve of its serialization in *l'Écho de Paris*, he was still moaning that it all needed to be done again. *La Rôtisserie* seems to suffer throughout from a confusion of purpose, as if France could not make up his mind even as he went along whether he intended to write a philosophical parable, a farce, a cloak and dagger novel, or a sulphurous period-piece with undertones of sorcery and satanic learning, for there are elements of all these in it. The one glimmer of light amidst the gloom encircling France as he wrote was, however, the character of Coignard who, France told Mme. Arman, seemed to be firming and filling out promisingly as he went along.

In fact, it was the Rabelaisian figure of the abbé – slovenly, drunken and lecherous – but possessing at the same time a massive intellect and a real integrity of the spirit, enclosed though it was in all too fallible flesh – who, in the end, carried the book to the success to which France was now becoming accustomed – carried it, too, over the not inconsiderable hurdles of an almost complete absence of plot, of some of the longest monologues that even France's characters have ever uttered and of an erudition which unusually – for France generally wore his learning lightly – became at times pedagogic and oppressive.

On his own, without the impediments which the design –
or the lack of it – in *La Rôtisserie* imposed, Coignard
showed to much greater advantage. His *Opinions* revealed
him as no respecter of persons, save possibly of himself.
Neither the army officers – 'What is this military gentleman
stiff with pride . . . except the degenerate descendant of
those wretched hunters whom Lucretius has depicted in
such a way as to make one doubt whether they are men or
beasts'; nor the Academicians – 'mediocrity triumphs at
the Academy . . . does one have to be an exceptional man
to work at a dictionary which wishes to regulate usage, but
in fact has to follow it'; nor the historians – 'Every time
they meet together they contradict each other' – nor any
of the others upon whom Coignard's tongue rounded, had
much cause to love him or his creator the more after reading
his opinion of them. Yet they would have been stupid to
take offence. For France was tilting, not at the individual,
but at the institution. For the ordinary man, caught in the
web of circumstance, becoming the more entangled the more
he struggled to free himself, France had nothing but compassion. It was the institutions – the Church, the Army, the
Courts, the learned Societies – who, to France, were responsible for much of the injustice, the prejudice and the
suffering in society. *Les Opinions de M. Jérôme Coignard*,
collected and published in the autumn of 1893, proved that
France was nearly, but not quite, as good a social as a
literary critic. All the same there must have been many
who regretted the change. France needed to be at one
remove from life to see it clearly and he was never again
to find so perfect a viewpoint as that provided by the books
on his study table.

France had also produced, under the title of *L'Étui de
Nacre*, in the autumn of 1892, a collection of stories, on
the whole, unremarkable, save for the first 'Le procurateur
de Judée'. In this France's sense of history and of irony
combined with a naturally and historically dramatic situa-

tion, to produce what is probably the best, and certainly the best-known, story he ever wrote.

On 3rd August, 1893, France's divorce was finally pronounced, on the grounds of his desertion of his home some fourteen months previously. Valérie was to have custody of Suzanne, although France was to have reasonable access to her, and to be paid monthly the not over-generous allowance of 350 francs. In due course the divorce was duly registered, and the sad relics of France and Valérie's marriage deposited without ceremony or mourners in the files of the Palais de Justice, Case 10, Folio 18.

Meanwhile, in May, France and Mme. Arman had anticipated the official pronouncement of France's freedom by going to Italy on a joint honeymoon with Gaston and Jeanne, now at last the bride he had married in May. For Jeanne, this joint honeymoon seems to have been something of a trial. Mme. Arman had always been an indefatigable sightseer. Her strenuous cultural upbringing had given her not only the inclination to spend long hours in museums, art galleries, churches, but the stamina to support them. It was inconceivable to her that one could visit a town without ferreting out all that it had to offer in the way of works of art, or leave it without plumbing to the depths any possible source of beauty or interest. Nor was it only the sights obviously on show that she sought out. She was equally tireless in her search through antique and curiosity shops.

But now Mme. Arman had an additional reason for scouring the towns they visited. She had decided that it was time that France should show that he could write a modern society novel. This was especially to be 'their' novel, and to carry the reflection of their own love-affair. France had at first groaned, but later agreed. Most of the action, Mme. Arman decided, should take place in the Parisian social world in which her salon was now one of the main meeting-points, but part should be set in Florence, whose romantic atmosphere had always appealed to her. So it was on Florence that she, France, Jeanne and Gaston centred during their stay in Italy.

With the thought of 'their' novel not so much at the back as at the front of her mind, and stimulated also by the pleasure of showing Italy to France for the first time, Mme. Arman was virtually unstoppable. Once France had agreed to the idea, he might as well have told Niagara to cease falling as attempted to stay Mme. Arman in her search for material. The greater part of every day was spent sightseeing or wandering about the streets in search of local colour. While they did so, Mme. Arman made copious notes which she stuffed into her handbag until they overflowed into France's pockets. The difficulty proved to be not so much the finding of material as its selection. For her enthusiasm made Mme. Arman over-susceptible to atmosphere. Every palace or church they visited, every street or square they walked through, seemed to her to demand a place in the novel. As the notes accumulated in his pockets, and the possible settings and scenes multiplied alarmingly, France grumbled to himself – not too inaudibly – 'Society novel in ten volumes'.

In fact, when he came to write the novel, France did not use a great deal of the material they gathered. The background to the Florentine part of *Le Lys Rouge*, as it came to be called, is only roughly sketched in. As is often the way, France's imagination seems to have been stirred by the stray detail more than by the great mass of collected notes. When, for example, Jeanne posted a letter home in a box in the Piazza San Michele, it gave France the idea of a scene in which the sight of Thérèse, his heroine, posting a letter, induced in her lover a mood of violent possessive jealousy. On another occasion they stopped on the Piazza Maria Novella before the shop of an old cobbler who had a tame sparrow with a matchstick tied on in the place of a missing leg, and who held out some basil for them to smell.

Jeanne suggested laughingly that France ought to put the cobbler, the sparrow and the basil into the novel. And he did.

This exacting routine, which filled up virtually the whole day, was hardly the ideal way of spending a honeymoon, and Jeanne wrote plaintively to her father that they spent ten hours a day running round the palaces, streets and shops 'thanks to the invincible ardour and even inspiration of my dear mother-in-law'. She was thankful, Jeanne went on, to have France as a travelling companion, since he had even less stamina than she did, and demanded some rest and meals at reasonable times. If she came back in a possible condition at all it would, she wrote, be entirely due to France. In general, Jeanne found France 'charming', and her mother-in-law 'touching' in the way she looked after her as if she were a little girl of six. She was, also, very 'diverted' by the 'disputes and dissensions' between France and Mme. Arman.

Through Jeanne's, in more than one sense, fair eyes, one can see that the character of France and Mme. Arman's relationship had already changed since the days not so far back when France, in Mme. Arman's absence at Saint-Gervais or Capian, would sit at café tables to write on paper filched from the Bibliothèque du Sénat, letters full of longing, love and jealousy. Partly, no doubt, it was the presence of the younger couple which tended to emphasize the relative age of the older one: partly too, that in bringing their liaison into the open, France and Mme. Arman were bound to some extent to change its character; but mainly one would think it was just that the years were passing, and since their affair had flowered so late, so it settled sooner than most into the shape of companionship. Perhaps, too, Mme. Arman was not altogether wise in suggesting that France should enshrine their love in a novel, for in writing about an experience, one is bound to some extent to pin it in its place in the past.

There was, of course, even on this gruelling first trip, a

private side to their relationship which Gaston and Jeanne never saw. Eighteen years later, France, after Mme. Arman's death, was to return to an hotel in Siena where he and Mme. Arman, Gaston and Jeanne, had stayed on that first visit. Then the insignificant details which always lodge in the crannies of memory – this time a stuffed deer and a 'horrific' inscription – made him miss Mme. Arman acutely. But he also remembered how on their first stay he had one night, on his way back to his own room from Mme. Arman's, fallen down a staircase which he had mistaken for his doorway. Returning 'in pain' to Mme. Arman, he had found her full of comfort and consolation. 'She was,' he remembered and wrote in his *Carnets*, 'the most charming of companions in those days of fine autumn.' But in public France and Mme. Arman had already assumed the aspect of a devoted but rather difficult couple, argumentative as well as affectionate, of whom time was to increase the differences rather than the dependence. One can see from Jeanne's picture that already at times France took pleasure in pulling against the harness, and that at times also, Mme. Arman drove him too hard.

Perhaps it was for this reason that France, on his return to Paris, did not immediately settle down to work on 'their' novel, but instead wrote at great speed a series of stories for which he, and not Mme. Arman, had gathered the ideas and the settings from their Italian trip. These were published as he wrote them in *l'Écho de Paris*, and collected, two years later, into book form under the title of *Le Puits de Sainte-Claire*. France hung these stories on the thread of the idea that while at Siena he went for a stroll after dinner out into the countryside 'on the wild road to Monte Oliveto . . . The clocks of the town sounded the peaceful death of the day; the purple of the evening fell with majestic melancholy over the low chain of hills . . . I went forward to meet silence, solitude.' He also met 'on the white road, in those transparent nights' a Franciscan friar who was also taking the air and enjoying the sight of the fireflies whose 'amorous light' darted about the bushes.

But in fact, although they showed considerable knowledge of Italian legend and history, these stories were not at all the sort one would have expected to hear from a friar; or that Mme. Arman can have expected of France. For they are full of a cynical mockery of people and beliefs. In them, France often seemed to be deliberately out to shock just as in *Sylvestre Bonnard* and *Le Livre de mon Ami* he had consciously set himself to charm. If France wrote *Le Lys Rouge* primarily to please Mme. Arman, did he write *Le Puits de Sainte-Claire* deliberately to displease her – in order to prove his artistic independence?

Whether he intended it or not, Mme. Arman was certainly displeased. But her annoyance vanished when France, in August, the month in which his divorce became final, really got down to write the novel she wanted of him. Once he got his teeth into it France became interested himself and the novel came more easily than anything he had so far written, probably because so much flowed from the fount of his own experience. He finished it in six months. During most of this time Mme. Arman was at his elbow, and in the final stages, far from encouraging France to delve deeply into the mysteries of love, she was actually toning down some of the passages, in which, she considered, he had described love rather too much in the raw.

But in the end *Le Lys Rouge* emerged very much as Mme. Arman wanted it, and, obviously to his surprise, very much as France wanted it too. For in spite of it being in origin more an exercise of duty and devotion than anything else, it was far from the dead weight which a work written under such conditions might well have been. Although rather overloaded with social occasions – France's table talk was such as was never heard even at a Parisian dinner table, and although English readers may take quite a while to recover from the frightful figure of Vivian Bell, the English poetess, yet the feel of genuine, passionate, un-predictable experience comes through. The brief moment of Thérèse and Dechartre is brought to the centre of the stage, and shown as something far from exceptional or extraordinary, an experience such as might happen to any-one, the cause of as much suffering as happiness, but all the same unquestionably one of the things that make life worth living.

Thérèse was younger, and possibly more beautiful, than Mme. Arman, but there was strong resemblance of character and background. It could, for example, have been Mme. Arman, and not Thérèse speaking when she is explaining to Le Menil, her previous lover, that their affair is over – 'What would you? I am avid and wilful. It is in my blood. I inherited it from my father. You know Joinville, you have seen the château . . . you would say that there is not a more beautiful one in France – but you have not seen my father's study: a table of white wood and mahogany. It is from there that everything has come, mon ami. On this table, in front of this fire, my father shuffled his figures for over fifty years . . . my father wanted to make money . . . I want to make and to keep what . . . I don't know – the happiness that I have or have not. In my fashion I am greedy – of dreams, of illusions. Oh! I know well that it is not worth the trouble that it gives, but it is really the trouble that is worth while, because it is my trouble, it is I, it is my life.'

Thérèse at Joinville had her own personal path, a path which she liked to think was hers alone – a path with the moon at the end of it – and Mme. Arman, too, had her 'petit chemin' at Capian, down which no doubt she often led France. And so throughout *Le Lys Rouge*, in many small and not so small ways, one gets glimpses of the path which France and Mme. Arman explored in the course of their love.

When *Le Lys Rouge* was published, in the spring of 1894, its reception was all that Mme. Arman could possibly have hoped for. The critics acclaimed it, the public followed their lead and agreed with them. It sold far more copies than any of France's previous books, although *Sylvestre Bonnard*, *Thaïs* and *La Rôtisserie* had done well enough by ordinary standards. For Mme. Arman it was undoubtedly one of the great moments of her life. She had the manuscript, grudgingly copied out by France, bound in calf, fitted with an enamelled clasp in the form of a red lily and set in a glass frame in her drawing-room. There it rested, the expression of their love – but also in a way, inevitably, its memorial too.

The spring of 1894, during which *Le Lys Rouge* was published, saw France and Mme. Arman off on another trip to Italy. But this time on their own, and this time without the need to look for copy. France, in fact, was never again to use these trips with Mme. Arman to gather working material. Sometimes on the long ones, particularly when on board the *Nausicaa*, the successor of the *Cymbeline*, he would do some writing, but never again, perhaps with recollections of the Florentine experience in his mind, did he allow a holiday to be spoilt by being turned into a working party. So one would imagine that on this second trip to Italy together, France and Mme. Arman were at last able to relax. France had become a devoted admirer of Italy long before he had even been there, and presence now made his heart grow fonder. It was not only the beauty and antiquity of Italy that appealed to him, but the gaiety of the people. 'I have a great need of gaiety,' France was to note in his *Carnets* when in Naples many years later, and in Italy he was able to satisfy that need. From 1893 onwards, a trip to Italy was to become a regular and essential part of France and Mme. Arman's year.

Over the rest of 1894, France's main personal preoccupation was to buy a house. The flat in the rue de Sontay was too small to be more than a place in which to sleep, and now

ANATOLE FRANCE

that he had his books again France needed somewhere to
house them and himself. Since his fortune had grown with
his success – he was already well-off and was soon to be
rich – he could now afford to look for something substantial in keeping with his position as a leading writer, and
suitable also to house his collections which were to increase
alarmingly now that he could afford to buy virtually anything that took his fancy.

France found his home in the Villa Saïd, a short line of
houses up a private road which opened out of the avenue
du Bois. It was pleasantly close to the Bois and conveniently
close to the avenue Hoche. France bought No. 5, Villa Saïd,
in the autumn of 1894 for 70,000 francs. It was a tall, thin
house with an impressive Second Empire façade, and a fine
room which occupied the full length of the second floor,
where France housed his books and entertained his guests.
But its amenities were not up to its appearance. Both the
bathroom and kitchen were in the basement. The heating
arrangements, also, were abysmal. With the house, France
took over an antiquated system of central heating – a
calorifère – by which smells were circulated round the
house on the pretext that they were hot air. France sup-
plemented this with wood fires, but these generally smoked.
He would not allow the installation of either gas or electricity, and so the house was lit by candles and oil lamps.
But in spite of its drawbacks and discomforts, No. 5,
Villa Saïd really suited France very well, and he was to live
there very happily for the next twenty years of his
life.

With France's establishment in a house of his own – he
moved into the Villa Saïd early in 1895 – his life settled into
the routine on which it was to run for the next fifteen years.
He and Mme. Arman seemed now to have evolved for themselves not only an agreeable daily round, but a satisfying
seasonal one also, with periods of work and social activity
at Paris, interspersed by trips to Italy and elsewhere, and

with always, in the autumn, a long, restful, recuperative stay at Capian.

France usually went also, some time during the summer, to stay with 'Gyp' at Lion-sur-Mer. This was a means of seeing Suzanne, for 'Gyp', the friend of both France and Valérie, now acted as the intermediary between them – in Paris it was at her house that France lunched most weeks in order to see his daughter. Amongst a crowd of children, for the villa that 'Gyp' rented was always packed to overflowing with her own and those of her friends, one would have expected France to feel out of place. But he seems, on the contrary, to have delighted in the children and to have been a favourite with them. When he bathed they formed a tug escort round him to see that he did not drift out to sea, for he could float but not swim. In the evening he would go for a walk along the sands and seems to have had a Pied Piper attraction, for generally not only the children of 'Gyp's' household, but other children whom they met on the way, followed him. Sometimes he was not back by dinnertime and then 'Gyp's' house would be beset by frantic parents wondering what had happened to their children. An hour or so later France would turn up, 'smiling and satisfied', with his youthful following, tired but happy behind him. 'Gyp' found France 'a delightful guest, always content with everything, good-tempered, equable, kindly'. Since France was not always like this, it can only have been that he was happy with 'Gyp' and the children at Lion-sur-Mer.

The most peaceful and therefore a most important period of the year was that of the weeks, sometimes months, which France spent at Capian, in the autumn, when the countryside around, which had been pressed down by the heat through the summer as if by a flat-iron, was beginning to revive, and when France's spirits and energies, after the exertions of the summer and the season, needed reviving also.

France had early succumbed to the charm of Capian and several of his articles of *La Vie Littéraire* had carried the reflection of the peace and pleasures he found there. 'The morning sun drinks the dew off the meadows, gilds the hill-sides, and pierces with its rays the already ripe grapes. The light air vibrates on the horizon. Sitting in front of my work-table, which I have pushed to the edge of the window, I can, by bending a bit, see the farm-workers thrashing the corn in the barn' – 'As the morning was warm and still, I carried my book into a small oak wood and read it under a tree. To read in such a way is to read happily; on the grass one does not think of taking notes. One reads with pleasure, with amusement and with honesty . . . the moving shadow which trembles on the book, the buzzing of the insects which flit between the eye and the page, merge with the author's thoughts to create a delightful impression of nature and of life.' Even when France had lingered too long and too late, and the winter's rains had come, he still seemed loath to leave. 'The cold and calm rain, which falls slowly from a grey sky, taps at the windows as if to call me . . . Everything is silent. The yellow leaves fall without a sound in the rides; the cattle stand dumb in resignation; one can hear only the rain, and this great silence weighs on my lips and my thoughts. I would like to say nothing. I have only one thought in my head, which is that I must leave. It is not the dark, the rain and the cold which are chasing me out. The country pleases me even when it no longer smiles. I do not love it for its joy alone. I love it because I love it. Those whom we love, are they less dear in their moments of sadness? I leave with regret these woods and these vines.'

Capian was a long, low house – cool in summer, cold in winter – which lay in the midst of its vines, close to the Gironde and some fifteen miles from Bordeaux. It was the particular love of Gaston, but for whose protests when still a boy, it might well have been sold, but they all, in their

France and Emma, his second wife

Anatole France in his study at the Villa Said

On his travels: at El-Djem, Tunisia, 1913

La Béchellerie

different ways, seem to have been happy there – M. Arman gathering the vendange in a pleasantly proprietorial way; France and Mme. Arman going for walks together and, one suspects, spending many so-called 'working' afternoons chatting happily in the sun, or if it was late in the year, in front of a fire of vine shoots.

Once a week, breaking the peaceful run of these quick-passing days, they would all go to Bordeaux by river, embarking at the little port of Langoiran and voyaging peacefully down the Gironde, to tie up at the *quais* of Bordeaux which were conveniently close to the Chapon Fin, one of the most famous and excellent restaurants in France. There they would always lunch. Afterwards France would spend the afternoon browsing through the bookshops and visiting the antique-dealers. Then in the evening they would make their way slowly upstream to Capian, only remembering when they had left Bordeaux well behind that they had forgotten the one thing they had particularly gone there to buy, thus providing the conventional excuse for their return the following week.

France was always loath to work at Capian – and rightly so, for it was essentially a place and a time for rest and recuperation. Nevertheless, it was there that France got much of the material, and possibly the inspiration, for his next book, intended to be something of a cross between a social commentary and a novel. France needed something to bind together his comments on the social scene, and he found it in the story of an ecclesiastical struggle for power in a provincial diocese. This had the particular advantage for France of bringing into the target area, two of his main institutional enemies – the Church and the State, whose relations were just then becoming the focus of much public concern and attention. Many of France's social views germinated as usual from conversations in Mme. Arman's salon, but much of the detail of ecclesiastical intrigue he based on local church gossip recounted to him by the curé at Capian, who, perhaps flattered by the attention of so distinguished a visitor, had been unwisely garrulous, without suspecting the use that would be made of his confidences. One can imagine his horror as he saw with each succeeding issue of *l'Echo de Paris* how far his folly had been stretched. But if the curé was horrified, France's Parisian audience was delighted. France seemed to have caught just the right tone of ironic but humane comment. The mellifluous roll of his prose served as the perfect foil for the often sharply critical views it expressed – and France's position and attitude, if no longer entirely detached, still seemed refreshingly independent and unaligned. This was the genesis of *l'Histoire Contemporaine*, the overall title of the series which was to run, first in *l'Echo de Paris*, then in *Figaro*, for seven years, and from which France was to draw the four volumes of *l'Orme de Mail*, *Le Mannequin d'Osier*, *l'Anneau d'Amethyste* and *M. Bergeret à Paris*.

For Mme. Arman, the years which followed the pronouncement of France's divorce were probably the happiest of her life. It was not only that she could now parade her love for France in public, but that everything she had hoped for her salon seemed now to be coming true. Everybody who was anybody now went there, and not only the stars of the literary firmament but politicians such as Barthou, Briand, Poincaré, the youthful Léon Blum, at that time a literary rather than a social critic, Jean Jaurès; editors such as Hébrard, Maynard of *Le Figaro*, Simond of *l'Echo de Paris*; aristocrats such as the duc Decazes, the prince Bibesco, Count Robert de Montesquiou; actresses such as Bernhardt, Réjane, artists such as Forain, Madeleine Lemaire; musicians such as Massenet; and, of course, a varied mass of *littérateurs* ranging from scholars such as Pozzi and Widal to lightweights such as 'Willy', Colette's husband. There were, too, occasional exotic birds of passage such as d'Annunzio.

Mme. Arman held her reception at five o'clock on a Sunday evening. Guests who went there for the first time could have been confused by the fact that the house had three similar porches opening on to the street. If they chose to enter the one on the left, they found themselves amidst a litter of dustbins: behind the one on the right lay Mme. Arman's magnificent dining-room, hung with tapestries and in which, on special occasions, a fountain played. If, however, they chose correctly and entered the centre door, they found themselves in a hall of classical character. Crossing a paved floor, they would then mount a fine, flowing staircase under which M. Arman at one time installed a stove hoping to bring some heat to the house, only to have it ruthlessly removed on aesthetic grounds by Mme. Arman. At the top of the stairs a small ante-room led into the long drawing-room which ran the whole length of the house. At the meeting and dominant point of these two rooms, Mme. Arman received her guests. The window of this ante-room opened on to a Russian Church and on most days of reception, since these were Sundays, the chants of the service next door would add to the air of religious reverence which surrounded France when he recited his anecdotes. Whilst he did so France was generally leaning up against the mantelpiece with Mme. Arman sitting on a small sofa nearby, controlling the flow of her guests and of conversation. Little in the way of refreshment was served at these receptions. This was not because of any meanness on Mme. Arman's part – on the contrary, as her dinners proved, she could be a most lavish hostess, but because on these Sunday evenings, it was the conversation, the mingling of minds as well as of people that mattered most. Mme. Arman did not wish to provide anything that might distract the attention of her more gluttonous guests.

A more serious lack in the winter months, was heat. For the same reason that made her remove her husband's stove from under the stairs, Mme. Arman refused to have central heating installed – simply because she could not bear the look of it. The only heat, therefore, in the drawing-room, came from a small open fire. As the room filled, the conglomeration of people in it generally produced enough body heat to thaw out the atmosphere, but in a cold spell, it was unwise to be amongst the early arrivals.

Every Sunday, France, on his arrival, went through a ritual that was as invariable as it was comic. All afternoon he had been writing, reading or possibly sleeping in the study on the floor above. Shortly after five o'clock, he would walk down the stairs, carrying in one hand his hat which he would hand to a servant, and in the other a bunch of violets which he would hand to Mme. Arman with the remark, 'Chère Madame, as I happened to be passing I thought I would call in to pay my respects.' Before France's arrival conversation had been general and noisy. At his approach it was immediately hushed and remained so until he had performed one or more of his party pieces. For these Mme. Arman would generally give him his cue – 'Tell us, Monsieur, about . . . ,' or 'What do you think, Monsieur, of . . .' France would then tell his anecdote, or discourse on some subject for which he had been prepared, and often rehearsed, beforehand. France on his own, un-prompted and unprepared, was still a hesitant speaker – 'You can hear me crossing things out as I speak,' he would say – but under Mme. Arman's tuition he learnt to put up a very creditable performance. When he had finished, Mme. Arman would generally nod her approval, but if he had forgotten anything or had been off form, he would be told. Sometimes even France's laggard speech got going of its own accord, and then Mme. Arman would wander amongst her guests, murmuring happily, 'How dazzling he is.' At such times – to one guest at least – it seemed as if twenty years had been taken off her age.

At this time Proust was an assiduous attendant at Mme. Arman's receptions, and an ardent admirer of France both there and elsewhere. So much so that he took to him some of his literary, and even linguistic problems. Thus he referred to France when reproached for saying 'Comme qui dirait', on the grounds that it was ungrammatical, by Laure Hayman, the beautiful Creole courtesan, who was the '*petite*', '*grande*' or '*belle*' *amie* of many of the most noble names in Europe including the King of Greece, the Duc d'Orleans, the pretender to the throne of Bulgaria – also of Proust's delightful great uncle Louis Weil. On this occasion she was Proust's – '*Belle, douce et dure amie* – Yesterday you made me listen to some brutal truths. They are very precious to me because they are friendly and come from you. But you will admit that if they are merely the fruit of friendship they are its bitter fruit – I want at least to exonerate myself from one reproach to which I am particularly sensitive since it is literary. I mean "*comme qui dirait*". Anatole France, with whom I happen to be at this moment, assures me and permits me to tell you, that this locution is irreproachable and in no way vulgar. I need hardly tell you that I sacrifice it to you with all my heart and that I would far rather make a slip with you than be right with the whole Académie. And France would too. Indeed it would be delightful to make a slip with you.' When in 1896, Proust published his first work, *Les Plaisirs et les Jours,* France wrote a perceptive preface for it, in which he compared it to 'a young face full of a rare charm and of a fine grace . . . Without a doubt this is a young book. It is young with the youth of the author. But it is old also with the age of the world . . . He is not at all innocent. But he is so sincere and so true that he becomes naïve and pleases thus.'

The year which thus saw the first faint glimmer of Proust's fame appear over the horizon, saw also the sun of France's fame shining at full strength. In the autumn of that year he was elected to the Academy. France later decried the point and pleasure of being an Academician, saying that the only advantages that he could see were that one could go to the

Opera in slippers and nightcap if one felt like it without being shut up as a lunatic, and that one could fondle one's *petite amie* in the Bois to one's heart's content without trouble from the park keeper. But in fact it meant a great deal to him and his election was the fulfilment of an ambition of which the roots ran far back into childhood, to the days when, listening to the Academicians in his father's bookshop, he had thought he could not conceive anything more 'splendid' than to be one of them.

Twice before there had been a possibility of his becoming a candidate. Renan had suggested it, but France had then judged it to be too early to present himself. On Renan's death he had also been mentioned as his suitable successor. But France had eventually stood down to clear the way for another candidate. Now it was Ludovic Halévy, now himself an Immortal, but who in his more mortal days had been one of France's colleagues on *l'Univers*, who suggested that France should stand, and who stood as his sponsor throughout the laborious ritual which any candidate had to undergo.

Every member of the Academy had to be written to and subsequently visited. It was, in fact a campaign, and as in every campaign, tactics and timing counted for a great deal. Halévy took charge of these, or so France used to delight in telling, to the extent that he rejected the first specimen letter which France produced for his approval, on the grounds that it was far too well written, substituting a much rougher draft of his own composition in which there were, deliberately, several grammatical faults. One of the supplicatory letters that France wrote in the course of his campaign as a candidate is in the Bibliothèque Nationale – 'It is your vote that I want at the Academy. If you give it me I will be proud of having the support of the most perfect man of letters and of the most gallant man that I know.' One does not know who was the recipient of this particular letter, but suspects many of the Academicians found themselves, at this time, possibly to their surprise, to be the most 'perfect . . . and gallant man' that France knew.

Every day Halévy would tell France whom to visit and what to talk to them about – thus with 'the dukes', the extreme right wing of the Academy, most of them members of noble families, very conservative and strongly catholic, France was adjured at all costs to avoid subjects of possible dispute, such as politics and religion, to remark only on the weather, or talk to the wives about the health of their dogs or of their children.

Yet, however much France and Halévy enjoyed creating an atmosphere of intrigue and uncertainty, the result of the election was really a foregone conclusion, as France showed by sending 'Gyp', the day before the election, a forecast in which he was only one vote out. On the 26th January, 1896, France was elected to the Academy at the first ballot by twenty-one votes to twelve. Thus, at long last, he completed the journey from his father's bookshop to the Institut: so short in terms of distance, so immeasurably long in terms of achievement.

But France's election was, of course, not only an honour to him, it was a tribute also to Mme. Arman – to the work she had done on his behalf, and to the social ascendancy of her salon. When, the day before Christmas, 1896, she sat amongst the distinguished audience in the crowded *salle des seances* of the Institut, listening to France delivering an evasive address on de Lesseps – the recollection of the Panama scandal was still painfully raw – she savoured a triumph that was her right as well as her reward.

FRANCE WAS FIFTY-ONE when he was elected to the Academy. For a late starter he had made remarkably rapid progress during the middle span of his life. At thirty-five he had been virtually unknown save to a close circle of friends. At fifty, he was the leading writer in France. Now when he stepped out from the Institut on the day before Christmas, 1896, after his reception into Immortality, it seemed reasonably safe to prophesy a period of peaceful productivity, untroubled by the demands of editors, necessity, or ambition. He was, too, one would have thought, ideally suited both as a writer and as an individual, to take full advantage of the freedom he had won for himself. The appeal of the attitude, underneath the charm and style on the surface of his prose, had always largely depended on its independence. France was subject to moods and humours, to likes and dislikes, but otherwise, or so at least his readers felt, to little else. Essentially he exemplified the detached but not disinterested commentator on human affairs, basically unaligned with any particular party, group, or even doctrine. Mme. Arman, or rather, the life she had organized for him, might have changed his attention from literary to social affairs, but he still retained the independence of his outlook. Now with the world as his oyster, it seemed that he had an inexhaustible supply of grit round which to form his pearls.

But already by the time of France's election to the Academy, a small cloud the size of a man's hand, the hand of the man who wrote the famous *bordereau*, had appeared in the political sky. Almost exactly a year before, on 21st December, 1895, Dreyfus had been convicted by a military court sitting in the rue de Cherche-Midi, one of the long streets on the Left Bank leading from the *quais*, and condemned to degradation and deportation, the heaviest sentence that could be imposed since by the constitution of 1848 the death sentence had been abolished for political crimes. In the social storm that was to build up from this small, and as yet insignificant, cloud, France was to lose much of the freedom of his position and the independence of his outlook, on which both he and his writing seemed so much to depend.

If, however, the Affair had started by the time France became an Academician, it was some time gathering way, and France was even longer declaring himself. It was not until January, 1898 that he came out openly on the side of the Dreyfusards. For France and Mme. Arman, the intervening years had filled out very much to the size and shape expected of them. In Paris France continued working on *l'Histoire Contemporaine*. Away from it, in the periods of rest and recuperation which the seasonal rhythm of their life allowed them, they enjoyed themselves and each other, letting the slow time pass quickly at Capian, or going on one of their sight-seeing trips abroad. Of these, the range had now been pleasantly and effortlessly increased by the fact that they now often used M. Arman's yacht as a floating hotel. Thus, in the autumn of 1896 they went on a long journey by land through Italy, and then by sea to Egypt, where France saw for the first time the scenery he had described so admirably in *Thaïs* eight years before. In July, 1897 they cruised down the Adriatic, using the *Nausicaa* as the base for several land journeys; and the following year went on what, for France, must have been a particularly exciting voyage – to Greece, where for the first time, France saw the fount of so much of his inspiration. On this

voyage they were shut up for a while by bad weather in
Messina, but France was a good sailor, and Mme. Arman
had converted a cabin for his use as a study. A letter to
Suzanne, of October, 1898, shows him in high spirits and
obviously getting a lot of work done while the storm
raged outside – 'The wind is strong. The sea is high . . .
What is miraculous is that I have masses of work, and that
I am blackening a lot of paper in my cabin.'

France had held over publication of the first volume of
l'Histoire Contemporaine (*l'Orme de Mail*) until after the
Academic election lest any sparks of clerical or anticlerical feeling should fire his hopes, but it appeared in
January, 1897 without any particular inflammatory effects.
Now he clearly intended to carry and chronicle further the
rivalries of the abbés Lantaigne and Guitrel in their quest
for a bishopric. But in fact it was one of the charms of
France's books that they often went their own, rather than
his way, and the second volume of *l'Histoire Contemporaine*
developed mainly into an account of the matrimonial
misfortunes of M. Bergeret, the provincial school-teacher
whom France had introduced casually at the end of the first
volume, on an evening stroll under the elms – 'very lax,
discouraged and full of chagrin', without apparently
other or greater interest than that his scepticism should
act as a foil to the abbé Lantaigne's fervent and faithful
views.

However, as the second volume grew, so too did Bergeret's place of importance in it, and in the end, as had
Coignard in *La Rôtisserie*, he took complete charge. Sore,
disappointed, disgruntled, but still hopeful of man even if
disillusioned with life, a savage defender of individual
freedom and man's right to be wrong, Bergeret showed a
side of France that had been little in evidence since *Servien*.
Considering how fortune had smiled on France, it was surprising that this side still existed, and even more that it

should appear now when the barometer of France's life seemed particularly to be set fair, but in the course of considering the wreck of Bergeret's marriage, France seems to have lanced the abscess of bitterness formed by the failure of his own.

France seems to have deliberately pinned the two experiences together by his choice of the title, *Le Mannequin d'Osier* – 'The Dressmaker's Dummy' – under which it was published by Calmann Lévy in September, 1897, for the episode which inspired it was known to be based on one which occurred in France's life. In the book, Bergeret, in a rage at finding Mme. Bergeret entwined on the divan with his favourite pupil, threw the dummy out of the window. In real life France, in a fury, not at any infidelity of Valérie's, but at the general domestic discord and disorder of his home, threw the dummy into the courtyard of the riding-school next door. Like France, Bergeret conducted against his wife a cold war which ultimately reached freezing point so that Bergeret, like France, would communicate with his wife only by written messages delivered by the servant. Like France, Bergeret claimed his wife thought she had married beneath her. Like France, Bergeret believed his wife scorned his work – in this case the patient translation of the classics. Since France was often at his funniest with his malice unfurled, his readers were delighted to forgo the fortunes of Guitrel for the misfortunes of Bergeret. But Valérie never forgave France for raking over in public the embers of their marriage.

Throughout the course of that year France was becoming increasingly involved in other misfortunes than those of M. Bergeret. However, in November, he was still undecided and evasive to a reporter sent by *l'Aurore*, recently founded by Clemenceau and Ernest Vaughan – 'I have never given an opinion on the Dreyfus case because I do not know why he has been condemned.' The moment of conversion appears to have come at a literary dinner, a 'diner Balzac', which took place early in December at a restaurant, Durand, in the Place de la Madeleine – a dinner attended by many distinguished men of letters, notably, besides France, Zola, Coppée, Barrès, Bourget and Alphonse Daudet. The conversation turning inevitably on to the Affair, it developed into an argument between Zola, putting the case for revision and Daudet, on the side of the judges. The majority were on Daudet's side, but it was noted with dismay that France, who had been expected to stay on his customary strip of no-man's land, applauded Zola loudly. A month later Zola's famous inflammatory article, '*J'Accuse*', published in *l'Aurore* of 13th January, 1898, was followed the next day by the 'petition of intellectuals' calling for a revision of the case, on which France's name was the first after Zola's. For this, France's signature had been sought by Marcel Proust, who, on the strength of it, claimed in a letter to Paul Sonday written more than twenty years later, to have been the 'first Dreyfusard, since it was I who went to ask Anatole France for his signature'.

By this action France threw the very considerable weight of his fame and his pen on to the side of the Dreyfusards. The importance of his adherence was quickly appreciated and at Zola's trial, which took place during the following month, he was called by the defence to testify to Zola's good character – a situation which had a certain irony, for Zola's work had long been one of France's blind spots. In the columns of *La Vie Littéraire* he had often castigated it, calling it, on one occasion 'obscene' and remarking of Zola – 'This terrible man has greatly angered me, and in various ways.'

At the time of France's declaration for Dreyfus, it was suggested, mainly by those former friends who now found themselves separated from France by his decision, that he had been forced into it by Mme. Arman and her Jewish connections. Barrès even went so far as to spread the totally untrue story that Mme. Arman, without France's know-ledge, had entered his name on the 'petition of intellectuals'. According to Barrès, France, when he learnt about it, went round to the newspaper office to withdraw his name, but found that it was too late and that the paper had already gone to bed. Yet it was unlikely that Mme. Arman was under pressure from her family. As Léon Blum put it – 'The rich Jews, the middle bourgeoisie, the Jewish public servants, were afraid of the fight . . . they thought only of going to ground and hiding.' Mme. Arman would never have been afraid of the fight, but it seems improbable that she was pressed to enter it by any of her Jewish relatives.

Nor, in fact, was it to her own interest to do so. Both M. Arman and Gaston were against Dreyfus. Mme. Arman, who had chosen to divide her house on other issues, would not welcome anything that divided it further. Nor, obviously, would she welcome a step that inevitably would bar a number of her most valued guests from her salon. This, then, seems to have been one decision that France did make on his own, possibly prompted to it by the desire to participate in what, in a famous phrase, he was to call when speaking at Zola's funeral 'a moment of the human conscience'.

France was never to play so central or controversial a role in the Affair as Zola, but he was always ready with his support, in whatever shape it was required, whether a speech, a signature, a letter to the Press. That autumn, for the first time in his life, he was up on a political platform, speaking on behalf of Picquart, who was threatened with arrest, and calling, most uncharacteristically, for 'no more vain words – actions.' His signature had been the first on the petition which a few days earlier had circulated on behalf of Picquart. A few days later, France was again speaking on Picquart's behalf at a meeting in the Freemason hall of the Grand Orient, which became so crowded that a second overflow meeting had to be organized in the courtyard outside –

'After a court martial has condemned one innocent man, and after another has acquitted a guilty one (Esterhazy), we must not allow another court-martial to confirm two unjust sentences by a third even more unjust.' Some of France's friends did not find him all that convincing in his new role of man of action, Blum for one – 'Both the sage and the critic seemed equally out of place in the public battle.' But there were others whose admiration was unbounded. Proust wrote him a letter of good wishes for the New Year of 1899 – 'Maître, I wish you a good year and good health . . . but no year can be so splendid for you as that which has just passed. "It was then that Alexander was called the Great." The courage which you have so nobly called for, nobody has had it in a greater degree than you . . . And in fact you have mingled in public life in a way unknown in this century . . . not to make yourself a name, but when you already had one, so that it should be a weight in the balance of justice.'

But if it was the Affair that brought France down into the arena of public affairs, it was the magnetic personality of Jean Jaurès, whom he met there, that drew him into the demanding hurly-burly of party politics. Until now France had played virtually no part in political affairs. In 1888 he had briefly flirted with Boulangism, but this was simply to flatter Mme. Arman, who was an ardent supporter of the General. Occasionally in 'Gérôme' he had trespassed on the territory of his other half, 'Richard O'Monroy' to give political comments, but always essentially safe, middle-of-the-road opinions that could offend no one, and were likely to influence them as little. In an article of *La Vie Littéraire* of the 3rd January, 1892 on 'Littérature Socialiste' he had struck a more genuine note – 'Instability, it is true, is the first condition of life. All progress is slow . . . let us expect no miracles. Rather let us resign ourselves to preparing slow but certain progress, which we will not see perhaps and which no human force can hasten.' But if France already had his socialist sympathies, he kept them well in check during the period of his climb to fame, and would probably have continued to do so had he not spent several days waiting with Jaurès in the vast Salle des Pas Perdus of the Palais de Justice, for their turn to testify at the Zola trial.

Chapter

8

FRANCE had met Jean Jaurès, already a visitor to Mme. Arman's salon, before the Affair started. But it was not until the two men found themselves fighting side by side in the ranks of the Dreyfusards that France really felt the pull of Jaurès' powerful personality. The process seems to have started at the Zola trial, at which both men were called as witnesses. Waiting for their turn to testify, they whiled away the time discussing literary subjects. France was astounded by the depth of Jaurès' devotion to literature, and astonished to find that his learning matched his love. He was particularly impressed by the fantastic memory from which Jaurès quoted 'the most beautiful verses of the epoch of Louis XIII', and by 'the exquisite taste' with which he commented upon them. This was the start of a quick-growing but long-lasting friendship that ended only with Jaurès' assassination on the eve of the Great War. It was over the bridge of this friendship that France was led to participate in a far wider sphere of political activity than he can ever have foreseen or imagined when he first entered the arena of the Affair.

Although Jaurès was fifteen years younger than France – at the time of their meeting in the Salle des Pas Perdus in February 1897 he was 38 – he had already played a promi-nent part in French politics for at least twelve years. When first elected as a Republican deputy for the Tarn in 1885 he had been the youngest member of the Chambre. Losing his seat at the 1889 election, falling out with the more hide-bound Republicans, and following the natural slant of his humanitarian inclinations, he had reappeared in the Chambre after the 1893 elections as one of a new bunch of deputies – some fifty in number but segmented into a number of mutually suspicious groups – calling themselves for the first time, plainly Socialists.

Across the gap in years there were several strands of similarity both in background and character which drew the two men together. Like France, Jaurès came of country stock, although his father had not come to Paris to seek his fortune – as Père France had really been doing when he joined the army – but had remained in the Tarn to lose what remained of it, first as a merchant, then as a farmer. As with France, a love of literature and a belief in the cultural values had come to be one of the main features of his character; although, unlike France, who had picked up most of his learning away from school, his had been acquired in the course of an extremely successful scholastic career. He had won a scholarship to the Lycée Louis le Grand, thence to the École Normale, where he had immediately become one of the star pupils. Jaurès' Socialism was based on a keen sense of the suffering lot of ordinary people. France, too, believed in the basic misfortune of mankind, although in his career so far, he had shown little sign of wanting to do much about it. Jaurès' faults were the exaggerations of his virtues. His respect for the things of the mind led him to become something of an intellectual snob; his liking for ordinary people and his desire to be liked in return, caused him to lean too heavily on the applause of his audience; and his basic idealism made him at times ineffective as a practical politician.

But although France and Jaurès were linked by these several points of similarity in background and character, the basic attraction between them was really that of opposites. Jaurès was a born orator with a magnificent voice and delivery. Once on a visit to England he whipped up to fever pitch an audience, most of whom understood little or nothing of what he was saying, since he was speaking in French, but who yet responded to the splendid sound of his voice, to the rolling rhythm of his phrases, and to the infectious enthusiasm which electrified his words. His power over his audience depended on his personal contact with them, and from them he drew both energy and inspiration. For all his cultural inclinations, for all the intellectual ability which lay behind the rhetoric, for all the sincerity of his Socialism, his real greatness lay in his oratory, in the spells he cast from his platform over his audience, or, in a closer circle, over his friends. He was a magnificent creative extrovert, and France, who in these ways was the complete opposite – introspective, a hesitant speaker and more likely to be petrified than inspired by his audience – fell, like many others, completely under his spell. Jaurès' liking for France was based, in part at least, on his admiration for France's writing, but he greatly respected also the subtlety of France's well-stocked mind and its greater profundity. Nor can one believe that he was so idealistic and impractical as to be totally unaware of the valuable catch that so large a literary fish would be in the hold of any political party.

Jaurès reinforced his personal conquest of France by taking him to many meetings at the École Normale, which from the start of the Affair had been a centre of Dreyfusist support, and where Jaurès as a Dreyfusard, as a Socialist, and simply as himself, had an enthusiastic following amongst both students and teachers. Then, as now, the École Normale belied its name, being neither an école nor normal in the sense of being typical of the general run of French scholastic establishments. It was much more of a university than a school, and its students were, as they are now, the pick of lycées and colleges from all over France. Since on its staff it had some of the greatest savants of the day, it was hardly surprising that it should have come to look upon itself, and be looked upon, as something of an intellectual élite, with its own customs, jargon and a traditional attitude which marked many *normaliens* for life. Since this attitude contained a strong element of scepticism, a liking for wit as well as wisdom, and a rather cynical approach to everyday affairs, France, although not himself one of them, was very much in their tradition, and was welcomed with open arms.

Always susceptible to admiration, France was particularly so to that of the *normaliens*, since they stood to him for those qualities of intellectual distinction and assurance which he had always particularly respected. Had circumstances and his schoolmasters been kinder to him in his youth, there can be no doubt that France would have much liked to have been one of them. At the time he was taken there by Jaurès, the École Normale was not only a centre of Dreyfusist support but of resistance to the wave of anti-Semitic, near-Fascist nationalism then sweeping the country. France was entirely in agreement with the views of his new friends, but even so was probably induced by their infectious enthusiasm to move a good deal faster along the road to political participation than he would have done had he been free to choose his own pace.

Jaurès did not only take France to meetings at the École Normale, he also took him to meetings of his own – the Socialist – Party; and to workers gatherings. Here again circumstances seemed to be contriving to hustle France rather faster along the political road than he may have liked. For at this time the desire, long-felt in Paris, for the spread of education, had resulted in the formation of a series of so-styled 'People's Universities' or workers' study-groups. How much these represented a robust do-it-yourself attitude on the part of the Parisian workers, how much a slumming gesture on the part of the intellectuals who had attached themselves to the movement but who were possibly seeking their own spiritual refreshment by contact with the masses as much as to help in widening the spread of education, it is difficult to make out. Certainly the original inspiration seems to have been genuine – the first study-group was started by a typographical worker, Georges Délorme, in April, 1898. But equally certain the programmes of many of these evening meetings seem to have been far too stratospheric to have been of much interest to an audience seeking primarily knowledge that they might use in their own lives. Typical of these was one over which France presided, consisting of a lecture on 'The Moral Ideas of Tolstoy', a poem entitled, 'The Muse and the Worker' read by its author, and a final section of music and poetry. Either way, however, these worker study-groups provided an obvious and easy lead-in for a writer who otherwise from the detached tone of his writing, the emphasis he put on the rare and the beautiful, and the little interest he had hitherto shown in political questions, might have seemed to have little to offer a predominately proletarian gathering. As it was, however, France, as one of the deities of the literary scene, was received rapturously by his audiences, few of whom had ever read any of his works and who might have found some disturbing thoughts in them if they had.

France first appeared in his new role on 21st November, 1899 when he presided – one imagines with some trepidation (was this the recorded but unspecified occasion when, out of nervousness, he started off by saying, 'La ouverte est séance'?) – over the inaugural meeting of 'L'Emancipatrice', the newly-formed study-group of the XV *arrondissement*. From this launching-pad he was shot into an endless orbit of similar activities. On 7th January, 1900 he was the main speaker at the fête of 'Soirées Ouvrières' at Montreuil-sur-Bois. On the 4th March he presided over the inauguration of another workers' study-group – this time 'Le Reveil' of the I and II *arrondissements* – giving an address on 'The Proletariat and Science'. Jaurès was one of the two other speakers. A month later France was speaking on 'The Unity of Art' at an evening organized by the

Theatre Civique – again followed on the platform by Jaurès. In June he addressed, at considerable length, a meeting organized by the French Federation of Book-Workers to celebrate the 500th anniversary of the birth of Gutenberg. A month later he was the principal speaker at a 'Fête civique' in the Salle Wagram organized by the People's Universities in honour of Diderot. France was also to inaugurate a co-operative restaurant in the XV *arrondissement* under the aegis of 'L'Emancipatrice', soon to be followed in the same district and, as it were, under the same management, by a co-operative printing-press, at the opening of which France made a delightful speech in which he told the assembled printers that by birth and upbringing he considered himself to be almost one of them – '. . . very young . . . I was concerned with the making of books. I corrected proofs. I corrected the proofs of others before I corrected my own.' He reminded his audience of the remark which Rabelais had put in the mouth of Pantagruel that printing had been invented by angelic inspiration as the counter-blast to the diabolically-inspired invention of gunpowder. France also supported a movement for the creation of a Théâtre Populaire.

But as well as all these activities into which, once he had taken the decision to enter the arena of public affairs, France's intellectual and literary interests seemed naturally to lead him (perhaps the co-operative restaurant can just be squeezed into them, since France would have been the first to maintain that if one eats well one reads better), France gradually became involved in a number of activities of which the motives and matter were much more purely political, and much further removed from his previous interests.

In February 1900, France gave his support to a meeting appealing for a reduction in the harsh sentences – from one to five years imprisonment – meted out to a youthful band, forming part of a general demonstration against the activities of the nationalists – organized by the Socialist Party throughout Paris, who had got out of hand, and broken up the contents of a church, l'Eglise St. Joseph, rue St. Maur. On the 16th June, he appeared for the first time on what was to become one of his most used and useful platforms, speaking at a meeting organized by the Ligue des Droits de l'Homme, formed some two years previously as a counterblast to the nationalist Ligue de la Patrie Française, on behalf of Armenian children orphaned by the Greco-Turkish war – a cause in which France had a more personal interest because of a visit he had paid to Constantinople at the end of 1899. In August he introduced, with a note of his own, to the readers of *l'Aurore*, a letter protesting against anti-Semitic measures in Rumania. He had already, in August, 1899, protested against the Russian domination of Finland, in a preface to a pamphlet produced on the occasion of the 'Peace Conference' at The Hague; and again in the spring of 1901 he was up in arms against Tsarist despotism, this time in support of demonstrations against the drafting of politically obstreperous students into the army. The students had carried their protests to the point of assassinating Bogoliepoff, the Minister responsible. Two days later, on 17th March, 1901, the Cossacks, in retaliation, had charged a crowd in St. Petersburg, killing ten, injuring over a hundred, and arresting more than a thousand. France's signature was last, but not least, on a list of protest and support published in Paris, and a letter from him also appeared in *l'Aurore*. In this he wrote – 'These workers, these students, are being deported and massacred because they have cried out for a little justice, a little liberty, a little truth. . . . Since a life of the spirit is inherent in Russians nothing will stop their intellectual and social emancipation. Their hour will come.' In September, 1901 when, on the occasion of the Tsar's visit to Paris, Laurent Taillarde, one of France's acquaintances from Parnassian days, published in an anarchist journal an article appealing for an assassin to make use of the opportunity and was consequently

charged with incitement to murder, France from Capian
sent a letter to the court in his support.

The champion abroad of Armenian orphans, of Ruman-
ian Jews, of Russian students, at home of rioters and
anarchists, France, in a short time had come a long way. But
he was to widen his experience even further when, for the
first time in his life, at the elections of 1902, he was hustled
out on to the hustings.

At the previous general election in 1898, Jaurès had lost
his seat, mainly because of his mishandling of a strike of
glass-workers in his constituency in Carmaux. Now he was
determined to make every effort not only to get back to the
Chambre, but to see that the Republican *bloc* of parties, of
which the Socialists formed a small but significant part,
were returned to power also.

It was a hard-fought campaign. Both sides, in preparation
for the struggle over the separation of Church and State
looming ahead, had closed their ranks for battle, although a
significant split in the Socialist party – over the right of
Party members to participate in the Government – an issue
brought to a head by the inclusion in 1901, for the first time,
of a Socialist deputy, Millerand, in the Cabinet – had not yet
healed. But, apart from the extreme Socialists of various
dissuasions, aiming at revolution rather than reform, but
differing as to the means of destruction, grouped behind
Guesde, all the parties from Centre to Left united in the
Republican *bloc*. On the other side, for the first time
the Monarchists made common cause with the *Ralliés*, the
nationalists of the *Ligue de la Patrie*; and the Catholic
Church, fighting for its livelihood more than its life, put
its full weight behind them.

France was one of the biggest guns produced in support
of the Republican campaign, and a 'Discours pour la
liberté' which he delivered to a mass meeting, a week
before the elections, was greeted with such acclamation that
it was printed as a Party eve-of-election hand-out. 50,000

copies were run off the Presses, and in whole or in part, it was reproduced in all the Republican papers, in the provinces as well as in Paris.

France himself seems to have entered into the electoral battle with zest. Not only did he become president of a 'committee for electoral action' in his own – the 16th – *arrondissement*, but he managed to insert some effective vote-catching propaganda into whatever speeches he was called upon to make at this time, whether they had anything to do with the election or not. Thus a large audience who had gathered in the Trocadero on the 2nd March, 1902, to honour the centenary of Victor Hugo, must have been considerably surprised to be told that Hugo, had he been alive 'in this troubled time when the enemies of democracy and of social justice are trying to restore the power of the Church and the rule of privilege', would undoubtedly have told them to vote Republican. France, by now generally accepted as the sage of the Socialist Party, was attentively listened to when, on the 21st December, 1901, he spoke on 'The Morality of Elections', counselling the intellectuals of his Party, evidently forgetting for the moment the Guesdists, the Blanquists and the Anarchists, all as eager to destroy Jaurès' Socialists as the members of other parliamentary parties, 'to remember . . . that you have no enemies on your left . . . without the proletariat you are only a handful of dissident bourgeois'. He was no less carefully read when in reply to a questionnaire, organized by the daily *Le Français*, after a deputy had brought up the ever-inflammatory subject of Capital Punishment by the roundabout method of proposing the removal of the 55,000 francs of executioners' wages from the Budget, he wrote 'An execution is a formal assassination. . . . The death penalty is a shameful and degenerate punishment.'

The results of the elections rewarded France for his efforts. The Republican *bloc* was returned to power with a majority of 148 seats. Jaurès regained his seat at Carmaux, although the swing was more in favour of the Left Centre than of the Left itself, and one of Jaurès' principal lieutenants, Allemane, was beaten in the 11th *arrondissement* of Paris. France attended at least three celebration banquets, presiding at two of them. The Socialists were still numerically a relatively small part of the Republican *bloc*, but the balance of power was so poised that their defection could seriously threaten the Government. With Jaurès as vice-president of the Chambre, and as the dominating figure of a newly-created committee, the Delegation of the Left, to supervise and co-ordinate the activities of the *bloc*'s deputies, they were in a position of greater parliamentary influence than ever before. To France, as to many other Socialists of longer standing, it must have seemed that the moment had at last come to take the first practical steps towards the achievement of the better world that was the Socialist ideal and dream. Yet, as on so many other occasions, this hope-awakening glimmer of light was to prove to be a false dawn, and the two and a half years of Republican rule which followed were to the Socialists to prove a bitter disappointment. The real reason for this was that the Socialists, for all their strong support of the Republican *bloc*, were at cross-purposes with the other parties who united in it – or perhaps not so much at cross-purposes as at divergent purposes. It was a question of priorities. For the Socialists, social reform was all important. For all other parties, not only in the *bloc* but in the Chambre, the vital issue of this parliament, whether they were for or against it, was the separation of Church and State. This had now replaced the Affair, which to outside opinion had seemed to be settled by the passing of the amnesty bill at the end of 1900, as the focal point of public interest. The previous Government under Waldeck-Rousseau had in 1901 passed the controversial Law of the Congregations, by which all religious orders as well as other associations had to apply to the Chambre for authorization, and those who did not apply or were not authorized were not allowed to teach. Although fiercely contested, this was, however, but a preliminary skirmish, and the real battle still lay ahead.

The Separation was not, to the Socialists, an issue about which they felt strongly. They had, in fact, opposed *la loi des congregations* in its original form since it had seemed to threaten the independence of their working-men's associations as well as that of the religious orders. But most Socialist deputies were prepared to give it their support if they were paid their price – by way of the passing of various much-needed social reforms – such as a scheme for workers' pensions, a subject which had been under parliamentary scrutiny for several years without producing any positive results. For once, too, they were in a strong bargaining position, for their opposition, as was later to be proved, could seriously embarrass, if not bring down, the Government. Yet not only did they fail to exact a good price, they failed to exact any price at all – a tragic failure, considering the circumstances and the consequences, and for which Jaurès himself was very largely to blame. Instead they allowed themselves to be side-tracked into what for them was a minor issue without achieving anything by way of compensation or reward. During the two and a half years of the Combes Ministry which followed, no social reforms of any consequence were passed; and the Socialists who started with a long list of reforming projects in their hand, ended with nothing changed save the smile on their faces.

In the difficult task of distinguishing the Socialist from the Republican ball and keeping his eye upon it, Jaurès may have found France little help. For while in most political matters France was very much the disciple and follower of Jaurès, on the subject of the Separation, his views were much firmer, more ferocious and forceful than those of his master. The issue brought out all the anti-clericalism latent in France since his unhappy schooldays. One is tempted to call it the worst side of his nature. It was certainly a largely destructive, revengeful and very personal urge which prompted his actions. Yet few are big enough to overlook, or to judge with detachment, the hurts of childhood. If the Catholic Church found the barbs which France now flung at it of any consequence or irritation, it had the Jesuits of Stanislas mainly to blame – the abbé who refused to associate with his one-time protégé because of the shame with which his ill-fitting tunic invested him; the original of the revolting 'Crottu' of *Le Petit Pierre* who all but succeeded in instilling into his pupil a dislike of learning as well as of himself; the many other masters who were not prepared to take trouble with an obviously difficult but equally obviously rewarding pupil whom they considered, and in fact was, socially inferior to most of the others.

In the course of the electoral battle France had already shown his claws when, in his 'Discours de la Liberté' he had written of his nationalist opponents – 'All these people are in the service of the monks. When they tell you they are republicans it is the Republic of the Monks they intend to give you; when they cry out for liberty it is for the liberty by which the monks can escape the law; what they call the liberty of teaching is liberty for the monks to teach children to hate.' Clearly, if that was what the monks – or rather the Jesuits – of Stanislas had taught France, he had well learnt his lesson.

Yet even if the Socialists were fundamentally at variance with the other parties of the Republican *bloc*, and even if France's attitude possibly hindered more than it helped him, Jaurès' failure to grasp not only the opportunity but what in the long term could well have proved to be the reins of power, would not have been so absolute and abject had he not suddenly found himself confronted with the formidable figure of Émile Combes, who, to his and everyone else's astonishment – he had only once before held a Ministerial appointment, that of Minister of Public Instruction in the Bourgeois government of 1895 – was, at the age of 71, nominated as Premier by the retiring Waldeck-Rousseau, who like a famous Oxford Vice-chancellor, seemed to find it 'time to make way for an older man'.

'Père' Combes was a formidable old man, full of energy and determination, but with only one idea in his head, the suppression of the Catholic Church, to which he harnessed all his activity. In his youth Combes had been trained as a priest, but had later defected to medicine. Like many renegades he was consumed by a rabid hatred of the cause he had deserted. The more moderate Waldeck-Rousseau, judging – probably rightly – that the time had come in the relationship of the Church and State to bring about some separation of their powers and interests, both to remove the rancour on the Republican side and also to purify the faith and simplify the functions of the Church itself, had put Combes forward as the man to carry this difficult measure through. But clearly even he had misjudged the extent of Combes's fanaticism, as the result of which what should have been a period of liberal innovation, which could have seen the implementation of many much-needed and long-promised social reforms, assumed instead the aspect of a crusade – but a crusade against, not for, the Church.

It was a crusade, too, backed by as sinister a system of personal espionage and individual intimidation as had been seen since the Terror. This was particularly evident in the War Department under André, who made use of the grape-vine of Free-Masonry to compile a series of personal reports on his officers, on which he based his promotions, in which it mattered little whether or not his candidates were good or bad soldiers, but only that they should be good Republicans. André's intermediary with the Free-Masons was his personal assistant, a Captain Mollin, a fact later to prove of considerable if coincidental importance to France, for Mollin was his son-in-law.

Mollin, himself a Mason, summarized the information collected by the grape-vine into a series of notes or *fiches*

– the famous *fiches* that were eventually to bring down the Government – which he passed on to André. To collect this information the Masons, from their headquarters at the Lodge of the Grand Orient in the rue Cadet, had quickly established an efficient but execrable spy system. Officers who were Masons were ordered to report the table-talk of their brother-officers. A watch was kept to see which officers went to Mass and sent their children to religious schools, both bad offences. Rivals for promotion were encouraged to denounce each other's shortcomings. Even shopkeepers were approached to find out whether the colonel or his lady had made rude remarks about the Government when making their purchases. Altogether it was as odious a system of inquisitorial intrusion into the privacy of the individual as could possibly be imagined.

Nor was it only in the War Department that this attitude prevailed, although in no other was it carried to such an extreme. Camille Pelletan, the Radical Socialist who had been made Minister of Marine, was also to be criticized in the Chambre for making appointments on Republican rather than naval merit; while the newly constituted Delegation of the Left, on which Jaurès sat, and which he in fact dominated, turned out not to be the sounding-box for deputies' wishes which he and many others had hoped it would be, but simply a disciplinary body keeping the deputies of the *bloc* in step and in line behind Combes. It, too, intruded far farther, and interfered much more with, the private affairs of the deputies than it had any reasonable right to do.

Yet for all the crusading fervour which Combes brought to his task, and for all the severity with which he dragooned his supporters, it is doubtful whether he speeded greatly the cause or the course of Separation. His uncompromising attitude and distastefully dictatorial methods provoked continual skirmishes, both inside the Chambre and out, which dissipated the energies of his forces and prevented the main battle being joined. When his Government fell, the bill had not yet come before the Chambre, and its passage would most probably have been delayed further if the responsibility of piloting its course had not then come into the much more skilful hands of Aristide Briand.

Combes's obsessional determination to wreck the influence of the Church in France led him to wreck much else besides. Amongst the most serious of the casualties were the high hopes of the more moderate Socialists, who had backed Jaurès at the 1902 elections, that he would achieve sufficient social reform to draw the dissenting wing of extremists behind them. As it was, however, the result was exactly the reverse. By his failure to secure social reform, by his submission to Combes's domination, and by the part he played in the activities of the soon-hated 'Delegation of the Left', Jaurès lost much not only of his reputation in the Chambre – he was not re-elected a Vice-President – but of his following there also – in March, 1904, Millerand and a number of other Socialist deputies voted against the Government. What was even more serious, Jaurès, by his inept leadership during these years, lost a great deal of support amongst the Socialist rank and file, so that when the schism in the Socialist party was resolved – a vote at the Amsterdam Congress of August, 1904 was implemented by the creation in April, 1905 of the United Socialist Party – rather than the moderate views of Jaurès, it was the extreme ones of Guesde that prevailed. It was the difference between reform and revolution. Because of this, as the result of a remote decision in which he had no say, France was to find himself a member of a party committed to a course of action aimed at producing just the state of affairs he most dreaded, for no one ever had a greater horror of revolution than he.

To France, of course, revolution meant primarily the French Revolution of 1788–93. His brief childhood experience –

when during the February days of 1848 he had been taken
to the front apartments of 19, Quai Malaquais, to watch the
mob milling around the Tuileries on the opposite bank –
had left its mark. But much more than this it was the long
years of browsing through the books and other stock on the
shelves of his father's shop that had conditioned his attitude.

What had brought the experience home the more forcibly
to the reserved but imaginative child that France had been,
was the fact that he was not reading about an epoch remote
either in time or distance, but about events that had happened on his doorstep and within living memory. Many who
were old men – and not so old as all that – when he was a
boy, remembered the Revolution, and most of the streets
around carried still some echo of Revolutionary times. The
Tuileries, the main target of the mob, stood just across the
river. The Place du Carrousel, the site of the guillotine until
it was moved into what had been the Place Louis XV, became the Place de la Révolution, and is now the Place de la
Concorde, lay just behind them. In the hinterland of the
quais on which France was born and brought up, the Abbaye
de St. Germain-des-Prés, in whose church France had been
christened, the scene of the September Massacres, was but a
short stretch of the rue Bonaparte from the quai Malaquais.
Haussmann had not yet bull-dozed the Boulevard St. Ger-
main over the Prison de l'Abbaye when France was a boy.
It would, therefore, have been that much easier to imagine
the scene in front of the prison gates when the pavements
of the rue St. Marguerite ran with the blood of 270 victims,
mostly priests, killed during the night of the 2nd September, 1792 – to see in his mind's eye the benches provided
by a thoughtful committee so that women could watch the
butchery in more comfort, the 84 lamps ordered from a
nearby candlemaker so that the corpses could be seen more
clearly. This was but one episode of many that must have
impressed themselves the more forcibly on France's mind

because they had happened just round the corner, not so long ago.

Many prominent figures of the Revolution had had their homes in the district in which France was brought up. Marat had lived – and died at the hand of Charlotte Corday – in a house in the rue des Cordeliers, only a few hundred yards from the Prison de l'Abbaye. He had printed his 'Ami du Peuple' nearby, in what is now No. 8, Passage du Commerce. No. 9 opposite was at one time the home of Dr. Guillotine. Danton and Desmoulins both lived at No. 1 Cour de Commerce. It would, in fact, have been difficult for France to take a walk in any direction from his home without passing a building associated with some Revolutionary character or experience, and often, after reading about some event of the Revolution, he must have found himself, by no particular intent but simply in the course of his wanderings, chancing upon the scene of its happening. It cannot, either, have needed a very wide stretch of imagination inflamed by such reading, to see in the black-clothed old women of the markets, the famous *tricoteuses*, which no doubt some of them had been – or to inflate the sound of some stray drunken brawl into the baying of an angry mob.

The fear of revolution instilled into France by his reading as a boy was confirmed by what he saw and heard of the fighting at the time of the Commune. That curious off-beat novel, *Les Desirs de Jean Servien*, which he wrote on return from his exile in Ville d'Avray, was not only a cry of adolescent anger against the injustice of the world, but also the nightmare of an innocent, such as himself, caught in the whirlpool of Revolutionary violence.

Witness Jean's end. In the final stages of the struggle, Jean was picked up and taken for a Versaillois spy, by a marauding band of Communards at whose head was a ferocious, furious Amazon – 'wild-haired, full-breasted, thick-thighed . . . she had the savage power of a magnificent wild-beast. From her little round mouth came a stream of obscene menaces; she waved a revolver . . . threw herself on Jean, spat in his face, shouted and threatened him with gestures of a frenetic obscenity – then put the barrel of the revolver to his temple. . . . The revolver went off. Jean's arms flailed in the air, and he fell face downwards. The men finished him off with bayonet thrusts – then the woman danced on his corpse, shouting with joy.' Just as for generations of Republican school-children the glory of the Revolution has been splendidly symbolized by Delacroix's magnificent bare-breasted Liberty, storming the barricades with a tricolour in one hand and a rifle in the other, so, for France, all the horror and capricious cruelty of the Revolution was personified in this revolting Fury, drunk with power and the lust for blood. Had France not succeeded in passing himself off on the Communard out-posts as a Belgian merchant; had he instead been caught up in one of the many cross-currents of violence which swept across Paris at this time, this was clearly the fate he had fore-seen for himself.

But together with the manuscript of *Jean Servien*, France put his fear of revolution into a drawer and firmly turned the key on it. It remained there for the next thirty-five years of his life. Now and again some recognizable emana-tion crept through a crack into his work. In 1884 he pub-lished in *Le Journal des Debats* a short story, 'Les Autels de la Peur', that was an attempt to evoke the atmosphere and mood of Revolutionary Paris and to show how easily the altar of patriotism can become the altar of tyranny. Now and again it strayed into his conversation when a good dinner or a pleasant evening stormed the barricades of his reserve. Barrès records in his *Cahiers* that at a *diner* Balzac, *chez* Durand on the 7th December, 1897, France said to him – 'What strikes me more and more is the stupidity of the men of the Revolution. Robespierre! He's the one I detest most. He wished to govern by morality. All those who have had this pretension have done the greatest harm. Morality is an artificial rule. One is burdening politics with an alien element if one tries to play it by rules that are not its own.' But in general, just as France's social conscience was firmly suppressed over the period of his climb to fame, so too was his fear of revolution. Now, however, when he had reached what should have been the safe anchorage of his sixties, he suddenly found himself a member of a party officially committed to Revolutionary action. Had the issue not been so serious, France, as an ironist, might have been amused to note how circuitous – or half-circuitous – a course circumstances had led him, so that he now found himself standing shoulder to shoulder with his Socialist colleagues, in support of a policy, the realization of which would also have realized one of his deepest fears.

France was not to see where he was going, however, until long after he got there. In the meantime he and Combes soon found that their mutual dislike of the Church brought them together – notably on the platform at Treguier, on the 13th September, 1903, when Combes was unveiling a statue to Renan and when France was one of the main speakers.

Treguier, a charming small cathedral town close to the north Breton coast, was for the occasion the scene of noisy clashes between anti-clericals and the supporters of the Church. France, now a large enough whale in literary waters to have attracted his pilot fish, took one of them, Nicolas Ségur, as well as Mme. Arman, down for the ceremony. Ségur has left an amusing account of their stay. On the eve of the ceremony, France attended a banquet. Ségur went too, but not Mme. Arman. When the banquet was over, at the relatively early hour of half-past ten, Ségur walked with France to the house where he and Mme. Arman were lodging. It was a fine summer's night. France was in a dawdling, pensive mood, thinking of his speech for the following day, which he had only finished that afternoon, and in the state of discouragement which usually afflicted him on the completion of any piece of work. The speech, he told Ségur, was 'spoiled, stupid and very bad'. Now and again the customary cloisteral calm of the streets was broken by the passage of one of the several groups of students touring the town, shouting 'Down with the Church.' At one point in their desultory return, France and Ségur nearly bumped into one of these bands. France hurriedly drew Ségur into a side-street. 'They think as we do,' he said, 'but it would be wiser not to meet them.'

On the day there were violent fights in the town, particularly in the square in which the ceremony was taking place. At one moment a pistol ball passed over the heads of those on the platform. This was the second recorded instance when France came under, or at least close to, fire – the other occasion being in 1870 when France, a National Guard on the ramparts, read Virgil while the Prussians made an effort to distract his attention by shelling the positions below. But in spite of these interruptions, France managed to make himself heard, and what he said was well worth hearing.

Far from being 'spoiled, stupid and very bad,' France's speech was one of the best he ever made. In it he paid tribute to the originality of Renan's thought, the patience and exactitude of his research – also to the courage and consistency of his character – 'Those who considered him irresolute and changeable had not taken the trouble to look at the world of his thoughts. He resembled his native land, over which the clouds run fast in an agitated sky, but the ground is of granite and the oaks plunge deep roots.' He also paid handsomely his own debt to Renan as a great writer who had considerably influenced the course of his own development. But at times there were signs of a conflict, not in Renan's thought but in France's mind. To France, Renan was the perfect example of the detached scholar – 'He considered the most noble use one could make of a human life was to seek to penetrate the secrets of the universe.' Yet here was France, who in many ways considered himself, and was considered by many, to be Renan's successor, engaged in a violent political campaign that left him little time for anything else – certainly not for penetrating the secrets of the universe. In his way, he had become as ardent a partisan as any of the demonstrators who had earlier been scuffling in the square beneath him, even if on this occasion he limited his criticism of the Church to some mild mockery – 'We will not attack the Church. We wish to believe she mellows with age. . . . Of her old habits there remains, it is true, the unfortunate mania of fulminating without cause. . . . Yet one can without too much inconvenience, leave her the freedom of her anathema and excommunications. Let her thunder roll so long as the State does not have to pay for it.' For all that France, on this occasion, seemed to be pulling his punches, surely the more thoughtful of his audience must have realized and pondered the paradox between his praise of Renan's scholarly detachment and his own presence in the forefront of a political battle?

France and Combes continued to keep closely in touch after this joint appearance, so much so that when Combes published, on the 5th January, 1904, a collection of his anticlerical speeches, entitled *Une Campagne Laique*, it appeared with a long preface by France, in which he retraced the steps by which Church and State had come to this parting of the ways, and which provided just as incisive and effective an argument for Separation as the text which followed. This preface was judged to be of such importance by the Separatists, that Clemenceau, one of the most ardent, had printed it in his paper *l'Aurore* eight days before the publication of Combes' book; and it was subsequently produced on its own as a pamphlet under the title of *Le Parti Noir*. Over the course of the next year, France enlarged and extended it to the point when it could stand as a book in its own right. As such it was published on the following New Year's Day under the title of *l'Église et la République*.

France showed in *l'Église et la République* that as a polemicist he did not altogether discard his personal style of writing. He would still sometimes appear himself in the midst of his arguments – on one occasion listening, during a debate in the Palais Bourbon, to Waldeck-Rousseau 'grave, insolent and glacial'; on another, telling of a visit he had made to a house near Bordeaux – presumably during a stay at Capian – which had formerly belonged to a Mme. Bouguey, who had hidden seven proscribed Girondins for a month during the Terror. In the end Mme. Bouguey had been guillotined for her courage and compassion. France quoted the remark of the priest whom he found in charge of the school that Mme. Bouguey's house had become, that he saw nothing really meritable in her action, 'no good works; only human virtues' as an example of the Church's 'saintly inhumanity'. Yet for all France's formidable powers as a polemicist, there must have been many readers of *l'Église et la République* who remembered regretfully the sharp satire of the early volumes of *l'Histoire Contemporaine*, and who found France not only more readable but more convincing when he was considering the Church in the guise of M. Lantaigne or the abbé Guitrel than when he was fulminating as if he was himself in the pulpit he was trying to pull down.

By the time *l'Église et la République* was published, the Combes Ministry was on the point of falling. Yet even so – and perhaps the more so – it gave an invaluable boost to the Separatist cause. In fact throughout the last eighteen months of their campaign, which came to a successful conclusion in the summer of 1905, France, with his preface and his book, had provided two of the most effective weapons in their armoury.

The active ally of the Combes Ministry during its life, France was also to be closely and personally linked with its fall. This had been foreseeable for some time. Incredible though it was that any democratic government could institute so despotic a system of coercive control, it was just as unbelievable that it could think it would long get away with it. The inevitable explosion came in the Chamber on 23rd October, 1904, when a retired army officer, Guyot de Villeneuve, now an Opposition deputy, rose to his feet clutching in his hand a bundle of what turned out to be Mollin's *fiches*. He proceeded to read out some of the more outrageous; for example, one that described a general as 'a Jesuit, a dirty Jesuit, a threefold Jesuit who soils the army'. These *fiches* had been sold by an assistant at the Lodge of the Grand Orient to Gabriel Sylveton, an Opposition deputy who was also secretary of the *Ligue de la Patrie Française*, for 40,000 francs.

In the storm which broke when Guyot de Villeneuve sat down, the Government all but foundered. It was saved only by an impassioned appeal by Jaurès from the tribune and by the narrow margin of four votes. The storm was stilled, however, only for the moment. In a subsequent debate, the vote on which showed the Government's slender hold on life cut to a majority of two, Sylveton walked across the Chambre and struck André repeatedly on the face. This, he explained afterwards, he intended as a deliberate declaration of 'civil war'. If put on trial for his brutal assault – which he was – he intended to enlarge his exposure of André's methods.

The day before his trial, however, Sylveton committed suicide when suddenly confronted with two charges – of embezzling the funds of the *Ligue de la Patrie Française* and of committing sexual offences with his daughter-in-law. Sylveton may well have been guilty on both counts, but this sudden revelation was suspiciously convenient for the Government. However, even so, it did not survive for long. Mollin's enforced resignation on the 30th October – in considerable bitterness that he was being made the scapegoat for the mistakes of his master – was followed after the interval of a few days by that of André. Combes, himself, tenacious though he was of power, could not hold out much longer, and resigned on the 18th January, 1905.

What really complicated things for France was not that Mollin was his son-in-law, but that he was not likely to be much longer. Mollin's marriage with Suzanne was on the point of breaking up. Suzanne and Mollin had married in December, 1901. The year before, Valérie, France's first wife and Suzanne's mother, had married again; this time to a man considerably younger than herself, Réné Dussaud, already, in spite of his relative youth, an eminent archaeologist, who, curiously, was to become a regular visitor to Mme. Arman's salon where, however, he always kept himself at the far end of the room from France. It may have been the removal of this prop to her security that had induced Suzanne, at the age of twenty, to rush into a marriage with a man much older than herself, for which otherwise she seems to have had little inclination and of which the success was short. In fact, France seems to have become much more attached to Mollin, a painstaking, not very bright but thoroughly decent army officer, than his daughter ever did.

France only heard of his daughter's intention to divorce Mollin after the storm over the *affaire des fiches* had broken. He did everything he could to dissuade her from it, not only because he liked Mollin, but because he feared that the divorce, coming at such a time, would be interpreted as an act of political as well as personal defection. However, together with her father's large and eloquent eyes, Suzanne had inherited 'le petit grain de folie' which France, in a different mood and moment, had wished for all those he loved. She could neither be dissuaded from the divorce nor induced to delay it, and it duly went through in May, 1905.

But if he could do nothing with Suzanne and nothing for Mollin, who had lost not only his job but his career as well –

he had been forced to resign his commission – and now his wife, France could at least show that his support of the Socialist Party was as strong as ever. He took every opportunity that offered to do so. When, for example, a vacancy occurred on the committee of the *Ligue des Droits de l'Homme* – due to Salomon Reinach's resignation in disgust at Ministerial methods – he allowed his name to be put forward, and was unanimously elected, thus involving himself in a further round of political chores, if incidentally, as it turned out, in some of his most useful work, and throughout the closing stages of the campaign for Separation he was always ready with a helping hand or article if either was needed, as they often were.

This desire to make amends for any political harm that Suzanne's divorce might have done, combined with his concern to achieve Separation to keep him in harness and blinkers throughout the greater part of 1905. But by the end of that year Separation had been achieved, Suzanne's divorce was forgotten, and he had time to take stock. France found then that he belonged to a very different party from that to which Jaurès had introduced him. Gone were the high hopes that the new century might usher in a new world; gone the belief that it was only a question of disseminating culture throughout the masses and all would be well; gone the illusion that the workers even wanted the cosy, comfortable, cultured welfare state that Jaurès and France believed in. Instead he found himself a member of a hard-headed, hard-knit political force, committed to class war and determined, if it could not get what it wanted through parliamentary channels, to achieve it by whatever means it could; a party that not only did not shrink from violence but chose it as the means by which it was most likely to achieve success; a party that had already given its allegiance to the Workers International, thereby surrendering much of the individuality and independence which seemed to France to matter as much for a party as for a person.

Thus the uniting of the Socialist Party, and its emergence in a much more extreme form than he had ever imagined, forced France to face up to the fact that its aims and his were now far from the same – if, indeed, they had ever been. Where in a strictly utilitarian philosophy was there space for the belief in beauty for its own sake that had for so long been France's guiding star; where, in a party that had surrendered the right to make up its own mind, room for the respect for the individual of which France had so long been champion; where in a policy of violence, place for the desire for peace that was to become an increasingly important part of France's political make-up?

Even if France accepted the possibility of a revolution without violence, it was still easy to envisage it degenerating into mob rule, always his particular nightmare. Nor was it only that France dreaded revolution: he did not believe in it either. His reading of history had led him to think that all that most revolutions changed was the people at the top; while his study of the French Revolution in particular, seemed to him to show that revolution provided the opportunity for the release of all that was worst in human nature.

Yet France's attitude towards the working-people who formed the bulk of the party to which he belonged, remained as before a mixture of fear and fellow-feeling. The proportions might have slightly altered. Now that the Socialist swing to the Left had brought the possibility of revolution that much closer it was that much easier to imagine the audience beneath the platform as the mob surrounding the tumbril. The element of fear in his attitude was in consequence correspondingly larger. But with it went still a genuine feeling of sympathy for the wretched conditions under which many, if not most, of those listening to him still lived. It was very much a 'there but for the grace of God' feeling, stemming most probably from those days in the wilderness in the garret in the rue Pré-aux-Clercs, when, on his own for the first time in his life, France had seen, as well as the vertiginous drop into the street below, the gulf of failure yawning beneath him. Since then, more because of what he had seen than what he had experienced, France had always been afraid of poverty, conscious of the crippling pressure it could bring to bear; conscious, too, and afraid also, of the inevitable erosion through excessive hardship of much that he valued most in both life and people.

His success had been to a certain extent an escape, and France never forgot from what by the grace of God, a good style, a lot of hard work and a bit of luck he had escaped. It was this consciousness of the basic hardship, even injustice, of life that gave the edge to his pessimism, a pessimism of surprising depth for someone so perceptive and appreciative of life's pleasures, and so skilful at catching their reflection in his work. His belief in beauty, his collections of beautiful things, his desire to create beauty in his work as well as his amusing worldly life in Paris, were all simply shelters from a prevailing wind of great strength and bitterness – shelters in which it was possible for a moment to catch and enjoy a bit of the sun.

France had done his best, during the period of his climb to fame when he was still unsure of himself and of his success, to avoid exposing himself to this wind. Even when established as one of the most famous of French writers, both living and dead, he had still been reluctant to don his overcoat, and emerge from the comfort of his study or the shelter of his garden into the main blast. But when through his connection with Jaurès and the immersion in politics which had resulted from it, he found himself facing the social problems of poverty, inequality, hardship – many more – his response came from a core of social concern that had long lain concealed within him, and which, even if long suppressed, was a genuine and important part of his character. This concern, diminished though it was to some extent by his increased fear of revolution, was still enough by itself to tie him to the Socialist Party, which continued to provide its obvious and easiest outlet.

France, however, was also bound to the Socialist Party by other more personal bonds, of which the strongest was still his friendship with Jaurès. It was a friendship that had changed its character. So, too, for that matter, had Jaurès. His failure during these decisive years had had a deep effect upon him. This shows clearly in an impression of 1904 recorded by Charles Péguy, originally, one of Jaurès's most admiring *normalien* disciples, and the strong supporter in a *Cahier* of 1900 of Jaurès's policy of reform as opposed to Guesde's advocacy of open class-warfare. Péguy, of late, had become more critical, accusing him of developing into a demagogue. In consequence they had not met for some time until, in 1904, Jaurès made a surprise visit to the printing works which produced Péguy's *Cahiers*. Péguy happened not to be there, but thinking Jaurès might have something important to say – which as it turned out he had not – paid him a visit in return. Not having seen Jaurès for so long, Péguy was struck immediately by the change in him. – 'He was a different man. No one could imagine how aged and changed he was. . . . He was all-in, bent, his face was ravaged. I had never seen so sad, so depressing, so depressed a human-being as this professional optimist.' The spell which Jaurès had cast over France, and many others, with his wonderful gift of speech and his magnetic personality was broken, but in its place France was bound just as tightly by a feeling of almost protective affection.

France was now, too, closely linked to Jaurès by professional collaboration. For, also in 1904, a group of Jaurès's friends and supporters had managed to raise the 800,000 francs needed to enable Jaurès to start a paper of his own. Thus *l'Humanité* was born – to become and remain the mouthpiece of authoritative Socialist opinion until 1921 when, at the time of the split between Socialism and Communism, it took the Left, and not the right turn. France was *l'Humanité*'s first literary adviser, being too distinguished and too easily distractable a character to be tied down to the more menial position of literary editor. He was also far the most considerable and constant of its contributors. For its opening number he had specially held over for eighteen months a long political–philosophical dialogue, subsequently published as *Sur la Pierre Blanche*, and for the next eighteen years most of his journalistic work appeared in its pages. But as well as its chief contributor and literary adviser, France was important to *l'Humanité* as a presence. As literary adviser he had to pay frequent visits to the rue Montmartre where, at No. 142, *l'Humanité* had set up its offices.

Jules Renard, famous already as the author of *Poil de Carrotte* and later for his bitter, boomeranging Journal, also paid a visit shortly after the appearance of *l'Humanité*'s first number which, to the astonishment of those concerned, sold 120,000 copies and to which Renard had contributed a *récit*, 'La Vieille'. Renard was warmly received – 'Jaurès, Briand, Herr, cover me with compliments. Never have I been so well received in an editor's office . . . France talks. Mirbeau laughs. Jaurès listens, his head moving about as he watches first one, then another. Briand jokes. I dare to say nothing in front of these men who lead France. So many celebrities in one corner.' Renard's picture shows France already very much at home and at ease in Humanité's offices. Each visit there, as each contribution, strengthened his links with Jaurès and with Socialism.

Thus, gradually over the years 1904–6, as the air cleared with the end of the Affair, the downfall of Combes and the achievement of Separation, France was to find himself facing a difficult personal dilemma. For while his fear of revolution, combining with the resurgence of his beliefs in individuality and in the importance of artistic independence, seemed to be drawing him out of politics in general and the Socialist Party in particular, his social concern and sympathy, together with his friendship for Jaurès and his work for *l'Humanité*, held him as tightly as ever in the Socialist ranks.

In such a situation most people would have made a choice. Either they would have come out of politics altogether, or they would have given up any remaining hope of independent writing – and France had already an impressive body of work on which to fall back if he had chosen to do so. France, however, was incapable of making a clean cut or a clear choice. He had dragged his first marriage through several, long, quite unnecessary years of suffering – years that for both France and Valérie must have been amongst the most unpleasant of their lives – simply because he could not bring himself to cut the bonds between them. Again, France had continued with his job at the Bibliothèque du Sénat long after it had ceased to be any good to him, or he at it, and at the cost of a long and wearisome campaign of running warfare with his superiors, simply because he could not make himself make the break.

Now he resolved the dilemma very much in his own way. He released the tension between the two conflicting, even contradictory sides of his nature, not by cutting, but by untying the knot which bound them together. He made no choice, or even compromise, between them, but allowed each side its head and its freedom. Henceforth his writing was to be at liberty to go its own way, no longer bound by the inhibiting necessity to serve France's political purposes, or even to express his political views; while, at the same time, he continued to contribute regularly to *l'Humanité* and to serve the Socialist Party and the Socialist cause in quite as many various ways as before.

From now on France the writer of books and France the political journalist and Party supporter could have been two different men, each going his own way regardless of the other. The inevitable disaccord and frequent disagreement between them was to cause France to be variously charged with hypocrisy, falsehood, senility and, simply, confusion. Yet as France had written in *Le Genie Latin*, 'Our contradictions are not the least true part of ourselves.' In allowing his contradictions their heads, France was being entirely true to himself, and, being so, could not, as Shakespeare pointed out, 'be false to any man'.

9

---◆---

ON JULY 21ST 1906, France and Mme. Arman attended a small and unpublicized ceremony in a courtyard of the École Militaire. As his only compensation for eleven years of the most intense physical and psychological suffering, Dreyfus, once again an officer of the French army, was decorated with the Légion d'Honneur, fourth grade. After the ceremony, France approached Dreyfus, and, stammering slightly, as he was still liable to do in moments of emotion, offered his hand and his congratulations. 'I am very happy and very moved. I do not know how to express my admiration of the constancy which you have maintained throughout so much suffering, and which has enabled us to accomplish the work of justice and reparation, of which today's ceremony is the climax.' It was the end of the Affair.

France had well earned his place amongst the select group of family, friends and supporters who witnessed Dreyfus's rehabilitation. At each stage of the Affair he had been ready with his support, his signature and, if necessary, his presence. By itself the weight of his famous name had provided valuable ballast for the Dreyfusards who were short of distinguished and distinctive public figures of his sort. 'Thanks to France,' wrote one of the opposition, Léon Daudet, 'the Dreyfusards can boast of possessing a man after our own heart . . . and one of our *premiers crus* . . . It is extremely tiresome.'

But if France in his way had an important effect on the course of the Affair, it was as nothing compared to the effect the Affair had on him. It radically altered both the trend of his work and the shape of his life. France's writing had quickly followed the slant of his political participation. With one exception, during the decade that followed his entry into the Affair France published no book of any account that was not subordinated to a political purpose. Even the last two volumes of *l'Histoire Contemporaine* – *l'Anneau d'Améthyste* published in 1899, and *M. Bergeret à Paris* published in 1901 – although they still contained moments when France's charm, wit and ironical interpretation of the human comedy broke through, had now been loaded with so strong a bias that they failed altogether to run true to the line of independent observation essential to a social commentary of this sort.

Of the other books France published during this period, *Opinions Sociales* (1902) was a collection of his political speeches and articles; *l'Église et la République* (1905), ammunition for Combes's campaign against the Church; *Sur la Pierre Blanche* (1905), a vain attempt to graft his new political purpose on to the old form of political argument which he had used so successfully in *Jérome Coignard*; *Vers les Temps Meilleurs* (1906), a more comprehensive collection of his political work. Although published in 1899, *Pierre Nozière*, some sketches of childhood hurriedly produced to quieten Lemerre who still considered he had claims on France, cannot fairly be considered in this period since it was mainly made up of earlier work; and *Clio* (1900), a slim volume of poetic musings, was too slight to be considerable anyway.

The one exception in this period of political preoccupation only served to prove the rule. In *l'Histoire Comique* (1903), France expanded to novel length the slight story of an actress, obsessed by the suicide of a spurned lover, who thus obtains over her in death a power he never achieved in life. France's main idea in writing this melancholy love-story may only have been to turn the public's mind, and his own, away from an unhealthy preoccupation with the Affair.

He was successful, however, only in his background evocation of the stimulating, superficial atmosphere of the theatre – in this, in fact, rather too successful, for he aroused Mme. Arman's suspicions that he had been doing more in the *couloirs* and *coulisses* of Parisian theatres than simply gather material. But otherwise France seemed so little interested either in his characters or his story that not surprisingly, he failed to rouse much interest in his readers either. Subsequently, showing a compensatory paternal preference for a neglected child, France declared *l'Histoire Comique* to be his favourite work, but it was all too obvious throughout the greater part of it that his mind was on something else.

On what, showed clearly in his other works of this time. In one of them, however, his political purposes seems to have coincided with a genuine creative impulse. *L'Affaire Crainquebille* (1901), the story of a street-merchant arrested and condemned for an offence he had not committed, was not only a parody of the Affair, it was also an attack on the system of man-made justice which lay behind it. Crainquebille himself, the simple-minded street-vendor, could easily have been made into a sham figure of maudlin misfortune, but as France portrayed him, he emerged a totally credible, if totally confused human being, quite unable to comprehend what life, or anything else, was about – utterly bewildered that at one moment he was being arrested for insulting a policeman when he had not, and at another was not being arrested for insulting a policeman when he had.

The astringent thought which lay behind this apparently simple cautionary tale, told in France's most accomplished manner, and in his most deceptively simple style, was aimed not only at the judges and jurists who, over the ages, had made justice what it was, but also at the social cruelty of ordinary people such as the housewives, Crainquebille's customers, who accepted the court's judgement and added to it the far heavier penalty of their own ostracism. Only to maintain the minimum requirements of social order and human safety would France admit that man had the right to judge his fellow men. He utterly condemned those, who, without reason and without authority, chose on their own account to do so. Crainquebille was fired by the strike of France's political purpose on the flint of his social compassion. Lit by this spark it is the one work of this politically dominated period to have outlived it.

The effect of the Affair on France's private life was as great as on his work. His declaration for Dreyfus had cut like a knife across many friendships. 'Gyp', Barrès, Lemaître, Bourget, Coppée – these, and many other friends of long standing, were now in the opposing camp. Attendance at most of the famous Parisian salons had, too, split up strictly in line with differing sympathies. Even Mme. Arman, who had hitherto prided herself on drawing the cream off the whole churn of Parisian society, had reluctantly to confine her receptions to those who thought as she did, and much of the spice of her salon in the old days had, of course, come from the presence and conversation in it of those who did not.

In the upper strata of Parisian society, France and Mme. Arman, as Dreyfusards, found themselves at first in a minority. France was particularly conscious of being the odd man out when amongst his Academic confrères. Here he had always been suspect to the strongly conservative, strongly Catholic right wing – 'the dukes', whose votes he had courted by talking to their wives, as Halévy had advised him, about the weather and their dogs. In spite of his conversational efforts, or possibly because of them, they had only elected France with reluctance, and continued to look upon him with suspicion. Now, by declaring himself for Dreyfus, he gave them the opportunity to show their hostility openly. It was, almost certainly, his resentment of this that lay behind an incident which occurred in 1901, and which led to France shaking the dust of the Institut off his feet, and refusing it a chance to resettle there for fifteen years.

One of the successful candidates that year had been Paul Hervieu, well-known both as a novelist and a dramatist. Some thirteen years younger than France, Hervieu had long been his close friend, almost his protégé, and France, acting as pilot, had steered him through the socially treacherous channels of his candidature, just as five years before Halévy had guided him. France had been generally expected, therefore, to be chosen by Hervieu as one of the two 'parrains' by whom every new member has to be presented, and of whom the selection is generally interpreted as a gesture of acknowledgement and allegiance. Hervieu, however, had an attack of cold feet and chose two less controversial figures to be his sponsors. He then made his ingratitude much worse by going round to France and excusing himself on the grounds of the hostility most Academicians felt towards France because of his Dreyfusism.

France took deep umbrage, and, at the same time, the pretext for easing himself out of an increasingly disagreeable situation. He sent a message to the Academy saying, in effect, that if that was the way they felt about him he would no longer give them the displeasure of his company. In spite of periodic moves for a *rapprochement*, generally scuppered by the insistence of Mme. Arman, who had taken equally deep offence over the incident, that he should first receive a personal apology from all Academicians who might have been thought to have been at this time in any way hostile to him, France did not again attend a meeting until 1916. He had already, some years earlier, also because of the Affair, discarded his other official honour, when in protest at the expulsion of Zola from the Légion d'Honneur, he had, in 1898, removed for ever the red rosette from his buttonhole.

France may not have minded too much his self-imposed exile. He had never been much of a club man, and it had been for the label, not the company and comforts it offered, that he had sought membership of the Academy. In a way, too, he had now the best of both worlds. For even if he never went to the Institut, he remained an Academician, and thus, in the eyes of the outside world, still one of the Immortals. Yet his action made him appear also something of a rebel, and so increased his appeal to the younger generation who might otherwise have been tempted to dismiss him summarily as just another member of the Establishment. But he undoubtedly did mind very much – as did many people at that time – the chill and hostile atmosphere rising like a ground mist from the Affair, which permeated all levels of Parisian society, and penetrated even the august precincts of the Institut.

France may not have missed his fellow 'Immortals' but he missed his friends and, in particular, one. Etienne Charavay, France's childhood companion, and throughout his adult life by far his closest friend, had died in 1899 and, in part at least, his prematurely early death had also been due to the Affair.

For Charavay, who, in the course of becoming an eminent bibliographer and archivist, had become also an expert on handwriting, had been called upon as such, at Dreyfus's first trial in 1894, to give his opinion on the handwriting of the incriminating documents. On the evidence then available, which did not include a specimen of the hand of Esterhazy, the real traitor, not yet under suspicion, Charavay had declared that the writing could possibly be a disguised version of Dreyfus's hand. Five years later, by which time he had seen a letter of Esterhazy's, he had publicly withdrawn this opinion and declared that he was now certain that Esterhazy, not Dreyfus, was the author of the *bordereau*. No one questioned Charavay's integrity or expertise on either occasion; or blamed him in the circumstances for his mistake. But, on so honest, high-minded and well-meaning a character, the thought that he might have contributed, even if inadvertently, to Dreyfus's condemnation, weighed heavily; and the worry of it undoubtedly hastened the break-up of his health.

France spoke at Charavay's funeral on 6th October, 1899, in the cemetery of Montparnasse. He left it to others, he said, to retrace Charavay's career and achievements. He intended only to make his adieux to his oldest friend. Charavay had never really changed. Throughout his life he had retained 'the same gay and witty eyes, the same benevolent smile, the same air of distinction and goodness, the same youthfulness of heart.' Charavay's life had 'flowed like a stream which widens insensibly . . . without ever losing the limpidity of its source.' For France, Paris was never quite to be the same again without the benevolent, bear-like presence in the apartment of the rue Furstenberg, whose tiny rooms had always seemed much too small for so large a personality.

Less obviously, but no less certainly, the Affair had a hand, also, in losing France his daughter. But for the political connections and political responsibilities which he had acquired as the result of his entry into the Affair, France would never have been hurt so badly by Suzanne's refusal to postpone her divorce. As it was, however, the effect of her act of defiance on their relationship was utterly catastrophic – far worse than she, or anyone else for that matter, could have possibly foreseen.

France never forgave Suzanne her disobedience. It made no difference to him that the reason she wanted the divorce was that she had fallen in love with Michel, the eighteen-year-old son of two of his oldest friends, Jean and Noemi Psichari. Noemi was the daughter of Renan. She and her husband had been delighted and delightful members of that small, intimate circle which had surrounded and supported

France in those far-off, forgotten, now almost unimaginable days of domestic happiness in the rue Chalgrin. They had remained close friends ever since. Only the year before, France had written a flattering preface to Michel's first book *Index raisonné à la mythologie d'Horace*, a work of precocious erudition, written while Michel was still at college.

Suzanne and Michel had to wait three years before they could marry – for Michel to finish his studies and come of age – and this long delay, contrasting with the apparent urgency of Suzanne's demand for divorce, threw salt into France's wounds. He refused to go to the wedding, when it finally took place in 1908, and he never saw either Suzanne or Michel after it. Save that a son, Lucien, was born of it, Suzanne's second marriage proved, in fact, little more successful than her first. It may have been she was simply unlucky in choosing first, a husband who was too old, and then one who was too young, for her; or her unsettled upbringing may have unfitted her for domestic happiness. For whatever reason she and Michel separated after only a short time together. During the war, as the general ordeal flattened personal difference, the possibilities of a reconciliation between them, and of one between Suzanne and her father, came closer. But before either was, in fact, realized, both Suzanne and Michel were dead – Michel, killed at the front in 1917; Suzanne dying of an epidemic of Spanish influenza which swept through Paris the following year.

So France's unforgiving anger, which one can only lay at the door of his political sensitivity, and of which the severity seems out of all proportion to the offence – and totally out of character with the clear line of affection which shows in his earlier letters to 'Ma petite Suzon chérie' – lost him his daughter for ever.

The Affair also had its effect on France's affair with Mme. Arman. Although it was undoubtedly by his own decision that France became a Dreyfusard, Mme. Arman had staunchly followed him into battle. There was no difference or divergence of opinion between them over this. Nor, although she did not herself share it, did Mme. Arman seek in any way to check France's swing to socialism. Monsieur Arman might make barbed remarks from the other side of the fireplace about France's new friends, but Mme. Arman made it quite clear that in this sphere, at least, France had his liberty.

But when Jaurès cast his spell over France, he was quite unintentionally and unconsciously usurping some of Mme. Arman's authority. Until then France had always needed someone or something to make him write. At first it had been financial necessity; then, a desire for fame. For the decade before he became an Academician, Mme. Arman had served him admirably in the difficult dual capacity of taskmistress and Muse. But when France subordinated his writing to a political purpose and a political party, he shifted his allegiance from Mme. Arman, who obviously could no longer inspire or even supervise his activities in such a sphere, not so much to Jaurès as to the various political tasks which Jaurès represented and imposed.

This, in fact, was to be the last yoke France imposed upon himself. When eventually he cast it off, he was for the first time in his life to need nothing more to make him write than the desire to do so. But this was not to be of much use to Mme. Arman, who, these six years or so earlier, had been deprived by this unexpected turn in France's development, of one of the most important of her functions, and that at a time when other links between them were becoming noticeably strained. For now the weakness always inherent in their relationship began to appear. Without a shared home, and without the bond of marriage, there was little except habit to hold them together if other things began to draw them apart – and habit by itself can become the most resented of jailers.

What really brought this weakness to the surface was the sad but unalterable fact that as France and Mme. Arman entered what Renan called '*les faubourgs de la vieillesse*', they fell out of step. Until recently the two of them, of much the same age, had seemed to be progressing at much the same pace through life. But now Mme. Arman began to age very much faster than France, who, contrariwise, having seemed so old for his years in his youth, appeared now, in his relatively old age, exceptionally youthful and vigorous.

Fame had agreed with France. At no time in his life had his appearance been so distinguished as it was now that he was in his sixties. His beard was grey, but it was trimmed so that it did not drop venerably from his chin, but seemed rather a sharp, assertive appendage of it. The long, Cavalier moustache which he wore above it gave him a gay, even a jaunty air, endorsed by the lively look of the large, limpid eyes, always the most striking feature of his face, but which so often in his youth had carried a sad, soulful, 'big boy lost' expression. His hair, although he always wore it cut short, generally *en brosse*, still grew vigorously, and had not thinned, receded or disappeared altogether as had that of most of his contemporaries. The tall soldier's figure he had inherited from his father had straightened up with success, and no longer spoilt its effect by the obsequious stoop he had learned at Stanislas. Late though it might be for most people, this for France was undoubtedly the prime of life.

But for Mme. Arman it was, sadly, a very different story. Conscious of the increasing disparity between them, she did her best to cover the gap. She dyed her hair, and bespangled it with diamonds. She wore large, youthful hats, full of fruit. She liked lace and used it to garland her flowing spring-like dresses, and with these she often wore red-heeled white suede shoes and sometimes silver stockings. Her general appearance prompted Brousson, France's secretary, in a particularly malicious mood, to write that

'Mme. Arman, on the threshold of old age, dressed herself as if she were Queen of the May.'

The effect, of course, was the opposite of that which Mme. Arman desired. The diamonds, the dye in the hair, emphasized not the intelligent, lively look in the eyes which had nothing to do with youth or age, but the full cheeks, the double chin – while the youthful dresses served mainly to show that there was no longer a youthful figure beneath them. After Mme. Arman's death France, on his fifteenth visit to Italy, his first without her, wrote sadly in his notebook, one sunny day in Naples, 'She would never give anything up.' It was true. Mme. Arman was incapable of renouncing anything – even her youth, and certainly not France.

With so gradual a process it is difficult to pin-point the exact moment when France and Mme. Arman fell out of step. But it seems to have occurred by the time of their visit to Treguier for Renan's centenary celebrations in 1903. For in Ségur's account of their stay the contrast between them comes out clearly – particularly in his description of that night when he had accompanied France to the banquet in Renan's honour, on the way back from which they had narrowly missed running into a band of student demonstrators.

When, after their escape, France and Ségur arrived at the house where France and Mme. Arman were staying, they had some difficulty in getting in, for the owner – in France's description 'an old and batty Tregoroise' – firmly closed her doors at ten and quite as firmly believed that no one, not even an Academician, was out for any good purpose after that hour. When eventually after a great deal of coaxing in France's smoothest manner she was persuaded, much against her will and her principles, to unlock the door, France invited Ségur to come up. Mme. Arman was lying in bed looking ill and old, and the contrast between her appearance and that of France, full of himself and of an evening which in its various ways – the banquet, the escape from the students, the battle with their landlady – had provided excellent and exhilarating entertainment, struck Ségur forcibly.

The break-up of health which lay behind Mme. Arman's decline was not helped by the austere conditions in which she lived in her large and luxurious house. Maurel visiting her when she was ill, found her crouched over a badly-burning fire. When he asked where was the fire-plate, a normal piece of equipment in Parisian homes at that time, so that he could try and draw the fire up, she replied that she did not possess one as they were so ugly. She often refused to have the *calorifère* lit because, understandably enough, she disliked the smell. But while the sacrifice of comfort to her aesthetic ideas was all very well while she was in good health, as she became older its absence became a serious lack, and a bad attack of pleurisy that she had at this time was certainly aggravated, if not caused, by the climatic conditions of her house. However, Mme. Arman's pride was as indomitable as her tenacity. She would not give in any more than she would give up.

Imperceptibly over these years the centre of gravity – and, for that matter, of levity also – had been shifting from the Avenue Hoche to the Villa Saïd. France still went daily to Mme. Arman's house, but mainly now to eat. Usually after lunch he would, as in the past, be taken up to the room on the second floor which served as his study and set to work at his desk while Mme. Arman worked at hers and occasionally M. Arman at his would play with the figures of his stocks and shares. But now that France no longer needed Mme. Arman's supervision he no longer wanted it either, and it became something of a game to see how he could avoid doing any work at such times even under Mme. Arman's vigilant watch. He would build a barricade of books on his desk, and go to sleep behind it until his snores gave him away. He would slip a light novel in amongst the heavy books of reference on his desk and read it happily, while Mme. Arman, thinking he was studying his sources, left him in peace. If it was a fine day and there was half or even a quarter of a chance of playing truant, he would contrive some quite implausible, highly imaginative excuse, such as that he had forgotten his thinking cap – he always wore some sort of hat or cap on his head when working – at the Villa Saïd, and had to go and fetch it. Then he would spend the rest of the afternoon browsing through the bookstalls, drowsing in the antique shops, or simply wandering along the *quais*, which still probably he enjoyed most of all. In these various ways France made it abundantly clear that, apart from the convenience of her excellent meals, his visits now to Mme. Arman's house, were more in the cause of duty than of pleasure, and that the important part of his life, as of his work, was achieved in the Villa Saïd.

Here in his own kingdom he had now his own court. It was held every Wednesday and Sunday morning. On Sunday it was a smaller affair, confined to his closer, more intimate friends, but on Wednesdays it was a considerable gathering. To keep Mme. Arman happy it was purely a 'salon mâle' but otherwise, both in the numbers and distinction of the guests, it rivalled her more famous and formal receptions in the Avenue Hoche.

The company was often curiously mixed. Old friends such as Calmettes, Plessis; distinguished men of letters such as Mendès, Marcel Schwob, Charles Maurras; journalists such as Maurel; artists such as Steinlen whose illustrations for Crainquebille had become almost as famous as the text itself; eminent philosophers, historians, politicians, would find themselves rubbing shoulders with ragged exiles from Eastern Europe, turned out of their own countries for their revolutionary activities, come now to pay homage to the great French writer who, by his political activities seemed to sympathize with their efforts. Young *littérateurs*, on the way up and in, might well find themselves chatting to some of France's Socialist colleagues, or helping to thaw the reserve of a workers' delegation bringing a petition to be signed, an address to be accepted.

But whoever they were, whether they were old friends or new acquaintances, whether this was the first or the umpteenth time they had come to pay their respects, they must all and always have been astounded at the incredible décor with which France had surrounded himself. For the Villa Saïd was by now much more like a museum than a private house. The tone was set even before his guests had entered the door, by an antique Florentine head in bronze which served as a bell-push. In the hall they might have been in a church, for the windows of stained glass let in only a dim religious light and every corner and niche had its piece of statuary or carving – not, however, always, although often, of religious subjects. The air was heavy with the scent of leather, of wax, of dust – with the aroma of age.

The Villa Saïd was a tall, narrow house with only two rooms on each floor. The kitchen, little used save to prepare France's breakfast and for his housekeeper's requirements, was in the basement. So, too, was the bathroom, never used for its proper purpose, although the actual bath was utilized by France as a receptacle for countless 'complimentary' copies that he was sent. When the bath was full he would sell the contents by the bath-load to a bookdealer.

On the left of the entrance-hall was the salon, in which the rather sombre effect of some heavy Renaissance chests, was countered by a table with a beautiful sixteenth century Venetian carpet laid across it, and by two great glass Italian show-cases, painted green, in which a display of Brussels and English lace, of golden chasubles and embroidered silk waistcoats formed a gay background to the rare and precious objects picked up by France on his travels round Italy and the *quartier Latin*. On the walls were pictures of the time of Henri IV, Louis XIII and XIV, and a Boulle clock in green lacquer. Stretched across the ceiling was an immense plan of Paris, *le plan de Turgot*, and this was a particular and perpetual source of delight to France who, settled in an armchair, would often take his guests on conducted tours round it.

At its far end the salon had an extension with a glass roof and a line of glass panes set high along the far wall. This was known amongst France's friends as 'the chapel', because its decoration, which included a floral design on the wall, centred upon a fifteenth century Madonna and Child carved in wood, set in a niche, backed with red silk, on a green painted pedestal. In the centre of the glass-roof, in order to give some illumination at night, France had hung a Venetian chandelier, and this was a chandelier in the true sense of the word in that it carried candles, not electric bulbs. Like the rest of the house, the salon was lit only by candles, and their light could have an enchanting effect on the many beautiful things in the room. Pierre Calmettes, the artist son of Fernand Calmettes, France's boyhood friend, who spent two years recording the interiors of the Villa Saïd on canvas, and a further considerable length of time describing them on paper for his book, *La Grande Passion d'Anatole France*, remembered in particular that, at the reception after Suzanne's marriage on the 10th December, 1901, the scene in the salon was like that from another age, another world, with the lights from hundreds of candles dancing about the room. But on other ordinary occasions, the night, when it came, could seem particularly dense and dark in this ill-lit house.

The décor of the dining-room on the other side of the hall was also sombre – its main features being an immense stone fourteenth-century fireplace with a frieze of carved faces and medallions, a vast fifteenth-century table with bulbous legs, and massive dressers round the walls, loaded with porcelain and pewter, copper and faience. France once told Calmettes that it was not entirely according to his intent or inclination that this heavy fourteenth- and fifteenth-century furniture predominated in his rooms, but because most of his buying was done in the company of Mme. Arman who always pinched the best pieces for herself, particularly if they were of the later, lighter periods of Louis XV or XVI. Thus anything in the nature of a Boucher or a Fragonard, a fan painted by Watteau, or some Sèvres china, was sent straight off to the Avenue Hoche, leaving France with his coffers and chests, credences and church carvings. Neither of these two rooms on the ground floor were much used in the normal course of events, but France would often wander through them, as through a gallery, examining and enjoying his possessions. Often, too, he would take his guests on conducted tours round the house.

The life of the Villa Saïd really revolved around the two rooms on the first floor, France's bedroom and his study. France's bed was magnificent, a vast four-poster, covered in velvet, standing on a silk-covered dais, with a sixteenth-century Venetian bedspread of crimson satin. At the head of the bed hung a small frame containing one of the few family relics France had in his house – a small piece of white silk, part of the royal flag torn up by the Duchesse de Berry in 1830 and distributed amongst her bodyguard – of whom Père France had been one – to thank them for their devotion. Amongst so much impersonal magnificence, this small expression of family pride provided a welcome personal touch. To tone in with the bed, the room was decorated in the style of the Italian Renaissance, mainly in purple and gold. There was a huge wooden fireplace which France had brought back with him from Italy, carved with grotesque, grimacing faces which he would see leering across at him when he woke up in the morning. Stretched across the ceiling was a large mythological scene. There was also an impressive bishop's throne, on which France sat to have his beard trimmed.

Generally, save for the full-scale receptions on Wednesdays, France received his guests in his study on the other side of the landing, across a passage in which stood two bookcases devoted to Rabelais and Joan of Arc. On entering, his guests passed through double doors, the outer covered in pleated parchment, the inner having a carved face. They would then find themselves standing, with on their left a sixteenth-century printing-press, in France's *'cité des livres'*. On the shelves were more than 8,000 books, many of them very early examples of printing, for France always preferred the ancient to the modern. His most prized possession was a Bible of Nuremberg. Also notable on his shelves were several beautifully bound arms-bearing missals with chased clasps. Later he enlarged his collection with rare editions of the sixteenth and seventeenth centuries, notably of Rabelais and of Racine. Many of these books were too rare to be read, and too delicate to be shown to his friends for fear of damage.

The room also contained what was probably France's most cherished possession – a headless, armless Venus, not unlike the Venus de Milo, and almost as beautiful. Of the many women in France's life, this was possibly the one to whom he was most constant. After fifteen years or so in the Villa Saïd, she went with him into country exile during the war, from which in a letter he wrote that he had by his side this statue 'so beautiful', which at other more propitious times had 'made him love life'. She was still with him when he died.

In between the fireplace and the window was a showcase entirely devoted to figurines from Tanagra. Close to it was France's desk, covered by a litter of papers, writing material and antique bronzes, and within his reach at the back of his leather-covered chair was a line of dictionaries, one or other of which was always open, for he used them constantly.

The fireplace in the study was again vast, this time of marble, ornamented with flowers and birds and occupying most of one side of the room. Considering their size, the amount of heat that came out of these fireplaces was disappointingly small. They smoked, drew badly and sent most of the little heat they produced, up the chimney. Since they were the only source of heat in the house, conditions in cold weather could be arctic.

From his study, an overspill of untidiness spread through the house. As his collections grew, so too did their demands on any available space. It would have needed a large and well-trained museum staff to keep everything clean and in its proper place. As it was, it was often difficult for his guests to find a chair on which to sit or even space in which to stand.

Most of the second and top floor of the house was taken up by the long room in which France held his main Sunday receptions. In this the furniture was entirely Gothic and included sacristy cupboards with painted panels, heavy iron-bound coffers, leather-bound chairs. There were a number of coloured wooden statues. The windows were of stained glass, with red and yellow panes. The ceiling – for most people a space to be ignored, but evidently always one of France's main concerns – was covered in Cordoba leather. The carved columns of the stone fireplace enclosed a multi-coloured background of Italian faience.

In this room France kept two of his most valued possessions – cartons containing engravings, portraits, sketches, designs by Proud'hon and Ingres, his two favourite artists. Often he would start his day by coming up and leafing through the contents, a process which seemed always to put him in a better frame of mind for starting his own work.

Ultimately France's growing passion for Proud'hon was

to lead to a major rearrangement of the house. For he had the idea of hanging his Proud'hons in his bedroom. He tried it out but they swore horribly with the existing decor. So he decided to give them a setting that would suit them, and in 1908 had his bedroom entirely transformed. The doorway was changed, the fireplace taken out – replaced by an elegant marble mantelpiece supporting a gilt Louis XVI mirror – the stained-glass panes removed from the windows, the woodwork painted grey, the walls hung with almond-coloured silk. The mythological scene on the ceiling was unstuck and sent to the Avenue Hoche for Mme. Arman's dining room where, having suffered on the journey, it had to be touched up by Calmettes. All the furniture, including his magnificent bed, was banished upstairs into the long room, from which the Sunday receptions were switched to the salon on the ground-floor. The change involved a great deal of trouble and expense, but once it was all over France could lie in bed in the mornings and look leisurely at his Proud'hons, thus sparing himself the effort of going upstairs.

The other room on the top floor was the extremely small mansarded bedroom of his housekeeper, who, over a period of some fifteen years, was Joséphine Boucard, described by one of France's friends as 'an old, haggard Swiss woman who laid down the law of the house and was the comic exasperation of France.' An important part of Joséphine's job was to repel callers when France was working, or in no mood to receive them, and many were the literary and social hopefuls who failed to penetrate the prickly barrier her person imposed. In various ways Joséphine did a great deal for France and in the end she came to think she did everything, so that she would grumble, 'Maître! Maître! . . . Why do they call him "maître?" Master of what? . . . Poor master, if I wasn't there he wouldn't be capable of changing his pants.' Joséphine might have been the personification of Thérèse, the housekeeper whom France created for Bonnard some thirty years before – Thérèse, who hid beneath her bleak appearance and gruff manner a heart of the purest gold and who looked after, and upon, Bonnard as if he were a child in her charge rather than her employer. The only difference between Joséphine and Thérèse was that with Joséphine one could not be sure of the heart of gold.

Sometimes when his guests arrived France had not yet dressed, and he would receive them in a long, chestnut-coloured woollen dressing gown, wearing bedroom slippers and on his head one of his splendid day-caps. Then in due course his guests would follow him into his bedroom, where, while he dressed, the conversation continued unchecked save when he brushed his teeth. At other times, if the weather was cold, France might be wearing a curious two-piece suit made of thick prison-grey cloth of which the coat buttoned closely up to the neck and of which the trousers totally enclosed the feet rather like an angler's waders, thus preventing the possibility of draughts whistling up his legs.

When he was working, France generally had one shawl over his shoulders, another over his knees, while his legs would be wrapped in a couple of blankets. Even so his feet would often get so cold that he charred several pairs of slippers through pushing them too far into the ashes of the fire to find some warmth. His guests, ill-prepared and equipped for such conditions, would often be seen stamping their feet on his precious carpets to keep their circulation going.

By contrast with his house, France was a warm and welcoming but somewhat disconcerting host – for he was bad at remembering names and faces. Generally his 'cher ami' sufficed, but if forced to the point of introducing his guests to each other he would often be reduced to an indistinguishable mumble. At times, too, he found himself in difficulties with admirers who produced copies of his work demanding a personal inscription. On such occasions his method of escape was to accept with apparent alacrity –

then, on the point of signing, to ask, 'Now, let me see, how is it exactly that you spell your name?'

Enjoying being king of his castle, and not simply the captive lion that he was in Mme. Arman's salon, France was generally pleased to see his guests. All that he held against them was that they would filch copies of his works from his shelves, so that even in his own house he often had difficulty in laying his hand on one of his own books. He particularly liked the young, and there was usually a generous element of would-be writers, aspiring artists and budding *littérateurs* amongst his guests, some seeking the stimulus of his conversation, others a leg-up in the literary or artistic worlds. Depending on which of these two grades they fell into they tended to find their attendance either richly rewarding or highly frustrating.

So long as they were content with the pleasure and interest of France's company, so, too, was he with theirs and he would do all that he could to spread his riches before them. At times, too, he was capable of charming and generous gestures towards them – as, on one occasion, when he was travelling in a cab with Myriam Harry, a young Jewish writer soon to make her name as a novelist, and her sculptor husband. She happened to mention that it was her birthday. Whereupon France spent the rest of the afternoon touring the antique shops to find her a present.

But, unlike Mme. Arman who would pull every string, beard every editor, bully every publisher, on behalf of her protégés, France would rarely make the slightest effort on their behalf in the outside world. At the root of this refusal lay a cynical consciousness of the irresistible force of the younger generation pushing up behind him. One day, he, too, grumbled to Brousson about the way everyone called him 'maître'. 'Maître! . . . I, too, in my day used to hand out "maîtres" to Academicians. I know very well what it means. Not, as one might think from the etymology "*Magister* – my good sir, you are worth three of me." . . .

What it really means is – "Poor old pedant, slobbering worse than a mustard pot . . . You are really going home . . . You repeat yourself. You are in the process of becoming God. Don't linger too long in this world. You have stayed long enough. It's high time to make way for the young." '

Some of those, however, who considered that by their attendance and admiration they had earned the letter of introduction to the editor, or the word in the publisher's ear that would make all the difference to their prospects, felt cheated when it was not forthcoming. One such was Henri Massis who, after several years of assiduous attendance, left with, as he put it, 'a distracted mind, a contracted heart and empty hands'. Brousson, too, when summarily dismissed in the middle of South America, was to feel that he deserved more than his fare home. Yet Brousson's time with France was to give him the material for his books, and even Massis had grudgingly to admit that France had given him some invaluable lessons in careful and correct writing. Few of France's young guests really went away unrewarded in one way or another. The trouble was that they were not always rewarded in the way they wanted.

Proust was no longer one of those who visited France in the Villa Saïd. This was not because of any feeling of disappointment or bitterness on Proust's part – of the many who in their time and their turn, brought their admiration to France, there can have been few less self-seeking. Nor was it because of any diminution in his respect for France's work and worth – in 1904 he sent France a copy of Ruskin's *The Bible of Amiens*, which he had prefaced and annotated, with the inscription 'in recognition of my infinite admiration, of my affectionate respect, and of my gratitude for a kindness impossible to forget'. Rather, the break seems to have come from France's side – the probable reason for it, Proust's conviction around 1899, when Suzanne was of marriageable age, but not yet engaged to Mollin, that France was trying to marry her off to him.

Whether there was any real basis for Proust's belief that France was eyeing him as a possible son-in-law, or whether Suzanne was simply part of Proust's phantasmagoric procession of 'jeunes filles en fleurs', one cannot know, but certainly Proust's alarm was real enough, for he wrote to his mother – 'Be very prudent if you are airing any matrimonial ideas for me. For it appears that France has been thinking of me for his daughter, and as I would not wish it, one must be prudent . . .' France's anger, too, was probably real enough when he heard, as sooner or later he was bound to, what Proust was saying and writing about his intentions for Suzanne. A spurned father-in-law is just as touchy as a rejected daughter, and if, as seems probable, Proust's fears were entirely without foundation, the slight was no less. Certainly at this time, France rubbed Proust so completely out of his life that when a friend, Mme. Alphonse Daudet, some years later mentioned Proust in conversation, France spoke of him as one would of an amiable acquaintance one had met long ago on one's travels but not seen since – 'I knew him . . . I believe I prefaced one of his books. He was agreeable and full of wit. He had a sharp sense of observation. But I ceased to frequent him very quickly.'

There was to be a curious last link between these two great French writers, possibly the greatest of succeeding generations. When Proust died in 1923, a year before France, a friend, Jacques Porel, Rejane's son, slipped on to a finger of the corpse a ring that had been one of Proust's most cherished possessions. It was the ring that France had given Rejane in recognition of her admirable interpretation of Thérèse in the dramatized version of *Le Lys Rouge*.

If there were some of France's guests who left the Villa Saïd embittered, there were many more, however, who left it utterly bewildered. France was variously criticized, not only for surrounding himself with a profusion of riches that accorded ill with the egalitarian views he now expressed on political platforms, but also for the manner in which he bought them – since he bothered little about the price, simply signing a chit for Calmann Lévy, who acted as his banker, to honour, confident that if there was a lot going out, there was even more coming in – which, nowadays, there always was. This careless attitude to money was offensive to many who had not as much as he had, the more particularly since France's political views seemed aimed at taking away much of what they had.

As a penalty of his fame, France was carefully watched for discrepancy, indulgence and error. 'If you watch what he eats,' said one sharp-eyed and -witted woman at a lunch party, noting the obvious delight with which France tucked into the delicious dishes that were placed in front of him, 'you will not believe what he says.' And, of course, there was much that was puzzling. For all France's appreciation of beauty, the total effect of the conglomeration of rare and beautiful objects in his house, was far from beautiful. For all the money and time he had spent on his surroundings, France, in the dark, draughty, smoky rooms of the Villa Saïd, lived in conditions of extreme and almost austere discomfort. Even in his own home, France could not escape from his contradictions.

WHEN France in the summer of 1904 engaged Jean-
Jacques Brousson as his secretary, it showed clearly how
much smaller a part Mme. Arman now played in his life:
for until then, ever since France had dispensed with the
services of his secretary the long-suffering Jeanne Cantal
some ten years before, she had done virtually all his sec-
retarial work for him. Brousson did not, in fact, meet Mme.
Arman until he had been working for France for over a
year – which reveals how rarely by this time, during working hours, she went to the Villa Saïd.

Brousson, the son of a doctor of Nîmes, was a young
man of 26 who had followed his literary inclinations against
the will of his family. France engaged him at 100 francs
a month – not an unusually low sum for such a position at
that period, but the same salary, one remembers, that
Lemerre had paid France when he had first engaged him
forty years before. However, as well as his wages, Brousson's five-year period in France's service was to provide
him with the material for three books – in the first of which
he showed that he was a born Boswell, bringing France's
character brilliantly to life in a way that no other of his
chroniclers has succeeded in doing. Brousson had to wait
twenty years – until after France's death – before he could
publish *Anatole France en Pantoufles*, and its success, although considerable, seems to have come too late for him.
In the other two books he wrote about his time with
France – *Itinéraire à Buenos Aires* and *Les Vêpres de*

l'Avenue Hoche – he succumbed to a mood of personal bitterness, which spoilt both their spirit and their shape.

Brousson arrived for his first day's work at the Villa Saïd at seven o'clock on a fine June morning. He had been told to come as early as possible, but as a provincial new to Paris his ideas of the possible were very different to those of France or of Joséphine. For some time he could get no answer to his repeated rings on the bell, and so had to wait on the steps, watching the magic of the morning dissipate into day. Eventually the judas in the door opened, and through it a bleary eye peered out at him. It was Joséphine. 'So it's you, making all that row. Have you fallen out of bed?' But she let him in.

Brousson had to wait in the hall nearly two hours until Joséphine emerged from the basement carrying France's breakfast-tray, on which everything, except the food, was a work of art. When nine had struck Brousson followed Joséphine and the chocolate into France's bedroom. Out of the shadow of a huge bed came an irritable, nasal murmur – 'I thought you were dead. Believe me, I would have consoled myself quickly if it hadn't been for my chocolate. Everyone abandons me . . .'

When the curtains were drawn, Brousson saw before him a figure whose head was wrapped in a turban of Indian silk, and whose arms and shoulders were covered by a series of shawls. The sight made Brousson think of Molière's *malade imaginaire* – alternatively, of the wolf disguised as Red Riding Hood's grandmother.

France also saw Brousson. 'Ah. Forgive me, my young friend, for inflicting on you the sight of my shame. How have I passed the night? . . . Fever never gave me an hour's rest. If this continues I shall soon be on my monument.'

'Don't believe a word of it,' protested Joséphine, 'From my room below I could hear his snores. They sounded like the Trump of Doom.'

This was the start of an association which, on Brousson's

side, was not to inspire a great deal of affection, but a grudging respect, a lot of laughter – a certain amount of resentment also. What France needed as much as a secretary, was an audience, and Brousson listened long and listened well. According to Brousson, France had two sorts of conversation, his set speeches and his ordinary talk. Brousson soon got to know the set speeches so well that he could have catalogued them. In these – 'the anecdotes were immovably linked, the points were made at pre-arranged places . . . There were changes of tone . . . The words of the culmination were nasally enunciated in a sacerdotal tone. No matter who came in or what happened . . . the Master recited his couplet with the imperturbability of the gramophone.' By contrast, France's unofficial speech was 'laborious, painful, creaking, breathless, discordant, full of contradictions, of extemporizing expressions . . . – "N'est-ce-pas" . . . "Tout de même" . . . . "Possible que" . . . this sort of conversation is the opposite of the official set-piece. If it has not its majesty, it has not its monotony either. No one knows where it is going, not even France himself.'

Brousson's portrait shows France enjoying being a character, choosing one of his thinking caps, of which 'his collection is considerable. There are skull-caps of silk, of velvet, of *toile de Jouy*. Some vast, covering the ears . . . others like a fez . . . others again resemble the curious cap . . . which is stuck on the back of choir-boys' heads'; deliberately carrying a watch which would not keep time in order to give him an excuse for being late. To France, wrote Brousson, the world was 'a vast museum. He professes the most complete indifference for mountains, rivers, geographical features . . . He says, when one speaks of a beautiful scene, "Don't let your imagination run away with you. It is only earth, water and clouds. . . . Thus he made a pilgrimage to the Gulf Juan to see the place where Napoleon disembarked. But he did not notice either the Iles St. Marguerite or the silhouette of Antibes. He found, under the olive trees, on the edge of the sea, a large library on the Hundred Days . . . If it is not engraved, painted or printed, a landscape does not interest him.'

France gave Brousson his views on life – 'the best season for man is that of his desires and pleasures' – and on love – 'One makes love, all the rest is fiction, make-believe . . . Contrary to what they tell you in books, to make it well, one must have made it a lot . . . Amorous exercises need skill, persistence and practice . . . like playing the piano.

But if in *Anatole France en Pantoufles* Brousson tells us much about France's way of life, he shows us something also about his manner of working. France would throw off the first rough draft comparatively quickly. It was written on any oddment of paper that came to hand. Thus the printer was liable to find pinned together pieces of notepaper, followed by sheets of foolscap, followed by pages torn out of some cheap notebook, followed by a number of ill-assorted scraps of paper – bills, circulars, envelopes – on the backs of which France had completed his chapter.

When the proof returned France would set to work on it not only with a pen, generally a quill one, but also with a pair of scissors and a pot of paste. He would cut out paragraphs, sentences, even words – juggle them around, fit them wherever the form seemed to beckon beneath the surface, paste his corrections on to the sheets, and send the whole sticky mess off to the printer again. When a fresh set of proofs arrived back the whole process would start over again. Sometimes with a piece of work that refused to come easily he would exact up to eight sets of proofs. France excused himself by saying, 'What would you. I have no imagination but a lot of patience.' Although he was often photographed, in the traditional pose of the writer, seated at his desk holding his pen, he considered it would have been more appropriate, he told Brousson, had he been shown standing, scissors in hand, like a tailor.

Regretfully France admitted that he had rarely felt the

touch of inspiration. In consequence he said he had had to make do without it. But he was often pleasantly surprised by the reasonable result achieved in a morning, at the beginning of which he had sat down with a mind as blank as the paper in front of him.

France advised Brousson to avoid over-melodious, specious phrases – 'At first they rock you pleasantly but by the end they send you to sleep.' He counselled him also to be wary of the pretentious, the flowery, the obviously over-contrived – 'Méfiez-vous de la pâtisserie.' In his youth he had often striven to attain the sublime. Now he avoided it at all costs. More and more he inclined to simplicity – 'The most beautiful phrase? . . . The shortest.' Yet the simplicity of France's prose was, of course, comparable to that of the classical statues he loved, whose purity of line was achieved only at the cost of immense labour and patience. No one could possibly have taken more care over his writing – and not only over his professional work. Massis once saw him rewrite four times a letter to a shopkeeper because he could not get the rhythm to run as he wanted it. 'Caress your phrase tenderly,' France told Brousson, 'and it will end by smiling at you.'

The particular task for which France had engaged Brousson was to help him sift and shape the material for a life of *Jeanne d'Arc*, a work of a size and a sort that France had not hitherto attempted. The Maid in her saintly simplicity is one thing to most men. To France she was many things – a means of exorcising a long-lingering trace of schoolboy inadequacy – of proving to his masters at Stanislas, now mostly long dead, that he was a sound and solid historian; of evading Mme. Arman who was entirely bored by the whole project; of disentangling, without too much fuss, his writing from his political activities – for an iconoclastic interpretation of their country's patron saint would be acceptable to his Socialist colleagues, while the period was sufficiently remote to prevent them interfering much with it – of trying out what France quite mistakenly looked upon as his scientific approach to historical events on a subject shrouded by centuries of veneration.

France had long had the idea of such a work at the back of his mind. As it turned out, that is probably where it should have stayed. For France, the advocate always of the subjective attitude to life; the expert exponent of the dilatory, dawdling approach; the upholder always of the importance of the variable, capricious, personal element in human affairs, was ill-equipped to tackle a subject ringed with conjecture and controversy – a subject that required above all else an objectivity of outlook and a scholarly stamina he had never possessed. For all the wide spread of his knowledge, for all his intuitive understanding of detail, France had not the balance, the long-sight, or the persistence to make a good historian. Nor had he the ability to organize himself and his material for the long campaign that any full-scale historical work involves. It was to help him regain control of a subject already alarmingly out of hand that he called in Brousson.

Brousson was introduced to the Maid when Joséphine lugged into the room an enormous bundle that looked like an ill-stuffed feather mattress. In this, tied up in a dust-sheet, were the pages of manuscript France had already written, the notes he had taken over many years of spasmodic research, and an immense muddle of pieces and pages of material. When Brousson undid the dust-sheet an avalanche of paper swept out on to the floor. As well as the pages of manuscript and notes there was a medley of letters, visiting cards, bills, on the back of which France had scribbled a few lines, a stray thought or a reference.

France excused the disorder to the dismayed Brousson. 'The trouble is, I work everywhere – and above all in stations. Madame has a frenzy for travelling. She cannot stay for long anywhere. In the summer it is Quiberon, Brittany.

In the autumn it is the Gironde, the châteaux of the Loire. Three churches, two museums, ten antique shops per day ... During the winter she consents to recuperate for a bit in Paris, but as soon as spring comes we jump into sleeping-cars, and are off to Rome, to Florence, to Naples ... I am a vagabond. It does not matter so far as writing stories is concerned. It matters a great deal for Jeanne d'Arc.' France airily waved over to Brousson the amorphous mass of material on the floor – 'It's all yours. I could not bear to poke my nose into it again.'

It took France and Brousson a further four years to produce the two weighty octavo volumes that were eventually published by Calmann-Lévy in 1908. Their fate had long been foreseen – even by France. The style was much admired, the various set-pieces were declared to be the best reconstructions of the period hitherto achieved, but even in the reviews of critics favourably predisposed towards France the undercurrent was cold; while historians jumped joyfully on the errors that could be found throughout the text. Of these the cause was generally the long lapse of time that distanced France's original research from the final version. By the time France and Brousson came to correct the proofs they were often unable to find their way back to the original sources in order to check them.

A wider margin of error might have been allowed if France had managed to present a consistent and cohesive point of view. But here again his liking for the by-ways rather than the main roads, his inclination always to take the long way round, his delight in diversion – qualities that were often the most delightful features of other forms of his work – prevented him from staying long enough on the direct line of approach ever to come to any conclusion at all.

Léon Carias, one of the most clear-sighted and devoted of France's biographers, summing up the faults which underlay the failure of *Jeanne d'Arc*, has suggested that France worked on it too much – and yet not enough. So many years had passed since France had started his project that he had become stale of his subject. Yet at the same time, perhaps from boredom, perhaps from a temperamental incapacity, he had failed to give his material that final working-over it needed to be licked into shape. Most writers have their cross to bear during some periods of their lives. France's cross was clearly the double-barred one of Lorraine. But at least, with Brousson's help, he managed at last to get it off his back.

France was always sensitive to the direction and force of the prevailing wind, although he did not necessarily trim his sails to suit it. Some while before he and Brousson completed their task he seems to have realized that this time both the omens and the odds were against him. Yet, as he had proved in other moments of crisis and depression, France had in his character, for all his apparent vagueness and indecision, a core of surprising toughness and resilience. Now, instead of gloomily accepting and awaiting the fulfil-ment of this premonition of failure, he set to work, during the months when he and Brousson were struggling to tie up the last loose ends of twenty years' research, on another book, of which the character and intent were so totally different, even contradictory, to that of *Jeanne d'Arc* that one cannot but think that his main motive in writing it was to hedge his bets. He was determined that if he did not win, he was not going to lose either.

There are times in France's life when the contradictions in his character seem to be manipulated with an almost Machiavellian cunning. This was one of them. For while with *Jeanne d'Arc* he was staking an ambitious claim to be accepted as a serious historian, he was in *l'Ile des Pingouins*, as this other work came to be called, writing a biting satire not only of the historians who would crab the errors of *Jeanne d'Arc*, but of the whole course and point of History itself. If his forebodings proved unfounded, and *Jeanne d'Arc* had the *succès*, mainly *d'éstime* he hoped for, well and good. But if on the other hand it foundered as he feared, then he would make up lost headway in this pirate craft that would steal the wind out of his critics' sails – and possibly scupper them as well. And so it proved. *L'Ile des Pingouins* was published in October 1908, only a few months after *Jeanne d'Arc*, and the immense roar of amusement and appreciation it provoked drowned the carpings of the critics over France's ill-advised venture into serious history.

'In spite of the great number of amusements which tempt me,' began France in *l'Ile des Pingouins*, 'my life has only one object. It is entirely directed towards the achievement of a Grand Design. I am writing the History of the Penguins.' But before he started on his task, because he realized 'it is extremely difficult to write history . . . The problems commence as soon as an event is reported by two or more witnesses since their evidence is always contradictory and quite irreconcilable,' France's historian of the Penguins went for advice to the experts. First he visited the palaeographers and archivists who looked at him with pity – 'Do we write history, I ask you? Do we try to extract from a text, a document, the slightest particle of life or of truth? We stick to the letter.' Then he went on to a conventional historian who shrugged his shoulders – 'Mon pauvre monsieur, for what good are you giving yourself so much trouble, and why write a new history when you have only to copy the old as is the custom . . . Historians copy each other. They spare themselves thus much fatigue . . . Imitate them and do not try to be original. An original historian is the object of mistrust, scorn and universal disgust.'

But, in fact, the author of the History of the Penguins proved to be a most original historian – and the History of the Penguins a most original history. From the moment the short-sighted Saint-Maël, landing from his bark on an iceberg, mistakes the waddling forms of the penguins for human beings and baptises them, thus causing consternation in Heaven and innumerable complications on earth, the whole evolution of the human race is brilliantly satirized. *L'Ile des Pingouins* did not quite last the course – a fault that can be traced to France's journalistic training which encouraged him to have an ephemeral and episodic approach. But even so it still firmly takes its place, alongside *Gulliver's Travels* and *Animal Farm* amongst the greatest of social satires.

So the success of a work, whose composition had taken France a matter of months, balanced the failure of an effort spread over many years. Yet the two were probably not unconnected. But for the disheartening experience of *Jeanne d'Arc*, France would never have turned so savagely on the whole process and purpose of history, and but for the tension built up over these disillusioning years of wrestling with a subject that was really too strong for him, there might not have been so powerful a release of creative energy as that which animated the history of the penguins.

Chapter

II

FRANCE'S DECISION to separate his literary and political work brought into the open the contradictions which had always played an important part both in his character and his talent. At times the contrast was startling. France, for example, had inserted at the end of *l'Ile des Pingouins* a most pessimistic picture of future times, with industrial intensification increased to the point when the sun was for ever hidden behind a pall of smoke and fumes, with an entirely materially-minded society that considered money the only god, and with the moneyed classes deliberately corrupting the mass of the workers in order to assure a cheap and docile labour supply. France sub-titled this gloomy vision of things to come, 'A Story without End,' on the grounds that if such a society carried within itself the seeds of its own destruction, that destruction when it came would be followed by the slow regrowth of a similar society and the gradual redevelopment of a similar situation – hence, ultimately, of a similar destruction. It was an endless process, an endless story – and about as depressing a prospect as France, or anyone else for that matter, could possibly imagine. Not surprisingly, since it suggested the futility of man's efforts to improve society, conditions of life or even himself, it was not at all to the liking of France's Socialist colleagues, who were trying to do all these things.

Yet despite this personal pessimism, France's political speeches continued throughout the years which enclosed the writing of his 'Histoire sans fin' to express a radiant social optimism. Possibly because of disillusionment with the slow progress in France itself of social reform, possibly because his horizons were widening with his experience, France's outlook now was international rather than internal. It was the drawing together of the workers of the world in the Socialist sun to which he now looked forward – 'Universal solidarity is about to be born, or about to be reborn, since you will recognize the same ideal of human charity that Rome taught' (3rd February, 1905); 'The only way of distancing for ever all danger of war, is a strong organization of workers' (27th October, 1908); 'Universal peace will be realized one day, not because mankind has become better (one can hardly hope for that) but because a new order of things, a new science, new economic necessities . . . will impose a state of peace, just as in other times the conditions of existence imposed a state of war' (28th June, 1911).

At times something of France's old scepticism still dropped like a gentle but dampening rain upon his audience, as when, in February, 1905, he counselled a meeting made up mainly of students – 'It is wise to keep one's illusions . . . for it is illusions which give to the world its interest and significance, and illusions when they are methodical and rational have often the excellent result of creating a reality after the image. That is why I value highly the illusion which I shall carry from here that after us you will work for the peaceful re-organization of the world.' But in general such undertones of doubt were rare. Much more often France's speeches were characterized by the same hopeful idealism, which, a decade earlier, he had expressed through the mouth of Bergeret, whose optimism had so surprised his daughter Pauline, on that showery New Year's Day walk that she had stopped in her tracks, and turning to her father, had cried in utter astonishment – 'You are an optimist.'

Another even more bewildering and blatant contradiction also came to the surface at this time. For France, the arch-enemy of revolution which he was shortly to castigate comically in *l'Ile des Pingouins*, and later to challenge more seriously and savagely in *Les Dieux ont Soif*, showed him-self now in public as its ardent advocate and supporter – if, admittedly, of a revolution not in his own country.

The abortive Russian Revolution of 1905, sparked off by the St. Petersburg massacres on 21st January, when a crowd of strikers in front of the Winter Palace was fired on by order of the authorities, had from its start aroused a great deal of protest and support in Paris. This was in spite of the fact that the French Government was officially the Tsar's ally, had lent him over a period of some fifteen years some 10,000 million francs worth of gold, largely used to finance the disastrous war with Japan, and was to lend him further vast sums in the future, which were to be mainly used to speed the return of reaction.

France's voice was one of the first and loudest raised in anger, not only against the massacres, but also against the loans. Five days after the troops in front of the Winter Palace had opened fire, he told a meeting of 5,000 workers gathered in the Tivoli Vaux-Hall, despite a large and hostile deployment of police outside – 'The revolution is on its way, and will not be stopped.' Three days later he was denouncing the Franco-Russian alliance and the loans which supported it to a protest meeting organized by the People's Universities; two days after that, suggesting to another largely university audience that it was 'a sign of new times, comrades, that the bullets which struck down Russian workers on the banks of the Neva, have whistled past all human ears.' When *l'Humanité* opened a subscription list for the families of the victims of the massacres, France's name was the first upon it; and when a *Société des amis du peuple Russe* was formed, France became its first president.

As such, over the course of the next two years, he was active in many ways – protesting against Gorki's arrest, against the extradition of a supposed assassin from Sweden, and on several occasions, vociferously and at length, against the loans, trying various methods of dissuasion, including the suggestion, aimed obviously at the hard-headed rather than the hard-hearted, that to lend money to the Tsarist government at such a time and for such a purpose, was not only a moral crime but also unsound finance – 'If our citizens have ears let them hear. They are warned; if they again allow money to be lent to the Russian Government so that they can shoot, hang, massacre . . . it will not only be a crime, it will also be a very bad bit of business.' When the hopes raised by the grant of a constitution and the sumoning of the Douma were quickly extinguished by a returning wave of reaction, France made a notable speech of regret and remonstrance in which he showed that his sympathy had now spread to the point when he not only supported revolution in Russia but favoured its extension elsewhere – 'The Russian Revolution is a universal revolution. It has revealed to the workers of the whole world its means and its ends, its power and its destiny.'

Yet this was the man who, to go by his books, believed that revolution changed nothing but the people in power, and who hated, above possibly anything else, the violence that was the necessary concomitant of both revolution and war. It was this platform revolutionary who, within a few years, was to produce two of the most withering exposures of the revolutionary experience that have ever been written.

Largely for his efforts at this time – for when at the end of 1906 the activities of the revolutionaries and reformers inside Russia subsided, so too did those of their French friends – France was ultimately to be given his statue in the city that by then had become Leningrad, a city in which, under Communist conditions of life, he would never, as Sir

Desmond MacCarthy put it, have 'known a moment's happiness, and would probably have been shot.'

But while France was devoting so much of his attention to revolution abroad, what of the situation at home? Here Mme. Arman was having little success in regaining France's love, affection or even consideration. France was still the star of her salon, but he was now a star that rarely twinkled. Often now, on those Sunday afternoons in the long austere drawing-room of Mme. Arman's house in the Avenue Hoche, when conversation was stilled so that the Master's voice could be heard, France's response was slow in forthcoming, and sometimes he refused to perform at all. Marie Shekievitch, a young and talented Russian exile seeking in the distractions of the social world, consolation for the failure of an early and disastrous marriage, remembered that on the occasion of her first visit to Mme. Arman's salon, some time in 1905, when the moment came for France to show his paces and Mme. Arman gave him his cue by calling out . . . ' "Monsieur . . . Tell us that story I enjoyed so much yesterday." He turned about sharply. "Madame, I won't do anything of the sort." '

France and Mme. Arman still went on their trips abroad together; every year to Italy, and also – in 1906 to Austria and Germany, in 1907 to Greece and Turkey, in 1908 to Greece again. They still went on their strolls around Paris together. But France was now an impatient and irritable companion, resenting the ritual that was all that was left to him of their relationship, and expressing his annoyance by making fun of Mme. Arman whenever he could – a fun in which there was little amusement or kindliness and certainly no love.

Brousson was walking with them one evening when they came to the Pont des Arts. ' "Here," announced France, "we must halt for the ceremony. Go . . . follow Madame on to the bridge, and assume an appropriate air for the occasion.

It is the moment of dusk . . . See, Madame is already in ecstasy . . . It is fifteen years since I first saw that inspired look on her face, about six o'clock in the evening on the Pont des Arts . . . You don't look sufficiently moved, my son. Come, a little effort . . . If you lack feeling on the Pont des Arts at six o'clock in the evening you will never find the key to Madame's heart." '

They still went together for their periods of rest and recuperation in the country, either at Capian or at a property near Quiberon in Brittany that Mme. Arman had acquired in 1905. But even at Capian, where they had always in the past managed to rediscover each other, they remained now apart and on edge – France irritable and bored; Mme. Arman sorrowful and suspicious, wondering all the time that France was away from her what he was up to. For it was now perfectly clear to Mme. Arman, and to everyone else, that France was no more faithful to her in the flesh than in the spirit. France undoubtedly enjoyed spreading the legend of his libertinage, particularly as the antidote to the possessiveness which increasingly overcame Mme. Arman the further France moved away from her. Brousson has stories of a demure procuress, of highly respectable appearance, who called upon France once a month bringing with her an album of her wares, of stray nocturnal encounters which left France far too tired to do any writing in the morning, of Joséphine berating him, on the evidence of the flotsam that washed up in his bedroom, for behaving at his advanced age like an amorous adolescent. Some of these stories probably testify more to the creative talent of either France or Brousson than to the truth of the matter, but all the same there was undoubtedly a good deal of truth in the matter. While still far from his second childhood, France was clearly enjoying a second youth, in which he was behaving with much less restraint than in his first.

It is difficult to make out whether Mme. Arman minded more France's unfaithfulness, or the fact that he made no secret of it. Most probably she minded both a great deal, for certainly the wound was deep – in the end, mortal. For France, too, in spite of his vigorous and verdant enjoyment of whatever life now brought his way, the deterioration and destruction of this relationship, the most important of his life, was a depressing experience, and played its part in engendering the gloom that marked his *'Histoire sans fin'*. 1908, the year of its publication, marked also for Mme. Arman the start of a nightmare period during which she found she could not control events, France, or even herself. For much of the time she was ill and she had given up the effort to make herself appear younger than she was. She no longer bothered much about her clothes nor even to dye her hair. She was frequently in tears and could no longer restrain her reproaches – so that there were frequent scenes – nor subdue her suspicions, so that she would sometimes descend on the Villa Saïd in the middle of the night to make sure that France was not sleeping with someone else.

One morning Brousson arrived to find the door open, Joséphine, looking more haggard even than usual, sitting on the staircase weeping into the bowl of chocolate intended for France's breakfast, and an air of drama, disturbance and desolation hanging over the house. During the night, Mme. Arman had had an attack of jealousy and had come round to beat on the door at five in the morning. Storming into France's bedroom, she had torn open the curtains and ever since then they had been quarrelling. When Brousson went in there was a temporary lull in the battle. Mme. Arman had thrown off the fur wrap in which she had covered herself for the journey round, and, clad only in a heavy flannel nightgown, was staring gloomily into what remained of the fire from the evening before. France was standing at the window, drumming irritably on the pane, watching some workmen on a near-by piece of scaffolding. Neither Brousson's presence nor that of Joséphine, bringing in the chocolate, restrained them for long. When Brousson noticed and objected that the workmen were over-seeing and over-hearing everything, Mme. Arman flung the windows open, so that they could the better hear her abuse of France.

This, and other storms, passed, but it was an impossible and an intolerable situation, of which the strain on Mme. Arman's side was aggravated by the fact that she, or M. Arman, had lost some of her money. For the first time in her life she had financial worries which, if not serious in themselves, were very serious coming at such a time. Pathetically, now that the creative outlet in France's work was closed to her, Mme. Arman made an effort to open another of her own. She herself wrote a novel, *Le Roman d'une Demoiselle de Modes*, which she published in 1908 under the pseudonym of 'Philippe Lautrey'. She kept the secret of her authorship from France, and even arranged, at the time of publication, a lunch party in honour of the unknown provincial author, at which she handed round a telegram in which 'Philippe Lautrey' regretted his absence. But in the end the secret did not prove worth keeping and neither 'Philippe Lautrey' nor the *demoiselle de modes* attracted any attention at all.

On France's side, his irritation was aggravated by the fact that Mme. Arman was not, after all and so long, his wife. If Mme. Arman had not been willing, so many years before, to give up her world for his, by what right now did she demand this dominion without dignity, a dominion that would have been barely tolerable at the end of a long period of affection and marital service! A more perceptive and compassionate man than France might have realized that this was the behaviour of a woman in every way at the end of her tether and, perhaps on that account, forgiven it. But France, in his present mood, was neither perceptive nor compassionate, and his fury to get away blinded him for the moment to all else.

He took the first chance of escape that offered, a lecture tour in South America, arranged in conjunction with the presentation of a series of French plays by a French company who were to travel out with him. The tour was to last several months, over the summer of 1909. Mme. Arman did all she could to persuade France to take her with him, but for once he was adamant, on grounds which can have deceived no one, and certainly not Mme. Arman. Argentina, he asserted, was a highly respectable, highly religious country, which would be shocked should he travel around with a woman who was not his wife. But, declared Mme. Arman furiously, had they not been travelling together all over the place, all these years without shocking anyone? However, in the end she gave in, on condition that François, her valet, should go too, to look after both France and her interests.

As well as François, France took with him Brousson and Pierre Calmettes. On the 30th April, 1909, they embarked at Cherbourg together with the theatrical company. In Brousson's description it was a dramatic moment. The leading actor of the troupe accompanying France was declaiming Corneille; the leading actresses vying to show their dramatic talent in the role of Mary Stuart viewing for the last time the beautiful land of France. Yet, in spite of their efforts, none of them succeeded in capturing the centre of the stage. This was reserved for France and Mme. Arman, who had come down to Cherbourg to see him off. Discreetly, but none the less avidly, the crowd of passengers, porters and seers-off, watched to see how France and Mme. Arman would manage the difficult moment of parting. Mme. Arman raised her veil; France, his large and worn grey hat. Mme. Arman tottered and seemed about to faint, France held her and gave her a large bouquet of roses. She revived sufficiently to snatch the roses which France had laid with one hand on her breast while with the other he held her up, and to remark somewhat savagely – 'Do you think I am already in my tomb?' France kissed her hand – then turned and fled to the ship. He had earlier confided in Brousson his fears that Mme. Arman, when it came to the point of departure, would never let him go, and that she was capable of storming the gangplank at the last moment. But she remained on the quay, a sad, solitary and desolate figure. Even France, watching and waving his last farewells, felt a touch of pity, so that Brousson heard him murmur to himself – 'Pauvre femme . . .'

On his recent voyages with Mme. Arman, France had formed the habit of making a few jottings in a cheap notebook. On board the *Amazon* he made but the barest and briefest of notes – 'In the Bay.' 'Madeira. A steep street, the funicular over the valley. The fountains. The flowers . . .' 'An overcast sky, very great intensity and vibration of light.' '10th. Sports. Dancing in the dark night. It was charming. Rain during the night.' '11th. Ball. Fancy dress . . . on the bridge, Venetian lanterns.' '16th May. The lights of an invisible boat – signals. The green starboard light was very beautiful – shooting stars.' '17th. The coast. Green rocks in forms of pyramids. Arrival at Rio de Janeiro. Have a sore throat. Remained lying down in cabin.' Finally on 22nd May, they came to Buenos-Aires, 'white houses in a rose-coloured sky – buildings in the Italian style.'

These jottings reflect a normal passenger existence on board ship. From them one would conjecture that little had been happening to France outside the ordinary round of marine life – the dances, the concerts, the sports, the calls at various ports, and the patches of bad weather – which were the despair of Brousson who was a bad sailor – the more so because France, who was not, would delight in telling him that his sufferings were psychological and self-induced. But, in fact, quite apart from an incident at Lisbon – where the theatrical company invaded uninvited a banquet given to France by his Portuguese admirers and were so carried away by the occasion that they virtually appropriated it; and at Madeira – where France was held up to ransom, for a very small sum, by a rogue taxi-driver – quite a lot did happen to France on board the *Amazon* – as in his present mood it was more or less bound to.

France, who still retained his liking for theatrical people and the theatrical atmosphere, had settled quickly and with delight into the theatrical décor in which he found himself. He was soon an accepted star in their firmament, just as much as Silvain or Albert-Lambert, the two leaders of the troupe. But it soon became noticeable that his was a shooting star and that it was veering rapidly towards Venus, personified on this occasion by Jeanne Brindeau, a middle-aged actress, of long and wide experience. Within a few days the obvious attraction that she and France felt for each other's company was causing whispers to go round. Within a week, their *affaire* was the talk of the boat; and by the time the *Amazon* docked at Buenos-Aires, theirs was an accepted and established liaison.

Nor did it prove simply to be a ship-board romance that ended with their arrival in South America. In Buenos-Aires, France accepted the hospitality of an eminent judge who put his home and servants at France's disposal. France extended the offer, without further reference to the judge, who had moved upstairs into his mother's flat, to include Jeanne Brindeau, and installed her as *maîtresse de maison*. This created a particularly difficult and delicate situation, for the judge was a misogynist, a collector who valued his possessions highly, and a very particular man who liked everything in its exact and proper place. Jeanne Brindeau was, of course, a woman and an assertive one at that, with an incurable mania for moving furniture around. The judge had to sit back and say nothing while his rooms were turned upside down, his table invaded by all the members of the company who could not find a free meal elsewhere, and his house made the scene of an indecorous and undignified love affair. However, for the length of their stay in Buenos-Aires, Jeanne Brindeau remained enthroned – the delight of France, the despair of the judge.

France's lectures did not go all that well, the Argentinians being little interested in Rabelais, the subject he had chosen for them. Dwindling audiences forced France's sponsors to change the subject for the last two, and the only one, in fact, which went at all well was that in which France talked to the Argentinians about themselves. However, the affairs of the theatrical party went better and so too, did France's affair with Jeanne Brindeau. But she did not have it all her own way. Accounts from shops would turn up for goods supplied to 'Madame Anatole France' and be sent back with the sharp comment – 'There is not a Madame France and will not be for a long time.' France, also, got out of buying her a magnificent emerald offered for sale by a member of the party who had run into debt, and for which she was avid, on the grounds that an emerald brought bad luck, and he could not bear the thought of giving misfortune to someone of whom he was so fond.

But France told Brousson that his affair with Jeanne Brindeau had made him feel years younger, and in spite of his repudiation of 'Madame France's' debts, he did, at one moment at least, consider marrying her, although this might have been simply to evade the day of reckoning with Mme. Arman that was awaiting him on his return. He was restrained, however, by his remembrance of all that Mme. Arman had done for him – for absence, and possibly guilt, had undoubtedly made his heart grow fonder – also by Brousson, who disliked Jeanne Brindeau, and felt, and said, that France was making a fool of himself.

Perhaps Brousson said too much, for at the end of June and their stay in Buenos-Aires, he was abruptly dismissed, given his return ticket to Europe, but no money, so that he quickly had to find a means of support until the date of his departure. But for the kindness of an Argentinian writer who took him into his house and found him a job looking after two boys who were due to travel on the same boat, he would have had some difficulty in doing so. According to

Brousson, France had earlier tried to get rid of François, the valet whom Mme. Arman had sent with him, and whose presence must have been a perpetual reproach to France. But François had refused to leave, on the grounds that he was not in the service of 'Monsieur', but of 'Madame', that he had given his word to 'Madame' that he would accompany 'Monsieur' wherever he went, and that he intended to carry out her orders.

So, without Brousson, but with François, Pierre Calmettes, Jeanne Brindeau and all the rest of the party, France left to continue the tour in Uruguay and Brazil. Wherever they went they had a royal reception. For such occasions France had a set speech of thanks which he used with only slight climatic variations, part of which ran, 'I have admired your town so white (or 'so red', or 'so grey') under your clear (or sombre) sky. I have noticed the strength of your men, the beauty of your women, the grace of your children.' Several of the local papers which signalled their progress, reported the presence amongst them of 'Monsieur and Madame Anatole France'. It was not until mid-August that the tour ended and they sailed for home from Rio. On board the *Danube*, France once more started his jottings – '11th August. Departed for Europe on the *Danube*.' 'Bahia. Bright blue sky, the deep bay, the roofs of a hundred churches, the boats round the ship, full of parrots.' '18th. A great wind.' '21st. Very high seas.' '22nd. Frightful weather.' '23rd. Madeira. Beautiful sea.' 'Fine weather.' '27th. The coast of France sighted.' '28th. Arrived at Cherbourg.' Again, if there is something in these notes to show the state of the weather, there is little to show the state of France's mind. Yet, on the *Danube*, one cannot believe that he was in so carefree a holiday mood as he had been on the *Amazon*, and that not only because the weather was obviously unkind. In Paris, France would have to face up to things. He would have to face Mme. Arman.

During this fateful, and to Mme. Arman, endless summer,

her position in Paris was becoming increasingly painful and pitiful. France's departure had left her in so low a state that she had not the heart to continue her salon. On Sunday afternoons a few of her friends still went to see her, but she gave them little encouragement to continue doing so.

Princess Marthe Bibesco, who had recently met her for the first time at a dinner party – during which Mme. Arman had become so agitated that the piece of jewellery she was wearing in her hair had fallen in the soup – and at her invitation had called at the Avenue Hoche the following Sunday, found herself seized upon by Mme. Arman as someone fresh to whom she could talk about France and taken into the privacy of her study, to the total abandonment of her other friends. There Princess Bibesco was shown France's manuscripts. When they came to that of *Thaïs*, Mme. Arman told her France had first written it as a Christmas story for *l'Illustration*, but that when he read it to her she had said, 'Monsieur France, you should keep that and make a novel of it.' As she recounted this 'her shrill voice trembled; her eyes filled with tears. "I am enraged," she said, "that he is not here to receive you . . . Where do you think he is, the unfeeling wretch? Upside down in the Antipodes – in the country of monkeys." ' Mme. Arman gave Princess Bibesco the manuscript of one of France's short stories as a keepsake.

But in spite of chance encounters with sympathetic listeners such as Princess Bibesco, and in spite of occasional and very well-meaning if unrewarding visits by friends, Mme. Arman, for someone who had always been surrounded by a great number of people, was now very much on her own. France was away. M. Arman now lived almost entirely in the country, rarely coming to Paris. Gaston, angry with France for his desertion of his mother, and with Mme. Arman for the spectacle she was making of herself over France, also saw much less of her than he had been in the habit of doing. Mme. Arman wrote frequently to France, but had to content herself with a rare letter in return, and with François' reports.

France had been gone barely three weeks when she was reproaching him for the fact that in this time she had received only two short letters, declaring miserably that it was bad enough having to cross half the world to reach him, but what was much worse was that she had lost the confidence to open her heart to him, that the taste and fear of his displeasure had made her so 'timid' and 'fearful' that now she retired into herself for fear of incurring France's blame. Her maid had brought her a calendar, on which she crossed off the days. But was she perhaps stupid, she asked France, to look forward so ardently to 'the far-away and mysterious' days when France would be back. For what would that bring?

A week later some, at least, of her fears had been stilled by the arrival of a telegram from Buenos-Aires. *'Quelle bonne dépêche. Quelle jolie dépêche.'* The paper of the telegram was as blue as the skies of fair weather, and the words seemed to Mme. Arman wonderful beyond everything. She told France that he was not to laugh at her joy. For she had had no news since Bahia, and she no longer felt she was alive. At all costs they must not repeat these *'plaisanteries'*, for she found this period of waiting worse even than she had imagined. Anything else, any misery, was better than the terrible uncertainty of France's absence. *'Au revoir, au revoir . . .'* – the sound carried over the water like a joyful peal of bells. They would see each other again. Perhaps they would be happy again. *'Au revoir.'*

However, there were no more telegrams, and the letters became less and less frequent. Yet the absence of news was better than the news when it did come. Some time in June, Mme. Arman received an anonymous letter announcing the imminent marriage of France and Jeanne Brindeau. This was followed by a newspaper cutting which referred to the presence at a fête of 'Monsieur and Madame France'. The news of France's love affair reached Paris at about the same time and was quickly and widely spread around by the many who, in the years of her plenitude, had envied Mme. Arman her worldly success.

Mme. Arman did not know where to show her face, and when she did it was a tragic one. In her despair she turned first to God, although she had been an atheist all her adult life. Abbé Mugnier, her confessor, was now her most constant companion. She also enlisted the aid of man, and shortly before France's return she underwent a surgical operation in the hope that it would give her back some of her lost energy, her lost youth. She was still suffering from the effects of this operation when she met France again on his return.

There are various versions of their meeting. Brousson, who was not, of course, there, writes that France stalked down the platform, with Jeanne Brindeau on his arm, and totally ignored the stricken, supplicatory form of Mme. Arman who was waiting for him. Mme. Arman herself is supposed to have said that France came round in terror to the Avenue Hoche, seeking refuge and deliverance from the harpy who had got hold of him. Another source suggests that France and Jeanne Brindeau had separated, either before, or as soon as they got to Paris, but on the understanding that she would move into the Villa Saïd on an agreed date. When, however, she arrived, accompanied by several taxi-loads of her belongings, she found only Joséphine with a message that France had left on a trip with Mme. Arman. All that is really certain is that either immediately upon, or soon after, his return, France broke with Brindeau and that he and Mme. Arman made a final effort to revive their relationship.

It was a forlorn hope. France never liked acting under constraint or out of charity, and it seems most probable that it was only the sight of Mme. Arman's distress and of the rapidly deteriorating state of her health that brought him back to her. Clearly all the old irritations returned as soon as he did. Most of the time France was in a bad temper, which he made little effort to control or conceal. At the end of September, Mme. Arman wrote in a letter that she did not know what to do with this 'malheureux', who had become so irritable and bad-tempered, 'empoisoned', she feared, 'for ever'. One day soon after France's return, Marie Scheikevitch went for a walk with the two of them in the Bois. Throughout, Mme. Arman was 'nervous and sad', asking innumerable questions; whereas France, 'repentant' but 'irritable', hardly spoke a word.

On another day Marie Scheikevitch accompanied them on a drive to Versailles. France was again in a bad temper, which became worse when Mme. Arman, who had been pointing out the sights they passed without eliciting any response, said regretfully – 'Ah, Monsieur, you've lost your sense of beauty.' But he softened a little when Mme. Arman began talking to Marie Scheikevitch about the time of their first meeting.

'It was chez Mme. Aubernon. M. France was very timid . . .' She turned to France in the opposite seat – 'You were very touching, then, Monsieur. Give me your hand.' France gave it, but quickly took it back again. In distress, Mme. Arman asked Marie Scheikevitch for her news, and when she said she had none, Mme. Arman shrugged her shoulders, 'What would you, petite, there are no more men. There was once one; he still exists.' Mme. Arman smiled across at France who, however, took no notice.

They decided to go to Capian. There they would be on their own, for although it was the time for the vendanges, neither M. Arman nor Gaston had forgiven either of them for the figures of fun they were making of themselves and each other, and both deliberately kept away. They went there by a roundabout, rambling route which took them from

Tours to Toulouse, and round the South West of France as far as the Spanish frontier. It was an obvious effort to recover their lost habits as the first step towards recovering their lost happiness. But Mme. Arman's health remained very uncertain, and both of them were glad finally to reach and settle down in the calm of Capian.

There they had an unexpected encounter. On one of their outings to Bordeaux, they went as usual to lunch at the Chapon Fin, and found, sitting at another table, Brousson and his two South American charges, to whom he was showing the sights of the South West before taking them on a leisurely sight-seeing tour up to Paris. Highly embarrassed, France did nothing, but at the end of the lunch, Mme. Arman walked across and signed to Brousson to follow her outside. There she thanked him for taking her side in South America and made a valiant effort to get him to abandon his charges, to come back with them that evening to Capian and to start working once more for France. In spite of his ill-treatment he was, she told Brousson, at bottom still fond of France – like herself – and there was France's work to be considered, for the sake of which one had to put up with a great deal. But that evening Brousson went, not to Capian, but on to Paris.

At Capian, it seemed for a moment as if things were going better. France began to work again, and at the beginning of September – for this time they remained at Capian while autumn passed into winter – Mme. Arman wrote more cheerfully that he had started to work again '*et fort bien*'. But she could not bring herself to forgive or forget France's behaviour in South America. The lasting injury to her pride showed in other letters, in one of which she wrote that France excused his behaviour on the grounds that all men would have done as he had done. But, complained Mme. Arman, firstly, not all men had his celebrity; and, then, not all men would choose the moment when everyone was watching them to have an affair of 'the lowest sort'. If France did not owe her his fidelity, he at least owed her, she considered, 'decent and discreet' behaviour. In another letter she wrote that she would prefer it if he did not attribute the renunciation of his 'great passion' to his affection for her. He ought, she considered, simply to be disgusted with it, rather than to think and talk of it as something admissible in itself.

On his side, France, now genuinely concerned about her health, was kinder to Mme. Arman. He told her long stories, just as one would to a sick child, to get her to take her mind off herself. He had a specialist come down from Paris to see her, who said that she had congestion of the lungs and, for the time being, should take life as easily as she could. But it was, of course, almost impossible for Mme. Arman to take anything easily. In the interests of her health they should already have returned to Paris, for Capian was not a house to withstand the winter's cold, but they lingered over the end of the year – perhaps because they were loath to confront once again the many curious, cruel and quizzical eyes in Paris.

Princess Bibesco, who had herself been away from Paris for some time, and on her return had written asking when she might see Mme. Arman again, and hoping that it might be soon, received a reply, dated 27th December from Capian – 'As if I could have forgotten you . . . I hoped to see you every day, and now look at my bad luck. For two months I have been retained by illness far from Paris.' But, Mme. Arman wrote, she would be back in Paris at the end of the following week, and she hoped to see her then.

But they never met again – for although Mme. Arman came back, as she had announced, at the end of the following week, two days later she was dead. When she and France arrived back in the first days of the New Year, she was so weak she could barely walk. She was heard miserably murmuring to herself – 'Too old. Too old. It would be better to die. My death would settle everything.'

Unexpectedly, for in spite of the obvious failure of her
health, no one realized she was so close to death, she did die
early in the morning of 11th January, 1910. Her last words
were to call – 'Gaston, M. Fr . . .' France's last words to
her, the evening before, had been – 'My back is aching,
Madame – I am off.'

I 2

———◆◆———

FRANCE NEVER WENT BACK to Mme. Arman's house in
the Avenue Hoche, even to collect the books and the papers
he had left there. At the funeral in Saint Philippe du Roule
he sat not with Mme. Arman's family at the front of the
church but alone amongst the large and distinguished con-
gregation that filled the body of the church – a sorrowful
and self-conscious figure, aware that he was being closely
scrutinized from all sides. Princess Bibesco saw him for the
first time as he was leaving the church – 'an old man, who
took refuge in the depths of a carriage to hide his distress
from lookers-on'.

Watching the rapid decline of Mme. Arman's health,
France must have anticipated its end, if, possibly, not so
soon and, certainly, not so suddenly. One would have
thought, too, that their relationship during their last years
together had retained little that would be greatly missed.
All the same, Mme. Arman's death seems to have come as a
considerable psychological shock to France. For, during
the years that followed her death, he filled a number of
small notebooks with his thoughts about her – and this for
France was quite exceptional and extraordinary, for he had
never been anything of a diarist. The closest he had ever
come to it before were brief maritime jottings – 'grey sky',
'storm', 'sunset – wind – clouds the colour of pigeons'
throats' – the simplest of pegs on which to hang his memories. Nor had he even kept a 'work-book' in which to jot
ideas, observations, information that might later be of use

to him. But now he filled page after page of these school-boy's pocket-books, with their cheap card covers, coarse hairy paper and cross-lined leaves, with his beautiful, sloping hand-writing.

Was it the routine that he missed – or the presence – or the maternal comfort of which there had always been a large element in Mme. Arman's attitude towards him? Did some nagging sense of regret or remorse raise a spectre in his mind that demanded to be appeased before it would let him rest? Or, now that the tiresomenesses which had jarred their day-to-day contact had been removed by Mme. Arman's death, was it 'the first Mme. Arman', his accomplice of the hide-out in the rue Washington, that he remembered and mourned?

Some two months after Mme. Arman's death France went with two friends, Doctor Couchoud and Madame Komulska, a young Hungarian travelling as his secretary, on his six-teenth visit to Italy, his first without Mme. Arman. That he chose an itinerary which included most of the places which he and Mme. Arman had regularly visited – Naples, Rome, Perugia, Assisi, Siena, Florence, Bologna – places where he was bound to meet memories at every step and round every corner the powerful pull of association, seems to show that he was not so much seeking to forget Mme. Arman as to find her again – even if only in order to be able to forget her.

She was there as soon as they arrived at Naples – 'The same guitar in the cabaret, but she will not hear it. I have only seen Naples with her, I have only seen Naples through her. I am surprised when I find the world surviving her.' The next day he wrote – 'She makes me like death. O. has said the only words that console me. "We shall soon rejoin her." She would not consent to grow old, but that does not console me. Errors and my faults add to my pain.'

Yet even if Mme. Arman made him think of death, there were still many things which made him think of life. On fine evenings the sunsets, turning the slopes of Vesuvius rose-coloured, were a delight to him. Had he, somewhat belatedly, also acquired a liking for 'le moment crepusculaire'? One day some 'rose-coloured houses, surrounded by greenery' caught his eye – also, in the museum, paintings by Titian and Correggio – and a Schedoni which had pleased the President de Brosses, Voltaire's enemy and victim, and which France also found 'charming'. There was a 'light mist' early on; then 'sun'. But after the sun the shade of Mme. Arman returned – 'She would never give anything up. And now she has nothing, not even her rings. Yet now she misses nothing . . . Alive she missed everything – her fortune, her life, my love.' Two days later, on Easter Sunday, he wrote – 'I regret her not for the happiness I promised myself with her – her character . . . and circumstances held out little promise of that . . . but because in her I have lost my *raison d'être*, and, it seems to me, almost the possibility of living. And yet life takes hold of me by all sorts of curiosities and caresses (*la vie me reprend par toutes sortes de curiosités et blandices*).'

When the weather was bad he missed Mme. Arman the most. On a 'grey' day his mood matched it, and he regretted particularly that Mme. Arman was not there to pull him out of it – 'I miss her in everything because she loved and adored me. Emma (Laprevotte) said to me "No one will ever love you the way she did." ' The following day his thoughts were still in the same trough – 'I know well that her terrible illusion spoilt my life and hers, and that we could no longer be happy together. My stupidity in B. (Buenos Aires) became criminal by its effects. Her state of mind was compromised by her health but that does not console me.' One wonders what France meant by Mme. Arman's 'terrible illusion' – her belief that life and love did not change, that France was dependent on her, or, simply, her belief in the durability of such essentially transient things as her salon and her social success?

Shortly before he left Naples, France, on an evening stroll, wandered along a street that had several antique shops 'much frequented by her. Why does her absence suddenly seem to me like an abyss . . . Here it is not on seeing the bas-reliefs of Eurydice . . . that I weep for her the most. It is on seeing the soft-hat of —— that I burst into sobs. Oh, the force of little things. They repeat themselves. Life is made up of them.'

And so it was all through Italy as France and Mme. Arman made their last journey together. In the train France followed his thoughts as well as the line to Rome – 'the incredible and monstrous thing is that in my boredom after her loss I search out her faults, I reproach her with certain small contrarities, a few imperceptible failings.' In Rome he wrote – 'She must kill me. For I do not want to, I can not, kill her in me' . . . On the way to Perugia he jotted down, in very shaky writing, – 'Tyrannical, perhaps, but then I weep for my servitude.' At Siena he remembered her as she had been when they first came there. Between Siena and Florence he had the impression that he had 'left her at Paris, for I have the painful regret of seeing beautiful things without her.'

When he came to Florence, which since that first '*voyage de noces*' with Gaston and Jeanne, had, more than anywhere else, been 'their' town, he met the full flood of his memories. First he noted – 'This time I find her again', but then, as if not entirely certain, he crossed it out and wrote instead, 'her absence fills the town'. Here he saw her in his dreams – 'I saw her this night. I knew she was dead and I had less surprise than joy that she was given back to me. We went for a walk in a damp countryside.' On a day of bad weather he noted – 'Since she has been dead it seems I wrong her perpetually.' At Bologna this thought was still in his mind – 'What heavy and continued reproaches she makes to me for having come here without her, without her for the first time.' The next morning he saw her 'hardened in age and character. I do not regret her any the less.' By the time they reached Verona, France was finding that, 'now that she is no more, the sights of Italy have lost for me, not their beauty, but their intimacy and familiar charm which I shall not find again. They survive her too impassively.' The next day he added as an after- or continuing-thought – 'and then she departed unappeased.' Finally France came to Milan, their last stop in Italy and found one of their 'old hotels, but hotels do not keep memories and do not speak of the past'.

In the train on the way back to Paris he dreamed of her again and at Basle he noted the chestnut trees under which the last time he had gone there with her they had sheltered from the rain. As they approached Paris, France had the 'feeling that I am nearing her again. It is there that I left her.'

Yet even when seeking Mme. Arman through the cities of Italy, where they had spent perhaps their happiest moments together – only to find that he really felt closest to her in Paris – France still had his days of sun, his moments of pleasure which for all his pre-occupation and sadness he could not, and would not, deny. In Naples he had written – 'I have an insatiable need of gaiety which life can no longer satisfy' – but that was the beginning of the journey. By its end he must surely have changed his mind. In Rome there had been the Villa Borghese and a small temple that particularly pleased him. He had visited the antique shop where, on an earlier visit, he had bought a statue. This time he bought a fan. In Perugia there was an irritable note – a healthy sign – 'to keep up with Couchoud I wear myself out and cannot find a moment even to send a postcard'. At Assisi there was 'the little church of Duccio', which had 'pretty bas-reliefs'. An effigy, also, caught his attention – 'Sainte-Claire has a strong chin, and a robust air if one can judge from this made-up mummy'. In Siena there was, of of course, the cathedral, and a fine figure by Donatello. At

S

Bologna he noted some carving of 'an extraordinary quality', a very poor museum, and that 'K. (Mme. Komulska) had a pretty figure', but then added as if in immediate contrition for so unfaithful a thought, 'I keep in my heart a miserable emptiness like the pit of one's stomach.' There were the mosaics and a blue sky at Ravenna; at Verona the 'pretty doors' and painted houses as well as the 'noisy sadness of a Sunday'; on the way to Milan there was Lake Garda, 'very calm', and 'the sun on the mountains the colour of rose flame'. Like many of the women in France's life, and, for that matter, the men also, Mme. Komulska wrote a book about him, under her maiden name of Sandor Kemeri, in which this journey figured prominently. She detailed France in it as 'lively, youthful, ardent, impassioned by beauty, always interested and full of a gentle joy'.

Three years later, in 1913, France paid his last visit to Italy. This time all his notes were contained in a few pages, and only at Florence did Mme. Arman come into them. There, in the dining-room of the hotel, where they had stayed on their first visit, he was to remember her – 'How many times have I dined here with her! Old things last; old people do not.' It was an abrupt dismissal that had the finality of a slamming door.

Back in residence and at work in the Villa Saïd, France found no dearth of applicants for the post of *confidante* left vacant by Mme. Arman. Sandor Kemeri, Marie Scheikevitch and others, gave him youthful company, and, if one can go by entries in his carnets, which he continued to keep all that year, there were some who were prepared to give him more than this. In the middle of that summer he went for a few days to Burgundy for a romantic rendez-vous. However, Mme. Arman seems to have gone with him. At Macon he could think of little else but an earlier visit he had made with her. This may well have been part of the reason why the visit does not seem to have been a success. The morning after,

France admitted he had not found what he had lost and sought. A later entry shows him somewhat discountenanced to find that his partner evidently had not either.

Subsequent notes in his carnets show France trying to pluck up courage to write a letter of rupture to a matronly figure with whom he seems to have become entangled against his better judgement. She had a grown-up son – why the thought of the son should horrify France, who had been in the habit of telling Brousson that love began at forty, one cannot know, but obviously it did. In his notes France concealed his loves under the transparent disguise of their initials, and the number of letters cavorting through his carnets, although the shade of Mme. Arman still held her own, show that over that first summer of bereavement, France was not short of consolations. But by the autumn he seems to have got fed up with the lot of them, for he noted bitterly that only Mme. Arman was 'faithful' and 'sure'; all the others were only 'decoys'.

Perhaps France was now feeling the need of something other than love, missing the comfortable surround of a personal, not necessarily passionate, relationship. For it would seem that it was in answer to such a need that in December he performed what was to prove the most significant action of a turbulent year. He installed in the Villa Saïd, for the moment only as a housekeeper, Emma Laprevotte, Mme. Arman's maid, who had often accompanied them on their travels. Emma was thirty-nine, reasonably handsome but far from strikingly beautiful, not very intelligent although perceptive about people, but gentle, affectionate, quiet – France was once to say of her, 'Tico is a precious woman. She has an opinion on everything but never gives it.' Emma was a woman who knew her place and kept to it, and in consequence, that place, both in France's house and his heart, grew swiftly.

As with most innovations, however, Emma's installation was not trouble-free. The day she arrived, Joséphine left.

There was not room in the Villa Saïd for two house-keepers. At times in Joséphine's day there had not always seemed room for one. But Joséphine was not the only one incensed by Emma's arrival. Some of those who, over the last months, had been spreading the charms of their youth in front of the great man's feet, were extremely annoyed to see someone else in his house and in what they may, secret-ly, have considered their place.

But still Emma's presence, if it comforted France, did not, for the moment at any rate, restrain him. Perhaps it was for that reason amongst others, that France had chosen her to live with him. He would feel no obligation to behave himself in front of Emma, who knew all about his past as well as his present. In the year following Emma's arrival, France had what seems to have been his most serious love affair since he had lost the 'first Mme. Arman'. She was an American, Laura-Julie-Sterrette MacAdoo, thirty-five, twice married, and now Madame Gagey. She had literary tastes and some talent. France helped her with some articles and she was his audience for much of *Les Dieux ont Soif*, on which he was working at this time. So much so that when it was nearly finished, she wrote to him that it was in part hers for so much of it had been created under her very eyes.

Yet the liaison between France and Mme. Gagey, or 'la belle Floridienne', as he generally called her, was not only literary, and the course of it revolved around romantic rendez-vous, in the churches of Saint-Philippe-du-Roule – a macabre choice, since it was little more than a year since it had been the scene of Mme. Arman's funeral – and Saint-Germain-des-Prés. However, France jibbed at putting him-self under the obligation either of marriage or of another acknowledged liaison such as he had had with Mme. Arman. When his affair with Mme. Gagey had reached the point when he had to go forward into one or the other, or back – he went back.

For 'la belle Floridienne' this was a final disappointment

in a life in which she never seems to have found a firm foothold. Part of her feeling for France seems, in fact, to have been based on the belief that in France's talent she had at last discovered something solid on which to build. When France was beginning to back-pedal she wrote him a letter in which she told him that she no longer had much hope of happiness or even contentment. Her hold on life was very light and it would not take much to make her release it. This was a clear warning to France, but one that he did not take. He had, she continued, made her believe that she helped him to live and that in his own unhappiness he could not live without her. He had taught her not to be afraid, and that the essential thing was not to feel complete except in someone else. It was like that she had loved him, allowing herself to be guided by her instinct only.

France answered the letter but not the appeal, and on the 17th December, 1911, Mme. Gagey killed herself with an overdose of sleeping pills. France followed the coffin to the cemetery of Les Batignolles, and there had to face the accusations of Mme. Gagey's husband. A few days later he took Emma away to the South of France.

If Mme. Gagey, with some right, could lay claim to playing a part in the creation of *Les Dieux ont Soif*, so too, had she been able to, could Mme. Arman – for it had been begun in her lifetime and in her company. But even more than to either of these, *Les Dieux ont Soif* belongs to France himself. For, although of necessity as a historical novel it contained little that was strictly autobiographical – although France was writing about the stones and streets he had always lived amongst which inevitably threw back echoes of himself as well as his characters – it was in essence his summing-up. Into the revolutionary experience France transfused his own experience of life. In the tight, claustrophobic conditions of the Terror, France played out not only the revolutionary drama, but also his own personal drama, the conflict between his love of life on the one side and his fear of the various eventualities which he saw as pitfalls lying only lightly below the surface on the other – intimidation, injustice, poverty, discomfort, loneliness and, ultimately, death.

These two themes – the historical and the personal – run side by side through the novel, but they are closely interwoven. As the protagonist of the one, France chose Evariste Gamelin, a poor painter continuing courageously to support not only his artistic integrity, but also his widowed mother; of the other Maurice Brotteaux, a cultured aristocrat, who had possessed virtually everything under the ancien régime – rank, riches, innumerable beautiful women, beautiful pictures, lands – and now possessed nothing except a worn puce-coloured frock coat, a copy of Lucretius, and a philosophic attitude to life.

Gamelin, an idealistic and ardent supporter of the Revolution, becomes a juror on a Revolutionary Tribunal, and from then is swept away by the current of fanaticism which turned the Rule of Virtue into the Terror. France is at pains to show that Gamelin, if a somewhat cold character, is yet normally charitable and kindly – for example, he depicts him in an early chapter giving half the meagre ration of bread he has stood more than an hour in a queue to receive to a woman he passes in the street, a total stranger but obviously ill and in greater need than he. He emphasises also that the jurors, caught up in this frenzy of killing, are ordinary people, who in normal circumstances would be leading normal lives – 'They were men, neither better nor worse than others. Innocence, most often, is a piece of luck, not a virtue; anyone who accepted to be in their place would have acted as they did.' To France the Terror was an obsession and those in power were the obsessed. The problem was what should ordinary people do in such a moment of madness, when the ordinary balance of society is upset and it is the insane who are in control, the sane who are shut up in their power? France's answer seems to be – 'as little as possible, and wait for the storm to blow over. If one has a God, trust in Him; if not, trust in one's luck.'

But what of those whose luck is out? Brotteaux from the beginning is obviously a predestined victim. He has accepted philosophically the change from wealth to poverty, from distinction to insignificance, from a château to a garret, but clearly he is going to be asked to accept a great deal more. One has Emma's authority for thinking that France was imagining himself in Brotteaux's shoes, even if he did not model Brotteaux's character too exactly after his own. Some years later when she was considerably more to France than his housekeeper, but not yet his wife, she told a friend, Mareel le Goff – 'In *Les Dieux ont Soif* he has imagined what would happen to M. France in a time of trouble, deprived of his possessions, of his books, of his belongings – he was Brotteaux.'

Due to ill-chance, and the indiscretion of a former mistress, Brotteaux is traced to his garret, arrested, put through a mockery of a trial, and finally executed. France treats him with compassion – as well he might – throughout his ordeal. Brotteaux's philosophical attitude stands up to the test, but he cannot stop himself being physically afraid at the moment of departure – 'He wished to smile; but an atrocious pain took hold of his heart . . . He was close to fainting. He continued none the less, "Mon père, you see my weakness. I love life and cannot leave it without regret." ' A life-long atheist, Brotteaux yet asked the priest to whom he was bidding farewell, to pray for him. In all humility, Brotteaux – and France – were allowing for the possibility of doubt. They might be wrong, there might be a God and if so the prayers of Père Longuemaur might do Brotteaux some good. As he stepped into the tumbril, Brotteaux was welcomed by the young prostitute whom he had befriended – in complete disinterest and without even seeking to have the debt discharged – and as an experienced voluptuary, the sight of her

beautiful neck kept his attention on the way to the guillotine. If one's luck is out, France seems to say, and one has
consciously to go through the ordeal, the fates may still
relent and send some aid to see one over the awkward
moment – and it is only a moment, not the whole of life.

France's lifelong familiarity with the events and setting
of the Revolution, enabled him to bring it vividly to life – it
was, of course, to him not really an historical period at all,
but rather a backwards extension of his own life – and to
sketch in with complete historical accuracy many sub-
sidiary aspects such as the military miracle that was being
achieved, even as the political experiment headed for disaster.
Concerned though he was with death, France still showed
his love for life. Despite the Revolution the sun still shone,
and when it did, no one ever saluted it more joyously – 'It
was morning, and it was spring. Sunbeams, intoxicating
as young wine, danced on the walls, and played gaily round
the roofs.'

In the end and at last, France did, too, exorcise his fear.
Its passing was symbolized by that of Robespierre – 'Paris
in its grace and immensity, smiled at the sun; hope was reborn in the hearts of prisoners, merchants light-heartedly
opened their shops, business-men felt themselves richer,
young men, happier, women more beautiful – all because
of the fall of Robespierre.' It was the end, not only of the
Terror, but of France's particular personal terror also.
Fear, like suffering, had its place in life, but even in fearful
times it must not be allowed to dominate to the point of
obscuring one's interest in living.

Les Dieux ont Soif is not only by far the greatest novel
France ever wrote, it is one of the greatest of French novels.

France's Socialist colleagues did not at all like the interpretation of the Revolution which he put forward in *Les
Dieux ont Soif*. Remarks such as – 'Men will never be equal,
there will always be large and small, fat and thin', or again,

'One must govern men such as they are, not as one would like them to be', went very much against the grain, particularly of the idealists who still saw in Socialism not only the key to a better world, but also the clue to a better man.

Nor did they like much more France's next book, *La Revolte des Anges*, not published until the spring of 1914 but which like *Les Dieux ont Soif* had been started in Mme. Arman's lifetime. France had taken seventeen chapters of it on that voyage of self-discovery to Italy after Mme. Arman's death. One evening he was reading one of these chapters to Mme. Komulska when a street band started outside. Throwing coins down had the reverse effect to that intended, for either hopefully or gratefully they continued to play on. Finally the manager had to be called in to get rid of them. With the gravity of a bishop France accepted his apologies – and his assurances that he would not again allow such an intrusion on France's 'religious meditation' – it happened to be Holy Week.

La Revolte des Anges was concerned with revolt rather than revolution – the revolt of fallen angels against their Ruler – and much of it was simply an amusing account of their adventures in mortal form on earth – but if the treatment was lighthearted, the thought underlying it was as gloomy as that which characterized the *Histoire Sans Fin*. What was the point of change, since it always led to the same thing? Power corrupts, inevitably and absolutely. Men, and, it appeared, the angels also were bound by the chain of circumstance, and could at best hope, not to break their bonds, but simply to ease their chafing by not struggling too much. Borne on the crest of the wave formed by the success of *Les Dieux ont Soif*, *La Revolte des Anges* had almost as enthusiastic a reception, but it was really too much of a *roman à clef* to be appreciated for long outside the particular Parisian circles who held the key.

The strongest Socialist critics of France's books should, however, have been conciliated by his activities on their be-

half which were many and various. The years 1911–1914 saw
France still taking up cudgels on behalf of those he considered to be the victims of particular cases of social injustice – such as Durand, a trade unionist accused of arranging the murder in a riot of one of his rivals; Gustave
Hervé, imprisoned for his politically inflammatory articles;
Rousset, a soldier of the Foreign Legion sentenced without
a fair trial for the murder of one of his companions. He still
made himself the champion of the oppressed and suffering
in obscure, far distant places such as the Congo, Rumania
and Armenia. He still opposed the Tsarist despotism in
Russia. He still contributed regularly to *l'Humanité*. He
still attended countless banquets and other Socialist social
occasions. With these he still mingled other ostensibly
literary occasions, such as a meeting of the Amis de Montaigne, of whom he was subsequently elected president; a
gathering to celebrate the fifth anniversary of the removal of
Zola's remains to the Pantheon; another to pay a com-
memorative tribute to Tolstoy, who had died the year
before; an after-dinner speech to the Société des Études
Rabelaisiennes, which, if the dinner was worthy of the subject, must have been a considerable test. Even on these
occasions, however, his speeches tended to have a political
slant. His tribute to Tolstoy, for example, contained an
eloquent appeal for peace – 'He was the enemy of war . . .
on this grave question, the most grave of all, everyone
must accept his responsibility. This universal peace which
we desire with all our hearts . . . will not come at the call
of the weak who bewail their fate. Let us hasten its coming
by a continuous effort, keeping in mind the necessities on
which the world runs.'

Peace, perhaps because he sensed the approach of war,
seems to have become France's main political preoccupation during these years. With a violence surprising in so
generally undemonstrative a character, he opposed and
criticized any governmental measure that he deemed to be

provocative or escalatory. Thus an interview of 1912 appeared under the heading of 'Foutez le Camp' and contained a violent denunciation of the 'loi des trois ans', despite the fact that the Minister responsible for this measure of conscription was Poincaré, not only an old friend, but the advocate who, the previous year, had pleaded and won for France a tricky case in which he sought to restrain Lemerre from publishing, on the grounds that it was a work of immaturity and haste, the *Histoire de France*, the manuscript of which France had delivered as part of that famous and infamous contract of thirty years before.

Passionate and partisan though he was in his own country, France could still for the benefit of outsiders, size up the situation clearly and coolly. An article published in *The English Review* a year before war finally broke out, shows him pointing out differences between the English and the French attitude – 'What strikes me in the character of the French is their idealism, and the disinterest of their likes and dislikes. If the English dislike the Germans it is because Germany is her rival in the markets of the world. In France you will hear nothing, you will never read of any economic tension, rivalry or competition . . . There is something else between the two countries; animosity . . . This enmity must cease. We are no longer in an age when the victor destroys and reduces the conquered to slavery. Today a war would weaken more or less equally both victor and vanquished . . . It would be a useless disaster, a pointless crime.' It was a fine appeal, but like so many others at that time, unheard.

If France in public seems to have been as active as ever, so too was he in private, despite the ameliorating presence of Emma in his house. Even the tragedy of 'la belle Floridienne' does not seem to have quietened him down. His friends were trying hard at this time to get him to marry again, clearly hoping, as one might for a hot-headed adolescent, that marriage might cool his ardour. But their efforts may have been partly in self-defence, for the wives and mistresses of even his closest friends were far from sacred. Georges Brandès, the distinguished Danish philosopher, was one to suffer. André Rouveyre tells us – 'About 1912 Brandès received, full in his back from the hand of Anatole France, the cruellest blow of his life. It was one of those treacheries which appears of varying importance according to the latitude, but for which Parisians generally have only laughter. Briefly, Brandès was, by his friend, knocked head over heels in the most complete defeat.' Brandes' letters show that his reaction was one of absolute astonishment and complete despair – 'That on which I had built my life has fallen' – 'I imagined that he was my best friend: on every occasion, even in public, he declared, "I love and admire you"; his last letter ended with these words'. 'You must look upon me as half-crazy, since I, the least familiar of men, have told you the most painful secret of my life. But the news came to me in so abrupt, so unforeseen a fashion that I have lost all sense of balance, all reason.' If it was any consolation to Brandès, not all of the laughter would have been directed against him, for France, by his amorous antics, was making a ludicrous spectacle of himself as well as of his friends. This affair, did not, however, have as tragic an outcome as that with Mme. Gagey, nor does it seem to have been long-lasting. Brandès was eventually to forgive France, but not until he was eighty.

By the beginning of 1913, however, both time and the presence of Emma began to have their effect. It was significant that when France went on his annual trip to Italy he took Emma with him as his companion; even more so that he made a will in which he left to Emma, 'all . . . that the law permits me to withdraw from my normal heirs.' When France paid an official visit to London in December, 1913, he insisted, too, on taking Emma with him, much to the embarrassment of his reception committee who, in those days of strict social convention, did not know what to make of her, nor, in fact, what to do about her. J. Lewis May, one of those who met both of them on this occasion, tells us that France, 'when he went to visit "the great houses", could not for the life of him understand how it was they always tried to persuade him to leave her at the hotel, and at the banquet at which Lord Redesdale presided, she was a nice problem. She was dissembled somewhere in the body of the room.' Thanks to some forceful publishing by John Lane, and some excellent translations by Frederick Chapman, Lafcadio Hearn and Lewis May himself, France's fame was now almost as great in England as in France. His visit included a tea-party with Mrs. Asquith at No. 10 Downing Street, meetings with the Fabian Society and the Socialist Party as well as the immense banquet at the Savoy attended by the most famous of literary names, amongst them, Kipling, Barrie, Shaw, Arnold Bennett, Masefield, Galsworthy and Gosse. Even in his speech at the Savoy, France managed to include his puff for peace – 'The Roman people loved justice and established equitable laws and a just peace on the countries they conquered. It is no longer a question of conquering this world, but of pacifying it. Work, let us work together for the peace of the world.' Lewis May tells us that at the time he wondered why France ended on so exhortatory a note, but that eight months later he realized the reason only too well.

France's more mellow mood showed in his choice of the work to follow *La Revolte des Anges*. In 1913 he returned to his childhood and the *quais* and began the series of sketches that were eventually to fill his last two books, *Le Petit Pierre*, and *La Vie en Fleur*. France gave these a fictitious form, but at the end of *La Vie en Fleur* gave authority also for them to be considered largely autobiographical – 'These recollections . . . are true so far as the principal facts, characters and customs are concerned . . . When I started to recollect . . . many witnesses of my childhood were still alive. I therefore had to change their names and their circumstances so that I should not offend either their pride or their modesty . . . For my own part, I was not displeased to change on paper my name and state. I found it easier thus to talk of myself, to accuse myself, to praise myself, to pity myself, smile at myself, scold myself at my leisure. At Venice, in olden times, the inhabitants who did not wish to be accosted, attached to a button of their coat a mask the size of the palm of a hand, thus warning passers-by to leave them alone. In the same way, this assumed name does not disguise me, but shows my intention not to appear in public.'

For France this was a second childhood, unspoilt by any signs of senility, but showing on the contrary a remarkable reflorescence of youthful energy and high spirits. In fact, at that age and time, it was the perfect task for France, liberating him from the cares of the world at a moment when these cares were growing particularly heavy, and allowing him to wander, in the leisurely, unpredictable way he liked, along the *quais* into a different world, only his life's time away but immeasurably further off considered in terms of change. This venture into the past went so well that France, by the summer of 1914, had written a large number of the episodes that were eventually to form the bulk of the book. Several of these were printed in various Parisian papers. *La Revue de Paris* started to serialize *Le Petit Pierre*, which served to herald its forthcoming appearance in book form. In fact, however, *Le Petit Pierre* was not to be published for a further five years.

For the second time in his life, France was unlucky that just when his personal affairs seemed to be shaping towards a period of calm and creative contentment, outside events should decide otherwise. Eighteen years before, when his election to the Academy, confirming his position amongst the leading writers of France, and the string of critical and creative successes behind him, had seemed not only to promise, but almost to assure a period of peaceful productivity, he had run instead into the troubled waters of the Affair. Now, when in these childhood recollections, he had tapped an indisputably rich vein, and in his personal life had made a no less valuable discovery in Emma, both his prospects and his plans were brought to an abrupt halt by the outbreak of war.

For France, the great but impersonal tragedy of war was closely preceded by the more personally poignant tragedy of Jaurès' death. One of the most bitter opponents of war, and one of the most active in seeking to avoid it, Jaurès, during the evening of the 31st July, 1914 – a day which he had spent, like many before it, seeking both in the Chambre and outside it to find any means of at least delaying the outbreak of hostilities – was shot while sitting in his favourite café, the *Café du Croissant*, by a member of the Action Française, who had mistaken Jaurès' desire for peace for a lack of patriotism. He was killed almost instantaneously. France was shattered by the news and the shock showed in a letter printed on the front page of *l'Humanité* on the 2nd August – 'My heart feels as if it will burst. I can but stammer. My grief stifles me. Never to see again the . . . most noble of characters.' He recalled how important up to the end the things of the mind had remained, even for so occupied and preoccupied a man. On a visit less than a month before to Jaurès' house – 'a house . . . so modest, or to put it better, so poor – but so glorious' – he had found Jaurès reading a play of Euripides in the original. 'His great mind found its relief from study in study, and took its relaxation from one work in another.'

Jaurès' funeral took place on the 4th August, 1914.

———◆———

THE OUTBREAK OF WAR caught France entirely on the
wrong foot. It was not only that he was still suffering
severely from the shock of Jaurès' death; nor that war meant
the total eclipse of much that he had been working for over
the last few years; but also that he was, at that moment,
without a home of his own. The Villa Saïd was no more.
Over the years it had been becoming more and more un-
manageable as France's collections continued to grow. Nor
as the years passed did it become any less draughty, chill- or
smoke-swept; whereas France's sensitivity to these conditions obviously increased with age.

But the decisive reason for the Villa Saïd's downfall was
that it could provide no place for Emma that corresponded
with the position of importance she now held in France's
life. She was still living in the small housekeeper's room
under the roof, and for someone of her unsound health, this
was particularly unsatisfactory. It was more France's wish
than Emma's that she be provided with more suitable ac-
commodation, but the trouble was that as things were at the
Villa Saïd – and there were never more things that were in
any house – it was virtually impossible to change anything
without changing everything. So mainly for the sake of
Emma, France had eventually taken what considering his
fondness for the familiar, his basic inertia, his dislike of up-
heaval – and by any standards the problems posed by the
removal and rehousing of his possessions, let alone of himself and Emma, were major ones – was a most surprising,

if sensible, decision; and ordered the old house to be pulled down in order that a new and more convenient one could be built in its place.

In the timing of this decision France could not, as it had turned out, have been more unfortunate – or so it seemed at first. When war broke out, work was at the stage when the old Villa Saïd had been pulled down but as yet no start had been made on the new. Then, of course, all plans had to be shelved indefinitely, and France, who had hoped to be in his new house a year after the first pick had fallen on the old, saw his prospects of rebuilding recede into the far future. His possessions were scattered throughout Paris – most of his books in Calmann-Lévy's basement; pieces of his furniture, many of his pictures, prints and other items from his collections in store with dealers or friends. But the bulk of his belongings France had taken with him to Versailles, where he and Emma were still in the process of accomplishing a most difficult move into a most difficult house, that seems to have been just about as unsuitable a choice, even for a temporary refuge, as France could possibly have made.

The house had belonged to his old friend Dr. Couchoud with whom he had travelled in Italy on that journey of self-discovery after Mme. Arman's death. Couchoud had bought it relatively recently, as a professional speculation, intending to turn it into a convalescent home, but the growing threat of war had prevented him going ahead with his plans for its conversion. At the same time, and for the same reason, he found himself in financial difficulties through having had to produce the whole of the considerable purchase price on which he could now get no credit.

France has often been accused of being cool in his treatment of his friends and unnecessarily unconcerned with their affairs, but on this occasion at any rate he seems to have acted with great generosity. For he offered to buy the building off Couchoud, and to use it as his home until such time as the new Villa Saïd was ready. There may have been an element of irresponsibility in France's offer – an indolent acceptance of what on the surface may have seemed an easy solution to his problems as well as Couchoud's. Yet France's main object in making his offer was undoubtedly to help Couchoud out of his difficulties, even at the cost of some discomfort to himself. Couchoud, of course, was only too delighted to accept.

Yet, as France would have been the first to prophesy, the result of this generous and good-hearted gesture was utterly disastrous. The house needed a lot doing to it to make it habitable, and even then, with its institutional aspect and impersonal atmosphere, provided about as incongruous a setting for France's very personal possessions, and for that matter for France himself, as it would be possible to imagine. Calmettes has recorded the pain it caused him to see some of France's best pieces cluttered around a hideous modern conservatory, and all the outbuildings full of unpacked crates and cases, for either France had over-estimated the capacity of his new home or he had miscalculated the quantity of stuff he had in the old. If Calmettes reacted in this way, how much more agonized must France's feelings have been.

In one way, however, it was probably fortunate that the house was so obviously unsuitable and that France was so immediately and utterly unhappy in it; for the nightmarish prospect of staying in such surroundings for the length of the war when it came, and it was now only a few weeks away, stirred him into unusually swift action in search of an alternative. France and Emma had started their move to Versailles in June. By the time war broke out, France had not only made contact with a country house-agent in search of a country-cottage somewhere in the Touraine or Anjou, but had been offered what was in fact not a cottage at all but a small manor house – la Béchellerie, at Saint-Cyr-sur-Loire, only two kilometres from Tours itself. The coming of the war decided the deal and, on the

2nd September, France and Emma were escorted to the station by the Versailles Commissioner of Police, specially charged by the prefect to see to their safety, to set forth for this house which France had not yet seen but which, in fact, was to be his home for the rest of his life.

The journey, in the disorganized conditions of that moment, took several days; and, at the end of it, France and Emma found themselves in a cold, empty house in a bad state of disrepair, with no servants and no furniture. This, however, would have been supportable and remediable, for they soon managed to rake up a few chairs, beds and tables, a small black desk at which France could work, an armchair with broken springs in which he could, to some extent, relax, had not France at the end of September unwittingly brought down on his head a storm of terrifying violence, only really conceivable in, as it was largely attributable to, the hysterical atmosphere of those first frenzied days of war.

The Germans had shelled Rheims cathedral. France, as shocked as anyone, wrote a letter of protest that was published in *La Guerre Sociale* on the 22nd September. In it he declared furiously that 'barbarians, invoking the God of Christians, have fired one of the most magnificent of Christian memorials'. But he then went on, unwisely as it turned out, but quite unwittingly – for he had often in the past taken a similar line with impunity – to urge that when the time came for victory and French troops were standing on German soil, they should take care that they did not commit any similar crime against civilization and against humanity. In that glorious moment when they, 'had conquered the last army and reduced the last enemy fortress,' continued France, the French people should use their triumph 'to admit into their friendship the conquered people.'

There was nothing in this that could possibly have caused any balanced reader to doubt France's patriotism – he had probably added the last paragraph without much thought simply as a well-meaning attempt to channel the widespread anger, which included his own, at the shelling of a cathedral, into a more humanitarian outlet – but there were few readers who, at that time, retained any semblance of balance. Even to mention the possibility, however remote, of friendship with the Germans, was considered by the Parisian public in their inflammatory, belligerent mood of that moment, as tantamount to treason. Virtually the whole of the Press, from garret to gutter, rounded on France, and many of the public followed their lead. Even figures as distinguished as Charles Maurras – 'Anatole France . . . Your atrocious folly is the real source of these rivers of blood,' – and Barrès – 'Who speaks of friendship?' – both in their time devoted disciples of France, threw themselves into the attack. On a lower level France was accused of being a traitor, a secret agent, another Esterhazy; and his arrest, trial, and even execution, were variously demanded.

Even through the tortuous postal channels which led to la Béchellerie, France received a flood of abusive, often menacing letters, of which this one from Versailles was typical – 'Thanks, in the name of all Versaillois, for having disembarrassed us of your dirty carcass . . . Soon you will be judged as you deserve. Sale crapule, fripouille, va.' Nor was it only threatening letters that France received. Shouting bands appeared at his gates; menacing figures were seen, or thought to be seen, lurking round the outbuildings. France became so alarmed that he asked for, and was given, police protection.

On the individual level this was, of course, a splendid opportunity for the settling of old scores. Some of those who hated him because of the part he had played in the Affair, or because of his Socialism; others who were simply jealous of his success, were only too delighted to have the chance to heave their brick. But the main impetus behind this tidal wave of abuse was impersonal. It was simply France's bad luck that he had happened to stick his head up and his neck out at a moment when a mood of uncontrolled, and probably uncontrollable, hysteria was seeking a target.

Yet a bucket of garbage smells no sweeter for having been tipped over one by chance rather than intent. Caught in strange surroundings, without the support of his books or other belongings – which in times of crisis had so often in the past provided a refuge – at a moment of extreme fatigue and distress, France crumpled completely. On the 29th September, a week after the appearance of the original article, he sought to excuse himself, again in *La Guerre Sociale*, as a 'Frenchman concerned about the glory of his country'. The following day, in a pathetic but also ludicrous effort to prove his patriotism, he sent a letter to the Minister of War, Millerand, asking to be called up – 'Many people seem to think that in time of war my style is worth nothing. Since they may be right . . . make me into a soldier.'

France persisted that he was serious in this offer to the extent that he arranged an interview with a military board at Tours, made Calmettes search out in Paris the birth certificate that was necessary for it, and declared to a reporter sent down by *Le Petit Parisien* that he considered himself 'already a soldier', and that he had only a few formalities still to complete before he became 'a soldier, a simple soldier and proud to be one'. However, when on the 27th October Calmettes arrived at la Béchellerie with the birth certificate, he found France in bed, ill from exhaustion and emotion. In his place Calmettes went to the military board and asked for France's exemption on grounds of ill-health. With possibly a secret smile to himself, but keeping a perfectly straight face so far as Calmettes was concerned, the colonel in charge formally granted his request. So France, at the age of seventy, did not after all become 'a simple soldier'.

Mollified by the abject spectacle into which they had reduced the most famous writer in France; also by the interview reported in *Le Petit Parisien* of 21st October, in which

France admitted the error of his views – 'I spoke too soon . . . I have lived too much in the world of ideas . . . I feel a profound pain at the thought that anyone could believe I was not entirely in support of the unanimous uprising by which civilization has withstood barbarism' – the Press at last forgave him and called off its hounds. 'Anatole France,' wrote *l'Homme Enchaîné* on the 1st November, 'will not be a soldier after all. It is a pity; but Anatole France will write some heroic lines which will console us for having a soldier the less on the Front.'

It was less than a month and a half from the time the storm blew up until it blew over, but its effect on France was great, deepening the depression caused by the outbreak of war to the point when he wrote to a friend in Paris asking for poison, a request which even if clearly not intended to be taken seriously, was yet equally clearly meant to express an extreme of despair and distaste for a world at war. Ségur, visiting him at la Béchellerie some time afterwards, found him still a shadow of his former self, careful and circumspect in his conversation, pathetically polite and anxious to please – 'silent, constrained, reticent, falsely optimistic' – an almost unrecognizable relic of the irrepressible, incorrigible character who had delighted Ségur in pre-war years with his wit and wisdom.

Yet although at this time France must have felt that the fates as well as the Press were all against him, they may not, in fact, have been so entirely hostile as they seemed for they had led him, blindfold, to la Béchellerie – and if, with his eyes open, France had searched the length of Touraine, he would have been unlikely to have found a house that suited him better. It was a small, stone, Louis XIIIth manorhouse with a deep stone-slated roof from which the mansarded windows of the rooms of the first and only, upper floor, stood out. It had a good position on a small hill, with a pleasant view, from the terrace at the back, over the Choisille, a small tributary of the Loire, to distant hills. It had a fine spacious entrance-court which centred, when France and Emma first saw it, on a fountain mounted on artificial rocks. One of France's first actions was to have this removed and the centre of the drive grassed over, although in later years he was to incorporate in the middle of the lawn a small pool, the shape of a Venetian window, with round the side six urns bearing roses or pelagoniums, and at its head an elegant nymph on a plinth, preparing apparently to enter the water. Inside, the house had not many rooms, but they were mostly large and well-proportioned – on the ground floor, a salon, a dining-room, a smaller room that was to become Emma's sitting-room, and what had been a billiard-room and was to become a study and library – above, three main bedrooms.

The appearance of the house as it stood was spoilt by two iron-framed, glass porches, one at the front and one at the back – of which the iron was rusty and the glass broken; also by some Second Empire additions. But France soon had these removed, and when they were, la Béchellerie showed as a house as full of character as of years, mellow, peaceful, harmonious – the perfect setting for someone of France's age and tastes. France fell immediately under its spell. At first he had only rented it – but he was so quickly certain of his liking for it that only some eight months after he and Emma arrived there, he bought it – in April, 1915. By successive purchases in October 1916, May 1917 and November 1918, he added adjoining ground and buildings so that eventually he had enough land to ensure the pleasant round of his walks, enough trees to provide wood for his still considerable log-fires – he had brought down some of the immense fire-places from the Villa Saïd – and enough outbuildings to house the overflow of his possessions and his guests. In all the purchase of la Béchellerie and its various appendages was to cost him 80,000 francs, roughly the equivalent of £30,000 today.

A not inconsiderable stroke of luck for France in those first, otherwise luckless months of the war, was that Calmettes, while awaiting his call-up, had taken charge of a friend's removal business in Paris and therefore was well-placed to organize the transport, which for private use was then very much at a premium, of France's possessions from Versailles. There, in fact, they were no longer in Couchoud's convalescent home, but stacked anyhow in a flat in the rue de l'Occident. France had been fearful that Couchoud's house, which stood in isolated grounds and was on the main road into Paris through Versailles, would be one of the first to be pillaged by the invading German armies. He had, therefore, taken a flat that happened to be empty in one of the central districts of the town and had had all his belongings moved there. Unfortunately, the removal men had piled one thing on top of another, simply as they came out of the vans, regardless of their fragility or value. In consequence there was a lot of breakage and damage. Calmettes was horrified when he came to inspect, and found cooking utensils dumped on the exquisite silk seats of France's best chairs, his heavy bronzes piled in his china bowls many of which in consequence were cracked or broken. In Calmette's words, the scene was that of 'disaster, disorder and desolation'.

However, by the end of November the first vans from Versailles were arriving at la Béchellerie. Calmettes, who in the meantime, had been relieved of his command in Paris – possibly because of his preoccupation with the moving of France's possessions to the detriment of those of other clients – was there when they came and has recorded how the sight of his beloved belongings lifted France out of his gloom. According to Calmettes, France was like a child, jumping for joy as he found one after the other his old friends – 'Emma, look – our little table . . . the showcases, my table – they are bringing my desk. Here come the cases of Tanagra. It is the Fragonard – take care – and there is

Mme. Jaure, as beautiful as ever. See, Emma, here they all are – all our beloved *bibelots*.'

There were only five rooms in la Béchellerie fit to be furnished when the vans arrived – and these were soon so full that it was difficult to close their doors. The loft, the bathroom and again even the bath itself – for which France seems to have had no more use in the country than in the town – were all filled to capacity – even the kitchen, in which they ate, was stacked with piles of copper, brass and wrought-iron ware. But even so, a great quantity of stuff had, for the time being to be stored in the out-buildings. All France's Gothic furniture was put in the stables; other pieces which included fourteenth-century painted wood panels, fifteenth-century cabinets, and many of his antique statues and wood-carvings went into what had been the cowshed.

Calmettes, still awaiting his papers – he was eventually to become a sous-lieutenant in the Service de Ravitaillement – and regardless of the demands of his own family – stayed at la Béchellerie all through their first winter and the spring and early summer that followed. His main use was helping France arrange his furniture, hang his pictures, and prepare to receive the bulk of the books, which were still in Calmann-Lévy's basement. France often worked with him. He had always liked pottering about knocking nails into walls and moving things from one place to another. Brousson recorded his astonishment the first time he arrived to find France with a hammer instead of a pen in his hand. France noted his surprise – 'You look thunderstruck . . . Eh! Oui. It is the manual work which St. Bernard alternated with spiritual effort in his monastic rule. The change is excellent when I have had a little debauch. It doesn't happen often. However, it happened yesterday. Oh, my debauches would seem temperate to most people. But after a little escapade, nothing is more relaxing. Thus I am busy re-arranging the position of my pictures, putting on the right what was on the left.'

At la Béchellerie the chance of even a little debauch must have been slight, but France was still happy arranging his furniture. The interest and occupation of it provided just the restful, recuperative rhythm he needed to restore his interest in life and in living. As a collector France's main fault had always been that he collected too much. As a result the Villa Saïd had become overstocked to the point when he could not possibly or properly appreciate half that it contained. But this slow rearrangement of his possessions in la Béchellerie enabled him once more to make their acquaintance.

France would appear in the morning from his bedroom, clad in his long dressing-gown, wearing one of his housecaps, a hammer in his hand. From then on, he and Calmettes were hard at it for most of the day. It was a cold winter, so cold that Calmettes remembered his fingers sometimes stuck to the nails he was holding. In the evening, their work done, he, France and Emma would huddle around a vast stove which Calmettes had taken it upon himself to have fitted in the centre of the salon. France was rude about the stink of this stove; also about the draught-excluders which Calmettes had fitted to the doors and the windows, and which, France said, wrecked the appearance of his room. But, according to Calmettes, he, his stove and his draught-excluders saved all their lives that winter.

The only rooms which France and Calmettes were in a hurry to arrange in some sort of order, were the reception rooms on the ground floor. This was so that France could institute regular Sunday afternoon receptions after the model of those in the Avenue Hoche, but at which at first, of course, the attendance was extremely slight, only a few faithful friends from Paris – amongst them Couchoud, eager to do all that he could to make up for the disastrous experience France had had in his house at Versailles, and able to do quite a lot by way of looking after Emma's health; Leopold Kahn, a director of Calmann-Lévy, but who looked after

France's financial as well as his literary affairs – and a handful of local inhabitants, but amongst whom luckily was Courteline, who had also sought refuge in the district, and whose warm-hearted, warm-blooded personality often succeeded in cheering France up. With his house and himself in such a state, it is surprising that France should have attached such importance to these receptions that he first opened his doors in welcome less than a month after his furniture arrived. It can but show that France was feeling sadly out of things and that he greatly disliked it.

For the first eighteen months of the war, France and Emma remained peacefully at la Béchellerie arranging things and letting themselves be arranged by them. France had never lived in the country before – although he had stayed for long periods at Capian – but he came of country stock and his liking for the countryside grew in concert with his dislike of the war. Both are reflected in his letters of this time – 'The countryside – alas – is delightful' he wrote to a young admirer, Jacques Lion, in 1915 – his 'alas' presumably prompted by the thought that at such a time, to enjoy anything was clearly unpatriotic. But at the beginning of 1916 he wrote, 'Mankind horrifies me and I would find it difficult to say which I hate the most – its stupidity or wickedness.' By now comfortably installed at la Béchellerie, France was conscious that he was one of the fortunate few at that time, but that did not reconcile him to the folly of the world he saw around him – 'Apart from the fact that the meat is bad, the bread uneatable and the milk nauseating,' he wrote in October, 1915 – 'we live well and must be counted amongst the lucky of this frightful world. I do not know any other planets, but I doubt if there are worse than this.' Some six months before, he had written, 'It is not enough that the war causes frightful suffering; it turns into idiots all those that it doesn't make mad.'

But if France at this time, as he told Jacques Lion, was in general 'a misanthrope' – while not being a pessimist in that he believed in 'the ultimate triumph of our arms', he had nothing but compassion for many individual men. One such was Barthou, with whom he had quarrelled just before the war, and who lost his only son early in the fighting. Hearing of this, France not only wrote Barthou a letter of compassionate condolence but in another letter to Jules Couèt, old friend and eminent bibliographer and supposed to have been the original of the librarian Sariette in *La Revolte des Anges*, expressed his deep regret that they had ever quarrelled – 'Hearing that Louis Barthou had lost his only son, I cruelly regretted my quarrel with him. One should only pity men and never be irritated by them.'

During much of this time, France and Emma had the builders in. In October 1915 France wrote to Calmettes, by then back in Paris, that 'for the moment all communication is severed between the kitchen and the dining-room, and we receive our dishes through the window.' Calmettes had come down from Paris for the great day, a few months earlier, when France's books had arrived from Calmann Lévy's basement, and he and France were filmed arranging them by Sacha Guitry, then staying at Tours, and who had included France in a series of short films he was making – 'Ceux de chez nous'.

With the distress of the first months and the many distractions of those which followed, one would not have thought that France had much time to write, but in fact he quickly settled down to it. His first concern was to produce 'the heroic lines' which *l'Homme Enchainé* had called for, and he achieved this with a number of articles published in various Parisian papers, eventually moulded into a volume, under the title of *Sur la Voie Glorieuse*, and sold in the autumn of 1915 for the benefit of the war-wounded. France had used his splendid Jack-of-all-Trades, Calmettes, to collect the material for these articles, in which he was not only eager to prove his patriotism to those who were still doubtful of it, but also to express it, for in certain ways, in his concern for the buildings, the countryside, the independence of France, it was quite genuine. It was simply that he hated and feared war more than most people, and would go further than they would to prevent it.

It was particularly the wanton destruction of the beautiful buildings of France that roused his anger – 'I shall never cease to raise my feeble voice against the barbarians who have torn the beautiful robe of stone with which our ancestors clad France.' His feeling for 'the traditional France', not only its buildings, showed also in a picture he painted of a small country-town – 'From the top of the hill we saw a small town. Its name does not matter. It was a town of France peacefully settled in the hollow of a valley. It was charming, with its pointed roofs, its belfry set in the frame of its elegant church.' France imagined that the stones of this town could speak, and that they told why they were standing, and what they were standing for.

But France wrote other lines, less obviously 'heroic', that winter, for in a letter to Jacques Lion of the 11th February, 1915, he told that a wave of confidence, emanating from Paris, had had a tranquillizing effect upon him, so that he had set to and finished *Le Petit Pierre*, of which, he wrote, the title might have to be changed, for by the end of it, Pierre was not so *petit* as all that. However, although the episodic form of *Le Petit Pierre* encouraged France to think that it could stand on its own feet before it was fully grown – and he had always liked books to be short, particularly his own – in fact it was still far from finished and France was to pick it up and put it down many more times during the course of the war.

In 1916, as a token of his desire to do all that he could to patch up personal relationships at a time when the war was rending so many apart, France went to Paris and attended a séance of the Academy for the first time in fifteen years. Hervieu, and most of those who had annoyed France and

Mme. Arman, were now dead. All the same, it was an appreciable and appreciated gesture of rapprochement.

That year France had another and more important reason for going to Paris. Emma was taken suddenly ill and had to be operated on. The operation was entirely successful and a few days after it, France was able to write, 'The operation was in time and has been done excellently and suitable treatment should ensure our future.' While Emma was in hospital France had lodged at a nearby hotel, but when she was well enough they both went for a period of convalescence to a home run by Couchoud at Saint-Cloud before returning to la Béchellerie.

France's happiness depended a great deal now on the state of Emma's health. Early in 1917 he wrote happily, 'Emma has found her gaiety again.' But later in the same year he was anxiously querying Couchoud – 'Cheron is thinking of giving Emma injections. In strictest confidence, and for the love of Emma and myself, tell me what you think of this.' Emma on her side, was now entirely devoted to France. But she could never entirely forget that he was her employer, and the respect due to him as such mingled quaintly with her affection in her speech so that her normal form of address to him was, 'mon petit M. France, chéri.'

Emma was always at her worst in the winter and to get her to the sun, France would often take her to the South of France. A letter of New Year's greetings to a friend when he had just done so, shows the easy charm which characterized both his correspondence and his writing in this mellow period, and also the sadness which invariably tinged it in time of war – 'Bonjour, bon an, as they used to say in olden times. I write to you with the window open. I have brought to the sun, Emma, full of colds. The train had great difficulty in getting here. So much snow is between us that I have the impression that we are separated by uncrossable spaces. The snow will melt and we will see each other again. But what miseries and misfortunes will have occurred by then –

by that delightful day when, once again, we will exchange our thoughts.' France and Emma were at Antibes for the first three months of both 1917 and 1918.

However, they were at home at la Béchellerie in the summer of 1917, when Jean Guehenno, who was to make a name for himself after the war both as a writer and as an orator, but was then directing a school at Tours for the rehabilitation of the war-blinded, came over to ask France if he would lecture to his patients. Guehenno tells of his visit in his *Journal d'un homme de quarante ans*. 'I went to see the last of the sages . . . The house . . . had kept the air of another century. We entered. What quiet! But it was that perhaps of an antique shop . . .' In the centre of the salon stood the golden torso of France's beloved Venus; out on a veranda, Emma was lying on a chaise-longue reading. Guehenno and his friend were so over-awed by their surroundings that they found themselves talking in whispers. France came in, eyed their medal-ribbons and the stripes of rank on their sleeves; then smiled – 'the gods, if they exist,' wrote Guehenno, 'must smile thus when they judge our vanities.' His face becoming grave again, France told him, 'What you have done – I will not say it was necessary – let us say it was indispensable.' France did all he could to welcome them, but Guehenno found the atmosphere too rarefied, and felt so constrained that conversation was impossible. France showed them round the house; they met Emma and France made them feel the cloth of her dress as if to show that that, too, was authentic. Then he put on 'an incredible little hat' and accompanied them to the road. 'We descended into the valley,' concluded Guehenno, 'as if into the lower regions of passions and needs.' One can understand that in the midst of war Guehenno should find the apparent ease and elegance of France's house offensive. All the same, one cannot help feeling sorry for France who had done his best to be both courteous and co-operative, and had been rewarded by being written off as patronizing and archaic. Yet it was not only in Guehenno that France's way of life provoked this resentful reaction. The wave of antagonism which washed away much of his reputation in the years immediately following his death, was founded on just such a feeling. Perhaps France had made of his possessions too much of a refuge from life; and any refuge must to some extent be a barrier also.

Fortunately, however, there were some willing and able to jump the barrier. During this period France was to owe a great deal to his friends who kept him in touch with Paris and with life – to Calmettes and Couchoud, of course, Leopold Kahn, but as much as any, to Jacques Lion, a young artillery officer serving at the Ministry of War. Lion's devotion to France, both as a writer and a man, was to prove one of the mainstays of his life. France quickly responded, and his growing affection shows clearly in his letters, sometimes asking him to do some shopping, more often simply to be kept in touch – 'You have a heart to match your name . . . Your little letter is full of charm and of worth.' – 'My very dear lion-cub, you remain deaf to any appeals and do not reply to my letters that are without charm but full of affection.' The friendship between France and Lion was to remain firm until France's death. After it Jacques Lion was to spend much time, trouble and money, not only compiling France's bibliography, but collecting France's letters, which after Lion's tragic death in a concentration camp during the Second World War, were given to the Bibliothèque Nationale.

By now at la Béchellerie France had become one of the sights of the district – 'They come to see me,' he would say, 'as if I was a monument, after the cathedral, but before Charlemagne's Tower.' Anyone of any position who happened to be in the vicinity of la Béchellerie, and many without a position but who were simply curious, would pay him a visit, not so much as a matter of courtesy, but as a matter of course.

France accepted these interruptions and invasions with
good humour and good grace, regarding the hospitality
and patience they entailed as part of his war effort; but glad
also that he had become again part of things. He was now
an avid reader of newspapers, as he had never been before
the war. Few of his letters went unanswered; none was now
thrown unopened into the fire, nor did complimentary copies
pile up in the bath. Sometimes he went to extraordinary
trouble to reply to little or unknown correspondents who
wrote asking, for example, what he thought would be the
state of French literature after the war. In his reply France
covered several pages explaining that he thought French
literature would be in exactly the same state after the war as
it had been before. Age, the war, and particularly Emma, had
brought out the gentler, more mellow side of France, a side,
full of charm and comprehension if also of sadness that the
world was what it was, a sadness deepened now by the
thought that even such as it was, he would soon have to
leave it. Feeling his age, France was more prone to moods
of melancholy. In one of them he told Marcel le Goff that
'old age is difficult and my existence is disagreeable'; in
another, 'for most people life is without attraction and yet
no one wishes to leave it'.

Even, however, if it was more subdued, less in evidence,
the sharper side of France's character was still there. Jacques
Lacretelle, who met France for the first time at la Béchellerie,
wrote that he rarely knew anyone whose face could change
its expression more swiftly, more completely. One moment
France's face would be overflowing with kindliness. Then,
all of a sudden this 'old shepherd's gentleness' would give
way to an expression 'hard, angry, scornful'.

France had this 'hard' and 'scornful' side of his character
by now well under control. It could still find some outlet in
criticism of the Government, of the generals, of the conduct
and character of the war. The longer the war went on, the
less France liked it. Sometimes these private remarks,

intended only for friends' ears, went further than France intended. In 1918 France genuinely for a while feared that he might be shut up by Clemenceau who is supposed to have given him some reason for thinking that he might be, by remarking when told of France's critical attitude – 'Let him take care that he doesn't say a word too much.'

By 1918 France's receptions on Sunday afternoons had swollen to a size when they were almost the equal of those he had held before the war. A surprising number of Parisians came down, not only to see France but to get away from the war and out of Paris at the week-end. The mixture was almost as varied as before – artists, politicians, society-women, as well as authors, editors and journalists. Only the anarchists and revolutionaries, now mostly shut up, were missing.

From 1918 on, one of the most regular visitors to la Béchellerie was Edward Wassermann, a young American soldier, stationed near Tours, who came not only on Sunday afternoons, but on so many days of the week as well that he was more or less accepted by France as part of his household. When Wassermann first met Emma she was introduced to him by France as 'what he had most dear in the world'. Wassermann himself grew to like Emma as he got to know her – 'Many people laughed at her, judging her to be mediocre and boring, but I had the impression that her simplicity and goodness made her worthy of the fine position that M. France was to assure for her later on. Visibly he adored her, and while treating her like a child, allowed himself to be influenced by her.' Surprisingly, considering the efficiency she had shown in Mme. Arman's service, which had earned her the nickname of 'Mlle. Perfection', Emma was not all that good a housekeeper. She had difficulty coping with servants – once she and France came back from the South of France to find that they had departed *en bloc* taking a quantity of France's linen and silver with them – and with the scarcities imposed by the war. They several times ran out of fuel, once even out of food. Wassermann, who managed to get a loaf of white bread out of his service ration, was greeted as the relieving column must have been by the inhabitants of Mafeking. France immediately distributed pieces of the loaf to those present in the room and thereafter frequently referred to Wassermann as their 'Saviour from starvation'.

Wassermann at one stage tried to get a commission. France wrote him a warm letter of recommendation to be passed on to his examiners, and later when he had failed, another of condolence, in which he wrote that examinations had been invented by the mediocre in order to trap the intelligent. After the war he was more successfully to help Wassermann get out of the army – by applying to take him on as his secretary. Both these efforts show another change the war had brought in France – for in earlier days at the Villa Saïd, France would have done little to help his *protégés* in the outside world. One day in October, 1918 Wassermann visited la Béchellerie a few days after France had heard news of the death of Suzanne. Somewhat coolly he analysed France's reactions. France amazed him by being able, at such a time, to discuss the quality of the meal they had just had. But as Emma was to say of France, 'At the time, M. France has a lot of chagrin, but he consoles himself quickly.' The truth was that France had really lost Suzanne many years before. All he lost now was the chance of a reconciliation.

France's fame by now had come out from behind the cloud which at the beginning of the war had temporarily obscured it – to shine brighter than ever before. Round his figure, public opinion had raised an aura almost of veneration. When he went to Paris, as he frequently did, if it was known that he was on the train, small crowds would collect round the carriage in which he was travelling. Whenever he appeared on a public occasion, and on many private ones, also, he was long and rapturously applauded. But to France, now, fame probably meant little – much less than Emma, less than his friends, less than the pleasure of beautifying la Béchellerie, much less than his writing.

For a while in 1917 France had tackled a series of philosophical studies, dialogues on such subjects as 'Nature', 'Old Age', 'War'; but he only completed one on 'The Existence of God', which together with other fragments was to be posthumously published in *Dernières Pages Inédits d'Anatole France*, collected and edited by Michel Corday. His essay on God shows a brave determination to go down with all guns firing, but France's thought in the abstract, was liable to seem in the void also.

France's main task and interest throughout, not only the war years, but the last years of his life, remained the youthful adventures of his alias, Pierre Nozière. France had resisted the entreaties of his publisher to complete his manuscript earlier, saying that to publish such a book in war-time would be 'like offering buttermilk to tigers' – but as the war came to an end, so at last did *Le Petit Pierre*. It was published in 1919.

In his timing France was proved entirely correct. The book answered the need of a public weary of war, asking to be amused and shown that the world, and more particularly Paris, had been, and could still be, a pleasant place in which to live. Yet its success was not only opportunist, it was deserved also. For it was a remarkable achievement to be able to produce at France's age, and under war-time conditions, a work of such freshness, humour and humanity.

Once before France had caught the wind of a similar mood in his sails when a world-weary public, delighted by the gentle charm of *Sylvestre Bonnard*, had given France his first real success. That nearly forty years later, at the other end of a long writing life, France should be able to claim an even greater success with a book written in a similar key, seems to show not only that charm was not the least durable quality of France's writing, but that in itself charm has not only its uses, but also its importance.

POLITICIANS can resign and retire, writers stop writing, but for a public figure of France's eminence, it is always extremely difficult even to fade away. It was particularly so in Paris in those early days of peace when many conflicts which had lain dormant throughout the war broke surface again, and when there were many people, many causes, eager to use the lever of his famous name to push themselves forward. For a man of France's temperament, who always found it difficult to refuse – either an invitation or a tempta- tion – it was virtually impossible to resist the pull back into politics.

Coincidentally, as twenty years before it had been the magnetic personality of Jaurès who had drawn France into politics, so now it was a storm centring upon his now long- dead friend that provided the reason for his return. In- credibly, Jaurès's assassin, about whom there was no doubt, for he was apprehended on the spot, was not put on trial until the spring of 1919. Equally unbelievably, he was then acquitted on the grounds that he had acted from patriotic motives. At the time of the trial France had written for *l'Humanité* a long panegyric in which he considered Jaurès's life and achievements, but never for one moment the possi- bility of his assassin's acquittal. He was outraged by the verdict, and expressed his indignation in an appeal on *l'Humanité*'s front page – 'Workers ... Jaurès lived for you. He died for you. A monstrous verdict ... puts you out- side the law, you and all those who defend your cause.'

The trial brought France back, not only on to the front page of *l'Humanité*, but also into the front rank of Socialist defenders. For the rest of that year, 1919, he was active in many ways, on many platforms. So much so that he was asked to contest a seat at the November elections. He refused, on grounds of ill-health, but in his letter of refusal wrote – 'I believe that only socialism is capable of guaranteeing a stable society.' The Socialists were soundly beaten, but even so, the following year France was again politically active, although once again more on the international plane – denouncing nationalism, urging clemency for the vanquished in the war, succour for the oppressed and suffering – such as the children dying of starvation in Germany, the Jews persecuted in Eastern Europe – and liberty for political prisoners.

The end of 1920 saw the start of the break between Communism and Socialism. The real points at issue were not yet clear, and it seems probable that at this stage France had little idea of the significance of the split. For he allowed himself to be drawn in on the side of the Communist majority who submitted entirely to the control of the Central Executive in Russia, rather than supporting the minority who wished to retain a certain measure of independence, and whose ideas and ideals of humanitarian and egalitarian reform were much nearer his own.

France may, however, have been tricked into giving his adherence to the Communists. Jacques Lion was present when Rappoport, an old friend and one of the leaders of Communist movement, called to enlist his support. Lion remembered and recorded every word of the conversation, of which the relevant part went like this:

Rappoport – 'Monsieur France, will you give me fifty francs for a good work?'

France turned to Emma and told her to get a fifty franc note to give to Rappoport – which she did.

Rappoport – 'Thank you, Madame; thank you, Monsieur
France, it is for the party, for the good cause.'

At no time, however, did Rappoport specify for which party,
for which good cause he was asking France's help. Yet when
l'Humanité, now taken over by the Communist faction, published a list of those contributing to the funds of the new
party, and obviously advertising their adherence by so
doing, France's fifty francs came at its head.

France did not immediately disavow his adherence – at
any rate in public – but during the year (1921) that followed,
he was much less active on the political scene, partly because of ill-health, partly because he was finishing *La Vie
en Fleur*, and in February, 1922, *l'Humanité* did it for him.
When writing of a banquet that he was being given by the
Ligue des Droits de l'Homme, it remarked, 'without a doubt
the Communists will not be numerous at this gathering'. In
an article on France a few days later, it specifically mentioned
that he was not a member of the Communist party.

A month later France ran into trouble with Moscow,
by appealing for clemency for the leaders of the Social
Revolutionary Party, the champions of the Russian peasan-
try but the opponents of Bolshevism, then in power, and
so about to be eliminated. France was publicly rebuked, and
the reproach seems to have sunk home. For, that autumn,
to celebrate the fifth anniversary of the Russian Revolution,
he wrote a 'Salut aux Soviets', published on the front page
of *l'Humanité*, in which he declared – 'The Soviet Revolution has produced for the first time a government of the
people by the people.' Yet for those accustomed to reading
the nuances of his thought there was an element of doubt
even in this fulsome tribute, greeted by *l'Humanité* as a 'gift
of inestimable value . . . by our greatest writer.' 'At least,'
wrote France, 'they have sown the seed which, if fate favours
it, will perhaps, one day, fecundate Europe' – but the
inference of that 'at least' was that the seed, if sown, had not
as yet sprouted very strongly in Russia itself.

ANATOLE FRANCE

The following year, 1923 – France's last active one, for he was to die in the autumn of 1924 – the scales finally fell, or were forced, from his eyes. At this time the Central Executive Committee of the International were intent on asserting their authority, particularly over branches of the Communist Party in other countries. They had, also, come to the conclusion that in France the spread of their influence over the working-classes was hindered rather than helped by the activities of many of their so-called 'intellectuals', of whom France was the most notable, who tended to veer off in directions of their own rather than sticking closely to the Party Line.

These two segments of Communist thought came together in a motion, formulated by Trotsky, and passed at the 4th World Conference of the International on 22nd December, 1922, which not only asserted the supreme authority of the Executive Committee but specifically condemned in France the *Ligue des Droits de l'Homme* as a 'radical bourgeois organization', forbad its members to belong to Masonic lodges, and insisted that all 'intellectuals' should break other commitments, and submit themselves absolutely to the Party discipline. Several prominent French Communists felt themselves, for various reasons, unable to do this and were expelled. Amongst these were Victor Meric, editor of *l'Humanité*, L. O. Frossard, secretary of the French Communist Party, but also an ardent Free-Mason, Georges Pioch, a well-known poet, and several other writers.

France was not openly expelled, but the rumour ran around that he had been told to consider himself as such. Yet it is more probable that the break came from his side, for it was not in France's nature or his beliefs to submit to so dictatorial a demand. Certainly at this time he removed his contributions from *l'Humanité* to *Le Quotidien*, a new daily formed by the non-Communist element of the Left. *l'Humanité*, in whose life he had previously played so large a part, riposted by attacking him on his now rare public appearances. When he spoke at a meeting in honour of Renan it commented sourly that the workers had need, not of writers who sought to understand the world, but of writers who sought to change it. On his eightieth birthday in April, 1924, the occasion otherwise of widespread congratulations and a large meeting at the Trocadero in his honour, it blamed him for not supporting a workers revolution. Coming from such a quarter, so bitter a blast must have greatly hurt France – for a paper to which one contributes regularly over a number of years becomes part of one's personal life, almost of one's family. In the last year of his life France made his break with Communism quite clear by supporting the 'Cartel des Gauches', the non-Communist block of parties of the Left, at the spring elections.

After his death France was immediately appropriated by the Communists, given his statue in Leningrad and his minor place in the Communist sainthood. Since then his writings have often been quoted to support particular Communist contentions – sometimes out of context, sometimes in it, for France threw off his sparks in many directions, and himself once said that after his death his writings would be found to be full of 'crumbs of dynamite'. His views did not really contain the explosive force he imagined, but even so they have provided useful ammunition through the years for the Communist offensive.

Yet France made it perfectly plain in the last year of his life that he had broken with Communism, and it is greatly to his credit that he went to the trouble of showing this when, enfeebled and fatigued as he was, he could so easily have slipped into silence, letting the world, of which the affairs were unlikely to concern him for much longer, look after itself. It is no less plain that his basic independence, belief in individuality, and desire to make as large a place as possible for that individuality in a world already too contemptuous of its importance, were quite in-compatible both with the doctrine and the discipline of Communism.

Why then did France ride along with it for as long as he did? Most probably France accepted Communism – as he accepted anyone who turned up regularly at his house as a friend, regardless of whether he liked them or not, so that Mme. Arman once said he had no friends, only habits – simply because it was there. It must, too, have seemed but the modern and extreme version of the idealistic design for a better world which he and Jaurès had shared at the turn of the century. When it came to the point, however, France, like so many others, could not admit that the end justified the means. But it only really came to the point, to this particular point, in the last years of his life, for it was only after the war that Communism began to show, not only its strength, but its character.

In his political role, France was both used and abused a great deal, even by his friends such as Jaurès. At every election he was hauled forth like an ancient but still service-able cannon to pound away at the enemy. Over a period of some fifteen years, which would have been longer but for the interruption of the war, he was an indispensable part of virtually any Socialist gathering or meeting of importance. At most of these, and the countless banquets he also felt obliged to attend, he was probably the only person on the platform or at the high table without any personal political ambitions, and so, in a positive, practical way, uncompen-sated for the effort involved. When called upon to speak, as he almost always was on such occasions, he was generally more concerned with what his audience wanted to hear than with what he wanted to say. Altogether, as a party poli-tician France presents a slightly ludicrous spectacle for a man of his eminence, pushed here, there, everywhere, where-ever there was need of a speaker, a chairman or a star – and submitting indiscriminately to these pressures for obscure, not easily appreciable, reasons of his own.

Yet through the maze of France's political activities there began also to show, as the years went by, a line of conduct surprisingly consistent for so inconsistent a character. Particularly through his efforts on behalf of the *Ligue des Droits de l'Homme*, France found himself speaking out on behalf of the suffering and the oppressed whoever and wherever they might be. Whether the Armenian victims of Turkish massacre, the Jews persecuted in eastern Europe, or the hungry German children starving after the war derived much practical help as a result of his words, one cannot know. But the fact remains that France was beating a drum of which the sound sooner or later was bound to have some effect on the human conscience and which carried further and faster because of his eminence. France set the seal on the value of this work by his appeal to Moscow on behalf of the leaders of the Social Revolutionary Party, for this showed that his intentions were entirely impartial and that he could, and would, protest even against his associates, if they warranted it by their actions.

Nor was it only to alleviate suffering, to oppose oppression that France spoke out. Because of his hatred of violence he fought a long, if losing, battle against war. He was not logical or courageous enough to continue the fight when war had actually broken out, but then, for France, the big things were made out of the small – his desire for peace out of his love of the stones of Paris, of the beautiful buildings and countryside of France; and it was insufferable to him to think that these should be destroyed or damaged without raising a hand in their defence. As soon as peace returned he was again to the fore urging clemency for the vanquished, as the first essential step towards building a better and more peaceful world.

All of these activities accord ill with France's reputation as a selfish and self-limiting writer, who closed the shutters of his study and let the winds of the world roar outside; whilst he in his armchair browsed happily through his books in front of the fire of his self-sufficiency. France had such a tendency – and for him half-an-hour with a book of his choice was probably the freedom for which he fought – yet few crusading writers have in fact supported with such disinterest so many diverse and deserving causes. For these activities alone France deserves his statue, not necessarily in Leningrad, but in any city where freedom is valued, suffering sought out and succoured, and oppression opposed.

15

OVER THE LAST PERIOD OF HIS LIFE, France was
luckier in his private life than in his public affairs. In it
Emma continued to take an ever-growing place. France's
concern for her health, still worryingly unstable, often
banished all thought of the far more precarious state of his
own. His young American friend, Edward Wassermann,
paying a visit to la Béchellerie after the war, found France
distraught because Emma as ill. 'He was in tears and told
me that if anything happened to her he would kill himself,
that he could not bear to live without her.'

Emma recovered, and France, thinking of her future
more than of his, decided to marry her. Under French law
even a divorced wife had rights on her husband's estate if he
did not marry again. Unless she had the status and security
of being his wife, France could not be sure that Emma
would be adequately looked after when he was no longer
there to do so. Yet this was not the only, or probably the
most important, reason why France decided to marry Emma.
It was just as certainly a way of expressing his affection,
gratitude and, now, love. On the 11th October, 1920, in
the Mairie of Saint-Cyr, in the presence of a few friends –
amongst them Calmann-Lévy, Kahn, Couchoud and
Wassermann – and a delegation of young Socialist women,
carrying bouquets of red roses in their arms, Emma Laprevotte became the second Madame France.

That year, 1920, had earlier seen France's return to
Paris, where the new Villa Saïd, slowly reconstructed during

the course of the war, was at last finished. But it was a very half-hearted return, for France and Emma were happy at la Béchellerie and had no intention of deserting it altogether. 'When one has breathed the air of Touraine,' France once told Calmettes, 'one is no longer capable of inhaling the miasmas of Paris. How can I go and shut myself up in the Villa Saïd where I cannot even see the sky.' But in other moods he was impatient to be back amongst his old haunts, and over the last months before his return, was bombarding Calmettes, still apparently acting unpaid Comptroller of his Household, with queries as to when everything would be ready.

At last everything was. France went with Calmettes to pay his first visit to his new house. France had left everything to his architects, Thiers and Oury. He had no idea what he would find, and what he did find, he found quite unrecognizable. The new Villa Saïd was a fine, spacious, stone-faced, three-storey building, of which the entrance was now at the extreme right of the façade. Inside, the only obvious point of similarity with the old building was that the kitchen was still in the basement – although the bathroom no longer. A large, well-lit hall, clear but cold to the eye, occupied the space of the old dining-room, forming a striking contrast with the murky, mediaeval interior into which France's guests had formerly been shown. On the left lay the salon, from which a passage led to the dining-room, standing on the site of the 'chapel' and the little garden that had lain behind it.

The whole of the first floor was devoted to France's study, which, however, could be made into two rooms by dividing doors; the second contained the bedrooms of France and Emma; and, above this, to his intense surprise France found yet another floor which he had known nothing about. This consisted of a large, airy studio with windows on both sides – obviously intended by France's architects, remembering how his collections had overgrown

the old Villa Saïd, as an overflow for the rest of the house –
and some guest rooms. Altogether it was a beautiful house,
thoughtfully tailored to France's needs – well-lit and warm,
clear, capacious and comfortable, elegant and efficient – all,
in fact, that the old Villa Saïd had not been. Yet it did not
really suit France nearly as well as the dark, smoky, draught-
swept setting of his old house. France never felt at home in
it, or that it was his home. This remained, for the rest of his
life, la Béchellerie. The new Villa Saïd served him as a
comfortable refuge in which to escape the cold of the
country during the winter months, and as a convenient
place in which to stay for the odd days when his various
needs brought him to Paris. But even during the relatively
short time that he spent there, his heart and often his
thoughts, remained in Touraine. 'Tell me,' he wrote in a
letter of 1923 from the Villa Saïd to la Béchellerie, 'how the
grass on the lawn is growing . . . Is the courtyard in its full
beauty?'

France moved some, but not all, of his furniture, books,
pictures and collections, back from la Béchellerie to the Villa
Saïd. This, however, left gaps in both houses, the filling
of which was one of his main occupations over the next
couple of years. But, sadly, in Paris some of the spark
seems at last to have gone out of his collecting. Calmettes
noting this and remembering regretfully France's advice
to him of some years back – 'Love your belongings. Love
them well. They alone do not wrong us – even if, sometimes, the dealers do' – put it down to the fact that neither
France's judgement nor his eyesight were as good as they
had been. But a more probable reason was the extortionate
price that France was now obliged to pay for most of his
purchases in Paris and which offended someone even so little
regardful of the value of money as he was. Prices had risen
greatly, but not by the thousandfold which France judged to
be the difference between the prices he had had to pay when
he had first started collecting and now. Undoubtedly, to

some of the less scrupulous dealers, France was a 'soft touch', and they were now piling it on, not knowing for how much longer they would be able to do so.

But at la Béchellerie it was quite different. Prices were much more reasonable. Also, there France was working for something he loved, and not the cool, heartless, elegant, expensive mistress he had acquired more or less inadvertently at Paris. The beautification of la Béchellerie still provided the pretext for countless enjoyable visits to the antique shops of the neighbourhood. There was more now of la Béchellerie to beautify, for by his later purchases France had acquired 'la petite Béchellerie', an adjoining farmhouse, of much the same date, with three bedrooms and a fine period salon. He also modernized another building, seemingly as a sort of summer-house, and converted a barn into a magnificent library, whose walls were lined from floor to ceiling with books, but which contained no furniture other than a desk and some chairs. All of this took time, but now time could not run too slowly for him, conscious as he was that as it took its course it must soon now take its toll. Only in 1923 was he finally satisfied, so that he could write, 'At last la Béchellerie is finished and very beautiful.'

The beautification of la Béchellerie, the rebuilding and the furnishing of the new Villa Saïd, not only took time, they also took a great deal of money. But happily his books were still working well for him and there was an immense amount coming in every year, not only from their sales in France, but also from translation, dramatic and now even film rights. His fame, too, continued to grow, and during these years he had a double distinction which tickled his sense of irony perhaps more than his sense of humour. In 1921 he was awarded a Nobel prize and went to Sweden to collect it. The following year all his works were put on the Catholic Index.

On his appearances in Paris, France still sometimes showed signs of the incorrigibility which at other times had been the inspiration of Brousson, the exasperation of Mme. Arman and the cause of both delight and bewilderment to his friends. Wandering through the streets one day with Calmettes, he remarked that the only practical results the long agony of the war seemed to have achieved were Summer Time and short skirts. 'Bonheur appreciable,' murmured France, 'but, just my luck, they have come at a time when I can no longer see clearly.' Sitting for a portrait by an artist called Van Dongen, he could not take his eyes off a nearby painting of a nude which led him to remark that if he was perforce nowadays somewhat detached from the good things of life, it was very much in spite of himself. Van Dongen considered that he sat 'like an angel', but France was very much less appreciative of the finished portrait in which he considered he had the air of 'un Camembert qui coule', and which he would not have in the house. One evening France allowed Wassermann to show him the night life of Paris, which included a visit to the Casino de Paris and a night-club, but he had never been much of a night bird and found that he saw no clearer or more pleasurably in the dark now than before.

Wassermann, while he was in Paris, visited him most mornings – 'We hung pictures, we examined engravings, we talked of my life, because his, he said, was finished. His friend Prouté (the art-dealer) . . . came from time to time with drawings of every sort. Steinlen knocked often at the door, always with a pencil and a piece of paper. While we chatted he made numerous sketches . . . The life of M. France was very simple. He got up late, wandered about the house throughout the morning, and after lunch, which was followed by a siesta, went by car to Versailles or Saint-Cloud to see the Couchouds or to the other side of the Seine to see booksellers or picture-dealers.'

Not many months before his death, France went to the opening of a new maison de couture. The observant Jacques de Lacretelle was also there and studied France

keenly as he moved around complimenting the manne-
quins, most of whom he apparently knew, on their looks
or their dresses. His voice was 'low and caressing', and his
hands, as he talked, were always moving, tracing small
clouds in the air. The show started and after a bit the crowd
moved on into another room. But France, tired, remained
behind, alone except for the unseen Lacretelle. His eyes
wandered round the room, resting for a moment on some
details of discarded finery – a tulle dress thrown across a
chair, a piece of ribbon on the floor – before settling drow-
sily on the flame of the gas fire. To de Lacretelle his attitude
seemed so weary and abandoned that he was about to break
in on his solitude to comfort him when a noise from the
other room roused him. To de Lacretelle's surprise he saw
then in his eyes an expression 'firm, hard, almost triumph-
ant' – an expression which he interpreted as the 'wry joy
that the aging artist feels as he watches his body and his wits
being slowly destroyed by time, and yet knows that he has
put the best of himself in safety in his works.'

At la Béchellerie, of course, the tempo of life was much
slower, and France's letters show him following the vagaries
of his moods, the weather and his health, demanding little
of life in order that it should demand as little as possible of
him in return. 'We live in peaceful life at la Béchellerie, but
I feel painfully the assault of old age.' (27th September,
1921). 'Everything goes well at la Béchellerie and my
health is as good as one can expect at my age. One must
never ask much of life, and it is prudent to ask nothing at
all of old age.' (24th July, 1922). Inevitably there were times
when he resented his sentence, in one of which he wrote
bitterly, 'There is only one irreparable and cruel evil in
life – old age.' But in general his letters reflect the peaceful
background that la Béchellerie provided.

The circle of personal relationships which lay closest to
France was very happily enlarged over these years by the
presence of his only grandson, his only grandchild, Lucien

Psichari, Suzanne's son. While Valérie lived they had never met, but Valérie died in 1921, shortly after Emma had become the second Madame France, so that France's testamentary concern for Emma proved, as it turned out, unnecessary. It was then decided that France should become the guardian of Lucien, aged thirteen. For both of them the relationship was to mean much, but to France in particular it meant a personal link with the future; also with the past, for here was an opportunity to make amends for his long estrangement with Suzanne. His affection for Lucien did not take long to grow or to show itself. Over the last few years France had often turned to the young for friendship, and it was a delight now to have someone young of his own blood living with him.

France's letters to Lucien over the few years they were together are full of affection, of charm, consideration and concern for the small things that are as much part of an upbringing as the large, such as that Lucien should go to the dentist. They also show clearly France's desire to bring together the two people now closest to him – Emma and Lucien. Over this there was little difficulty, for the kindly, motherly Emma was delighted to have a child about the house, particularly if it was the grandchild of her beloved 'M. France chéri.' She became Lucien's 'Grand-mère' or, alternatively, and more frequently, 'Mère-grande'.

In a letter headed 'Babylon (Paris)' France wrote to Lucien on 3rd January, 1923 – '. . . We shall be miserable, your Grand-mère and I in Babylon, until you come to recall us from exile . . . you have taken away all our pleasure with you.' Some months later, Lucien had become, '*Mon cher petit Lulu* . . . thank you for sending us your news. You cannot know how everything which concerns you is dear to me. Your Grand-mère France (Emma) has given me a very great proof of her love for you, but as it is in making a will I cannot tell you more. She is keeping well, except that she has still some bees in her bonnet. And one can hardly hope now that they will fly away.'

The bees were still there some months later – '*Mon cher petit*, you have sent us a letter which does honour to your judgement. Your Grand-mère is well and, in spite of a few bees in her bonnet, is gay.' These letters were generally sent to la Béchellerie where Lucien was left when France went to Paris – now, unfortunately, as often to see doctors as friends. '*Mon petit, mon cher petit*, Ledoux-Lebard told me on Saturday evening at six o'clock, that Gosset refused to operate on me. Dr. Meugot is going to treat me with electricity. The first treatment will be on Friday next. I am not very hopeful about it and don't know when we shall be able to return to la Béchellerie. Your petite Mère-grande is gay, which is a good sign. I am keeping well enough for my age. We have seen the chef. He may be a good cook, but he is not handsome.'

Later letters show that the fondness of France – and of Emma – for Lucien, was ever-increasing – '*Mon cher petit, cher petit Lucien*, your absence and the bad state of my health have made it a painful stay in Paris. Your Grandemère France could not be happy in a house where she did not see you.' He was buying a new car, and looked forward particularly to its arrival because on the previous day they had been poisoned by the fumes of 'the Panhard which, in its extreme age, no longer has the pure breath of a virgin.'

'*Mon cher petit* . . . you wrote us a letter so tender and charming that it brought tears to our eyes. But you must know that everything we do for you, your Grande-mère France and I, gives us so much pleasure that there is no need to thank us for it.' In another letter when it is Lucien who is in Paris and France and Emma who are at la Bechellerie, he is arranging to meet him on his return – '*Cher petit*, it is understood – we shall be at Le Mans on Friday, 24th. We'll meet you at the station . . . and for us it will be a great day. We did not realize, your grandmother and I, the place you held in our life.' France had not always fulfilled his family obligations, but in these last few years, he clearly could not have done more for Lucien, and his affection for his grandson did much for him in return.

Throughout these letters, France's primary concern was always for Lucien, yet in fact, over this period, he had plenty of reason to be concerned about himself. He had had a slight stroke in 1920, which, with a momentary return to his Rabelaisian manner and, one would think, absolute untruth, he attributed to a moment of passion with a beautiful visitor. He suffered badly from headaches. He had trouble with his breathing. In 1922 he had a bad attack of urticaria. In 1923 an attack of neuritis in the right hand made him so miserable that he wrote – 'I suffer so cruelly as almost to lose my reason, . . . I count still on an operation. If that does not help there is nothing for it but to throw myself in the river.' The following year, the attack spread to his other hand. He was sleeping badly and he had intestinal trouble. Altogether he was clearly in a state of general, if gradual, decomposition; and no one realized it more clearly than he. But there were moments when for no particular reason, he felt better and more cheerful. One such came at the beginning of 1924 when, with the melancholy optimism of the condemned man granted a reprieve, he murmured – 'I believe I shall see another spring.' He did, and it was the spring that saw his eightieth birthday – the occasion for general congratulation throughout the Press, with the notable exception of *l'Humanité*, and the country.

Of the many miserable consequences of his age and his illness, perhaps the one that France felt the most was the handicap it imposed on his writing. In 1923, in one of his letters to Lucien, he wrote, 'My health does not allow me to work much.' For some time past France had not, of course, needed to work at all, save for his satisfaction and interest. He had long had as much money and fame as he wanted. Yet he continued to write as long as it was physically possible for him to do so. As late as September, 1922 he excused his bad hand-writing on the grounds that his hand was tired because he had been 'working a lot, these last few days'. Amazingly, considering the state, not only of his hands but of his health in general, his last book, published in 1922, *La Vie en Fleur*, a continuation of *Le Petit Pierre*, was one of his best.

La Vie en Fleur lived up to the promise of its name. It was an evergreen evocation of France's youth, in which he remembered again the old Paris he had known as a child – had he ever forgotten it? – the characters who had formed his own, the incidents which had engrained themselves in his mind and so become part, too, of his adult life. Far from growing stiff with age, France's style seemed to become ever more flexible and fluent; and his charm was as potent as ever. For the more thoughtful of his readers there was, too, much to ponder between the lines as well as along them, for France unobtrusively introduced into the conversations of his characters, by inflection as much as by insertion, much of his own philosophy of life.

But more than either his wisdom or his charm, it was France's zest for life that irradiated *La Vie en Fleur*. Here was a man who had always encouraged his readers to take life with a pinch of scepticism; who had counselled them to doubt, to question, even to mistrust; who had refused the helping hands that faith on the one side, and a doctrinaire approach on the other, held out; whose own experience had been far from easy; affirming triumphantly that life taken straight in this way was worthwhile, that his life had been worthwhile, and proving it by producing, at the extremity of his writing life, this work that was still full of the sap of youth as well as of the experience of age, and which, if full of affection, was entirely free from regret. It was particularly moving that so joyful a work should have been written by someone who must have known that he was close to death. *La Vie en Fleur* was not the most ambitious, or the most successful of France's works, but it was, in its way, perhaps his greatest triumph. If death still had its sting, where was its victory?

After *La Vie en Fleur* France still wanted to write another similar book, a book full of 'humour and philosophy', but he was conscious that he no longer had the strength to do so. Yet that did not mean that he stopped writing. All his books were very much alive to him, and being so, were always open to change and correction. He continued to go over them seeking to improve, to change here and there a word, a phrase, a paragraph that would clarify the meaning or add to the beauty. Since the war he had worked on *Le Lys Rouge*, *Thaïs*, *La Rotisserie*. Now it was the turn of *l'Histoire Contemporaine*. A young friend, Claude Aveline, suggested revising his youthful study of Alfred de Vigny. This was the last literary task he was able to complete. So his writing came full circle, and his first work was, coincidentally, to be his last also.

For a long time now France had written because to write was to live; and living, to him, meant writing. When he could no longer write he knew he had not long to live. Yet his last letter, dictated to Lucien because he was too ill to hold a pen, to a painter who had sent him some studies of himself, still showed the sense of style and the courteous charm which had become so characteristic of his writing – 'The portraits you were kind enough to send me pleased me by their style and their character. As to those of my extreme old age, which you wish to send me, they impress by their monumental quality. I only hope that time will lend my works a little of the force and grandeur which you impress on your compositions.'

France was ill for much of that last summer. In August he took finally to his bed. He was now on the point of death, but he was still reluctant to leave life. Generally he was barely conscious, but he had occasional moments of returning lucidity. In one of them he murmured – 'So this is what it's like to die'; then he sighed – 'It takes a long time.' Throughout September life lingered, as reluctant to leave him as he it. One day in October he said to Emma – 'I shall never see you again.' It was the 12th when France finally, with extreme reluctance, died.

Bibliography

Index

Bibliography

For France's own works there is a comprehensive bibliography in vol. VI of *Bibliographie des Auteurs modernes de Langue Française*, by Talvart & Place (Horizons de France), 1937.

Most of the letters I have used come from the considerable collection in the Bibliothèque Nationale, mainly in the Collection Lion. There, also, are France's *Carnets*, for the use of which I am particularly indebted to M. Lucien Psichari.

Amongst the printed sources I would particularly like to mention *Anatole France* by Jacques Suffel, Éditions du Myrte, 1946, a handrail that has often prevented me from falling; and the commentary by Claude Aveline and Henriette Psichari, to the three volumes of *Trente Ans de Vie Sociale*, France's political and social speeches, Émile-Paul 1949–63, which provides a remarkably comprehensive picture of the period.

Other books that have helped me are:

RICHARD H. BAKER, *Marcel Proust*. Faber. 1959.

MARIE-CLAIRE BANCQUART, *Anatole France, polémiste*. Paris. 1962.

MAURICE BARRÈS, *Mes Cahiers*. Plon.

E. BERGERAT, *Souvenirs d'un enfant de Paris*. Fasquelle. 1911.

ANDRÉ DE BERSAUCOURT, *Au temps des Parnassiens. Nina de Villard et ses Amis*. Fasquelle. 1911.

MARTHE L. BIBESCO, *Portraits d'Hommes*. Paris. 1929.

Une visite à la Béchellerie. Paris. 1925.

V. DU BLED, *La Société française depuis cent ans*. Bloud et Gay. 1924.

ANDRÉ BILLY, *Les Frères Goncourts*. Flammarion. 1954.

ROBERT DE BONNIÈRES, *Memoires d'aujourd'hui*. Ollendorf. 1885.

PAUL BOURGET, *Quelques témoignages*. Plon. 1928.

JEAN-JACQUES BROUSSON, *Anatole France en Pantoufles*. Cres. 1924.

Itinéraire de Paris à Buenos-Ayres. Cres. 1927.

Les Vêpres de l' Avenue Hoche. Editions du Cadran. 1932.

FERNAND CALMETTES, *Leconte de Lisle et ses Amis*. Lib. Imp. Réunies. 1902.

PIERRE CALMETTES, *La Grande Passion d'Anatole France*. Marcel Seheur. 1929.

LÉON CARIAS, *Anatole France*. Rieder. 1931.
Les Carnets intimes d'Anatole France. Paris, 1946.

PIERRE CHAMPION, *Mon Vieux Quartier*. Grasset. 1932.

GUY CHAPMAN, *The Dreyfus Case*. Hart-Davis. 1955.

H. CHEVALIER, *The Ironic Temper*. 1932.

RAPHAEL COR, *M. Anatole France et la pensée contemporaine*. Pelletan. 1909.

MICHEL CORDAY, *Anatole France, d'aprés ses confidences et ses souvenirs*. Flammarion. 1927.

E. P. DARGAN, *Anatole France, 1844–96*. Oxford University Press. 1937.

LÉON DAUDET, *Au temps de Judas*. Librairie nationale. 1920.
Salons et Journaux. Plon. 1917.

MAURICE DREFOUS, *Ce que je tiens à dire*. Ollendorf.

J. L. DIRICK, *Franciana*. Simonson. 1925.

EDMOND DE GONCOURT, *Journal des Goncourt*. Paris. 1887–96. Flammarion.

O. GÉRARD, *Académie française. Discours de Reception*. Firmin-Didot. 1896.

GEORGES GIRARD, *La Jeunesse d'Anatole France*. Gallimard. 1925.

MYRIAM HARRY, *Trois Ombres*. Flammarion, 1932.

A. HERMANT, *Souvenirs de la Vie mondaine*. Plon. 1935.

ALISTAIR HORNE, *The Fall of Paris*. Macmillan. 1965.

GEORGES HUARD, *Anatole France et le Quai Malaquais*. Champion. 1926.

SANDOR KEMERI, *Promenades d'Anatole France*. Calmann-Lévy. 1927.

J. DE LACRETELLE, *À la Rencontre de France*. Editions Tremois. 1930.

MARCEL LE GOFF, *Anatole France à la Béchellerie*. Delteil. 1924.

J. LERAILLANT, *Les aventures du scepticisme*. Colin. 1966.

JACQUES LION, *Bibliographie des ouvrages consacres à Anatole France*. Giraud-Badin. 1935.

P. MARTINO, *Parnasse et Symbolisme*. Colin. 1925.

H. MASSIS, *Evocations*. Plon. 1931.

ANDRÉ MAUREL, *Souvenirs de Litterature*. 'Oeuvres Libres'. 44. Hachette. 1925.

ANDRÉ MAUROIS, *À la Recherche de Marcel Proust*. Hachette. 1949.

CHARLES MAURRAS, *Anatole France, politique et poète*. Plon. 1924.

J. LEWIS MAY, *Anatole France, the Man and his Work*. Lane. 1924.

John Lane and the Nineties. John Lane. The Bodley Head. 1936.

A. MEYER, *Ce que je peux dire*. Plon. 1912.

M. MISSOFFE, *Gyp et ses Amis*. Flammarion. 1932.

E. MONTFORT, *25 ans de littérature française*. Librairie de France. 1925.

GEORGE MOORE, *Confessions of a Young Man*. Heinemann. 1888.

Memoirs of my Dead Life. Heinemann. 1906.

J.-M. POUQUET, *Le Salon de Mme. Arman de Caillavet*. Hachette. 1926.

MARCEL PROUST, *Correspondence*. Selected and edited by Mina Curtiss. Chatto and Windus. 1955.

H. DE REGNIER, *De mon Temps*. Mercure de France. 1933.

ERNEST RENAN, *Correspondence*. Calmann-Lévy. 1928.

Souvenirs d'enfance et de jeunesse. Calmann-Lévy. 1883.

JULES RENARD, *Journal inedit*. Paris. 1925–27.

HENRY ROUJON, *Au milieu des hommes*. Rueff. 1907.

J. ROUJON, *La Vie et les opinions d'Anatole France*. Plon. 1925.

JEAN SAREIL, *Anatole France et Voltaire*. 1961.

NICOLAS SÉGUR, *Conversations avec Anatole France*. Fasquelle. 1925.

Anatole France, anecdotique. 1929.

Dernieres conversations avec Anatole France. 1927.

E. SEILLIÈRE, *Anatole France, critique de son temps*. Nouvelle Revue Critique. 1934.

La Jeunesse d'Anatole France. Nouvelle Revue Critique. 1934.

MARIE SCHEIKEVITCH, *Souvenirs d'un temps disparu*. Paris. 1935.

MAURICE SOURIAU, *Histoire de Parnasse*. Spes. 1929.

LAURENT TAILLHADE, *Quelques fantomes de jadis*. L'Edition française illustre. 1922.

A. VANDEGANS, *Anatole France, les années de formation*. 1954.

MARJORIE VILLIERS, *Charles Péguy*. Collins. 1965.

E. WASSERMANN, *Anatole France vu par un Américain*. Editions Tremois. 1930.

I have also found useful information in *Le Lys Rouge*, the journal of the Société Anatole France, a flourishing body, eager to welcome English members, and which can be contacted at 133 rue de la Pompe, Paris XVI.

Index

335